THE BEDFORD SERIES IN HISTORY AND CULTURE

Margaret Fuller
A Brief Biography with Documents

Related Titles in
THE BEDFORD SERIES IN HISTORY AND CULTURE
Advisory Editors: Natalie Zemon Davis, Princeton University
Ernest R. May, Harvard University

THE BEDFORD SERIES IN HISTORY AND CULTURE

Margaret Fuller
A Brief Biography with Documents

Eve Kornfeld
San Diego State University

BEDFORD BOOKS   Boston   New York

For Tom and Anna

For Bedford Books
President and Publisher: Charles H. Christensen
General Manager and Associate Publisher: Joan E. Feinberg
History Editor: Katherine E. Kurzman
Developmental Editor: Phyllis Valentine
Editorial Assistant: Kate Sheehan Roach
Managing Editor: Elizabeth M. Schaaf
Production Editor: Ellen C. Thibault
Copyeditor: Barbara G. Flanagan
Indexer: Steve Csipke
Text Design: Claire Seng-Niemoeller
Cover Design: Richard Emery Design, Inc.
Cover Art: Margaret Fuller. Engraving by Henry Bryan Hall, Jr. Courtesy of the National Portrait Gallery, Smithsonian Institution, Washington, D.C.

Library of Congress Catalog Card Number: 96–86774

1   0   9   8   7   6
f   e   d   c   b   a

For information, write: Bedford Books, 75 Arlington Street, Boston, MA 02116
(617–426–7440)

ISBN: 0–312–12009–5 (paperback)
ISBN: 0–312–16387–8 (hardcover)

Acknowledgments

Willard P. Fuller, Jr. and the following libraries have granted permission to quote from the listed unpublished manuscripts in their holdings.

The Houghton Library, Harvard University: "Diary of Timothy Fuller," 15 November 1804, Fuller Manuscripts and Works [hereafter FMW], fMS Am 1086, 2:6. Margaret Fuller [hereafter MF], Journal, [ca. August 1838], FMW, 9:264. Eliza Rotch Farrar to MF, 25 July [1843], FMW, 17. Margarett Crane Fuller to Timothy Fuller, 17 December 1820, FMW, 6:102. Margarett Crane Fuller to Timothy Fuller, 18 and 22 February 1818, FMW, 6:16, 20. Timothy Fuller to Margaret Fuller, ca. 1823, FMW, 5:16. James Freeman Clarke, "Journal of People and Things," bMS Am 1569.2 (9), 12 September 1831, and "Journal of the Under-

Acknowledgments and copyrights are continued at the back of the book on page 245, which constitutes an extension of the copyright page. *It is a violation of the law to reproduce these selections by any means whatsoever without the written permission of the copyright holder.*

Foreword

The Bedford Series in History and Culture is designed so that readers can study the past as historians do.

The historian's first task is finding the evidence. Documents, letters, memoirs, interviews, pictures, movies, novels, or poems can provide facts and clues. Then the historian questions and compares the sources. There is more to do than in a courtroom, for hearsay evidence is welcome, and the historian is usually looking for answers beyond act and motive. Different views of an event may be as important as a single verdict. How a story is told may yield as much information as what it says.

Along the way the historian seeks help from other historians and perhaps from specialists in other disciplines. Finally, it is time to write, to decide on an interpretation and how to arrange the evidence for readers.

Each book in this series contains an important historical document or group of documents, each document a witness from the past and open to interpretation in different ways. The documents are combined with some element of historical narrative—an introduction or a biographical essay, for example—that provides students with an analysis of the primary source material and important background information about the world in which it was produced.

Each book in the series focuses on a specific topic within a specific historical period. Each provides a basis for lively thought and discussion about several aspects of the topic and the historian's role. Each is short enough (and inexpensive enough) to be a reasonable one-week assignment in a college course. Whether as classroom or personal reading, each book in the series provides firsthand experience of the challenge—and fun—of discovering, recreating, and interpreting the past.

Natalie Zemon Davis
Ernest R. May

Preface

Margaret Fuller, one of the most famous American women of her time, was known to her contemporaries as the first editor of the New England Transcendentalists' literary journal and the author of both a popular travel book and the feminist *Woman in the Nineteenth Century*. She was one of the first women to act as an editor, literary critic, and journalist for a major New York City newspaper and as a foreign correspondent during the Roman Revolution of 1848. Fuller was often in the public eye, yet she remained an enigma to most observers. Her determination to question, challenge, and cross conventional social boundaries left many mid-nineteenth-century Americans wondering about her identity, and perhaps their own.

Fuller's willingness to question the fixity and divinity of the boundaries that structured and ordered social life of her day provoked her generation and speaks powerfully to ours as well. Her desire to live a fully human life led her to develop a broad feminist and humanist vision for all men and women. Although she could not completely escape the language and constraints of her culture, she dared to dream of a world without class, racial, national, or gender borders. Her dream can still compel our attention.

This book also attempts to cross traditional borders between academic disciplines and discourses. It draws upon the insights of feminist and post-structuralist theory as well as the methods of intellectual history, biography, and literary criticism to explore the scope and limits of Fuller's vision. It offers a strong gender interpretation of her life and work but also provides a range of published and unpublished documents against which readers can test that interpretation and formulate their own. I hope that teachers and students of history, literature, women's studies, and American studies will all encounter in these pages a many-sided person who resisted artificial divisions and reductions all her life. She may yet inspire us to do the same.

ACKNOWLEDGMENTS

Many students at Harvard, Princeton, and San Diego State University have shared and supported my interest in Margaret Fuller. Hundreds of students in my surveys of early American history at SDSU have read Fuller with me and assumed her voice in role-playing debates among American reformers. Several seniors and graduate students have written theses under my direction about Fuller or her circle; of these, Melissa Marks of Princeton and Kathryn Fuller of SDSU were particularly stimulating intellectual companions. The first versions of this interpretation of Fuller's life were presented to history majors and graduate students at a *Phi Alpha Theta* colloquium and to students and faculty of the Women's Studies Department at SDSU. Their questions helped to clarify and reshape my thoughts.

Colleagues and institutions have also supported this project. Conversations over the years about intellectual history, gender, poststructuralism, biography, and teaching with John Clive, Donald Fleming, Edith Gelles, Jean Matthews, John Murrin, Dorothy Ross, Carl Schorske, Frank Stites, and colleagues in the interdisciplinary faculty seminars at SDSU, the Humanities Project of the American Council of Learned Societies, and the American Culture Association have been invaluable. A Research, Scholarship, and Creative Activity grant from SDSU helped to defray the costs of research for this book. My first exploration of Fuller's life and work, "Margaret Fuller: Minerva and the Muse" (coauthored with Melissa Marks), was published in the *Journal of American Culture* 13:3 (Fall 1990), 47–59. I am grateful to Willard P. Fuller Jr., custodian of the literary estate of Margaret Fuller, for permission to quote from manuscript materials. I am indebted to the Houghton Library of Harvard University, the Thomas Cooper Library of the University of South Carolina, the Boston Public Library, the Massachusetts Historical Society, and the Fruitlands Museum Library for permission to quote from unpublished manuscripts in their collections, and also to the institutions that granted permission to reproduce the illustrations in this book.

I could not write about Fuller's parents without remembering my own. Helen and Samuel Kornfeld caught only a glimpse of the trajectories of their daughters' lives, but their hard work and dedication to their family continue to inspire me. I hope that this book honors their memory. Despite her very different interests and busy career, Sally Carol Kornfeld has always found time to listen to my stories about the women and men of the past. She was and is the best of sisters.

Without Tom and Anna, this enterprise would have been far less joyful. My husband, Tom Simpson, provided moral and technical support at crucial moments and learned more about Margaret Fuller than any physicist should know. From her second to her third birthday, Anna Kornfeld Simpson asked almost daily what Margaret Fuller was doing, diligently searched Fuller's books for the best pictures, and announced that she, too, was writing a book about Fuller. (Hers, I believe, was finished well before mine.) Together they supplied the hugs necessary to complete the project. This book is dedicated to them, with love.

Eve Kornfeld

Contents

Margaret Fuller

A Brief Biography with Documents

PART ONE

Minerva and the Muse

1

A Question of Identity

Pondering the remarkable presence of "the unquestionably haunting Margaret-ghost" fifty years after Margaret Fuller's death, the American author Henry James concluded that her mysterious power came from "having achieved, so unaided and so ungraced, a sharp identity." Yet as he attempted to describe Fuller, James presented not one but two "sharp" identities. First she was "the talker," a "sparkling fountain to other thirsty young" people in Boston. Then she was the activist, known for "her plentiful life, her active courage and company" in Rome. The disjunction between the two portraits seemed only to add to the fascination of the "Margaret-ghost" for James.[1]

Fuller's contemporaries, friends and foes alike, agreed that she was an unforgettable, central figure in early-nineteenth-century America. Many felt compelled to define her identity for themselves and for posterity. The philosopher and author Ralph Waldo Emerson considered her one of his "luminaries," a shining light in his intellectual circle. "Wise, sincere, accomplished, and most entertaining," she was "one of the noblest of women." Her mind and spirit so impressed him that he was unable to imagine anyone "more variously gifted, wise, sportive, eloquent, who seems to have learned all languages, Heaven knows when or how, — I should think she was born to them, — magnificent, prophetic, reading my life at her will."[2]

Not all of Fuller's contemporaries stressed her inner life in describing her. The educational reformer Bronson Alcott claimed her as "a citizen and a socialist, by virtue of constitution, or by womanhood; and here in this particular, she was less American than Greek." The women who convened at Seneca Falls, New York, in 1848 to launch the American women's rights movement, lauded Fuller's feminist activism and longed for her presence among them. Decades later, two of the leaders of the struggle for woman suffrage, Elizabeth Cady Stanton and Susan B. Anthony, dedicated their *History of Woman Suffrage* to her and eighteen other women "whose earnest lives and fearless words, in demanding political rights for women, have been, in the preparation of these pages, a constant inspiration to the editors." They concluded that Fuller had "possessed more influence upon the thought of American women than any woman previous to her time."[3]

Others were less certain how to describe Fuller. Although he had admired her in the early 1840s, the author Nathaniel Hawthorne later privately recorded his view that Fuller "was a great humbug; of course with much talent, and much moral reality, or else she could not have been so great a humbug." After denying her womanhood for years, he contended, she "proved herself a very woman, after all, and fell as the weakest of her sisters might." Conversely, the conservative writer and editor Orestes A. Brownson, never an admirer of Fuller, doubted very much that she was a true woman at all. He considered her "wholly deficient in a pure, correct taste, and especially in that tidiness we always look for in woman." The author Edgar Allan Poe shared Brownson's professed confusion about Fuller's gender identity, if not his unwavering contempt for her ideas. "She judges woman by the heart and intellect of Miss Fuller," Poe objected, "but there are not more than one or two dozen Miss Fullers on the whole face of the earth." Faced with such contradictions, Fuller's old friend, the financier Samuel Gray Ward, could only ask, "How can you describe a Force? How can you write the life of Margaret?"[4]

Few were content to leave the question unresolved. Fuller's identity was sharply contested even among her friends and admirers, who cut and pasted her letters and journals—and their memories of her—to shape her image after her death. Was she the detached, pure intellectual of Emerson's circle or the social activist whom Alcott saw? Was she the most inspiring woman of her time, as Stanton and Anthony believed, or one of the most confused, as Hawthorne suggested? Or was she scarcely a true woman at all, as Brownson contended? In a country and period in which traditional identities had been shaken by political revolution and economic transformation—in which one could apparently assume a new or "counterfeit" identity simply by moving to a new town, living on credit, or adopting the latest fashions—the question of identity was of central concern. And Margaret Fuller raised that question more forcefully than most.

She did so deliberately and self-consciously. Dissatisfied with the boundaries that her society drew around her own and others' identities, Fuller openly explored and questioned those cultural constraints that limited individual development. She did this in person: her conversations, friendships, and teaching were considered the most engaging and challenging of her time. Her writing also carried this spirit of inquiry to her many readers. Her essays and books repeatedly inscribed her own struggle for full self-realization and recorded her efforts to analyze that struggle in order to free herself and others.

Overcoming as best she could the pain that such self-revelation and analysis inevitably brought, Fuller insisted on confronting the issues squarely. As she reflected at age nineteen, "When disappointed, I do not ask or wish consolation, — I wish to know and feel my pain, to investigate its nature and its source; I will not have my thoughts diverted, or my feelings soothed; 'tis therefore that my young life is so singularly barren of illusions." Her lifelong effort to reconcile the demands of inner and outer worlds, of thought and action, of empathy and judgment, made Margaret Fuller a compelling and haunting presence.[5]

2

Childhood and Education

Sarah Margaret Fuller was born in Cambridgeport, Massachusetts, across the Charles River from Boston, on May 23, 1810, to a middle-class family. The period in which she lived was characterized by the social transformation and destabilization that accompanied rapid growth, mobility, commercialization, and urbanization. In the year of her birth, Boston's population numbered almost thirty-five thousand. Its ethnic homogeneity and cultural conservatism made it seem much smaller. "Here a man is not as in London, lost in an immense crowd of people, and thus hidden from the inspection of his fellowmen; but is known, and is conscious that he is known," a visiting minister noted approvingly in 1810. "His virtues, and his vices, his wisdom and his folly, excite here, much the same attention, and are examined in much the same manner, as in a country village." Over the next two decades the city filled with mobile strangers who, for good or ill, experienced little of this traditional closeness. With more than sixty thousand inhabitants by 1830, Boston had been overtaken by the anonymity and social fragmentation characteristic of modern cities and commercial capitalism.[6]

The deep economic and social changes of these years touched many areas of New England life. Among the new demands of the market economy were the movement of production and exchange away from the household, and the resulting stark division between the "outer world" and the "home." This disruption of the traditional domestic economy could also lead to a new kind of alienation as personal relations were increasingly confined to the home and productivity to the ever more impersonal, competitive outer world. Contemporaries adapted to these drastic changes largely by associating them with a specific set of gender roles. The home, now designated the "private sphere" of middle-class women and girls, became physically, economically, and culturally separate from the male workplace, or "public sphere."

This separation was justified in religious terms. The public world of markets, politics, power, wealth, and temptation was men's realm, but it

State Street, ca. 1840. In the heart of commercial Boston, State Street reflected the social and economic transformation of the city in the early Republic.

was decidedly not a world of virtue. To act in it effectively, it was thought, men had to relinquish their traditional roles as moral stewards. Women, who lost whatever little economic and social autonomy they had gained in the Revolutionary period, were granted instead an enormous but privatized moral and spiritual realm. From her sphere, the household, a woman was responsible for the transmission of religious and moral values and the maintenance of social stability. Women, from the chaste circle of the domestic fireside—and only from that circle—were the presiding moral spirits of the world. This cult of domesticity silently reversed earlier Puritan and American Revolutionary traditions, which had assumed the spiritual and moral superiority of men and had excluded women from religious leadership and political participation on those grounds.

The enlargement of women's "sphere" and its potent restrictions were both apparent in sermons of the early nineteenth century. "My desire is to aid the design of the gospel, by impressing the female part of my auditory with a sense of their *worth,* and of the importance of their character; with the sentiment that in the appropriate duties of their sphere they are most acceptably serving God," the Reverend Joseph Richardson preached to his congregation in Hingham, Massachusetts, in 1832. "The world expects of you stricter virtue and a nearer approach to perfection than it does of men. . . . It concedes to you the honor of exerting an influence, all but divine; but an influence you lose the power to exert, the moment you depart from the sphere and delicacy of your proper character." A true woman had no need of the "power to rule by authority," he reminded his female listeners. "The graces of purity, gentleness, kindness, modesty, constancy, sincerity, resignation, and of a meek and quiet spirit are your bright ornaments."[7]

Other aspects of early-nineteenth-century American culture also fostered the belief in a dualistic opposition of "masculinity" and "femininity," which divided not only the sexes in society but the entire cosmos as well. Popular literature and science supported the idea that men and women each had an inherent, essential nature. Women were compassionate, self-effacing, and mentally inferior; men were rational, selfish, and intellectually superior. To challenge gender roles and boundaries meant to be branded unnatural, for these cultural constructions were taken to be immutable, natural, and divinely ordained.

The different methods of educating boys and girls reinforced these essentialist beliefs. Language itself became divided according to gender. In the public schools and private academies that prepared them for college or careers, middle-class boys studied the classics, mathematics, natural science, history, and theology; they learned an aggressive language suitable for debate. Those middle-class girls who attended an increasing number of female academies or finishing schools studied literature, art, languages, dance, and music; they were taught a docile language intended to soothe and to smooth over controversy. The different interests, talents, and modes of expression of girls and boys, carefully cultivated during their formative years at home and at school, were then taken as further proof of the natural gulf between the male and female worlds.

Paradoxically, their construction of more rigid gender boundaries reconciled many middle-class Americans to the tremendous social changes and fluidity of the early nineteenth century. Developed by and for northern middle-class men and women to anchor their own identities in a world of flux, the doctrine of separate gender spheres also formed their standard for understanding and judging the lives of others. Gender norms allowed an elite threatened by political democratization and economic mobility to distinguish itself from the rest of society. Clearly articulated gender spheres became a mark of worth and civilization in a confusing world.

Thus Indians were perceived as "savage" because of their refusal to abandon communal economies (in which women participated and sometimes dominated) in favor of private property held by individual males. All too visibly for middle-class comfort, Indian women made decisions and did work that violated the cult of domesticity. Similarly, the poor were condemned as indolent, immodest, and immoral for their failure to separate family life from public life and to keep their women and children out of the workplace, off the streets, and in the home. They, too, seemed unwilling or unable to assume the polarized gender roles that many middle-class Americans considered most natural, most civilized, and most their own.

In looking back on her childhood, Margaret Fuller remembered her parents as virtual archetypes of the polarization of gender roles. Timothy Fuller, a graduate of Harvard College, a lawyer, and a politician, seemed "a man of business, even in literature." Contemporaries described him as assertive, earnest, highly responsible, argumentative, abrasive, intelligent, industrious, and ambitious, despite his dislike of "petty" business and democratic politics. To his daughter, he represented a paradigm of practical intellect lacking emotion and spirituality. "To be an honored citizen, and to have a home on earth, were made the great aims of existence," Margaret Fuller noted in retrospect. "To open the deeper fountains of the soul, to regard life here as the prophetic entrance to immortality, to develop his spirit to perfection — motives like these had never been suggested to him, either by fellow-beings or by outward circumstances."[8]

Her mother appeared to Fuller and many others to be "the green spot" of Timothy Fuller's life. Also intelligent and determined, Margarett Crane Fuller added grace, modesty, sweetness, humor, and playfulness to those attributes. "She was one of those fair and flower-like natures, which sometimes spring up even beside the most dusty highways of life — a creature not to be shaped into a merely useful instrument, but bound by one law with the blue sky, the dew, and the frolic birds," her daughter thought. "Of all persons whom I have known, she had in her most of the angelic, — of that spontaneous love for every living thing, for man, and beast, and tree, which restores the golden age." While Timothy Fuller pursued a legal and political career, she suggested, Margarett Crane Fuller cultivated her garden and the spiritual lives of her children.[9]

Yet Margaret Fuller herself was startlingly atypical in her society, for several reasons. Besides being bright and eager, she was somewhat removed from typical feminine socialization. She was her parents' first and, until her fifth birthday, only surviving child; a younger sister died in infancy in October 1813. Both of her parents lavished attention and affection on her in her earliest years. She came to identify with both of them.

Timothy Fuller, who quickly recognized his daughter's intelligence, became unusually involved in her education (suggesting that he may have been less completely "a man of business" than she believed). He had read appreciatively the educational theories of his political hero and model, Thomas Jefferson, as well as those of Benjamin Rush and other early American educational reformers. Following their precepts, he decided to raise his daughter to become a virtuous republican wife and mother: although she would not participate directly in public life, she should be ready and able to guide her future husband and sons toward moral, patriotic service to the nation. But he far exceeded the Founders' vision of a proper education for girls when he offered her a college preparatory education similar to his own.

He taught his daughter to read and write at the age of three and then gave her a rigorous classical education, including Latin and Greek, grammar, history, and mathematics. By age six, she was translating Virgil. The sentimental novels and etiquette books usually given to young girls were strictly forbidden, and all plays and novels were banned on the Sabbath; eight-year-old Margaret was once severely chastised for reading Shakespeare's *Romeo and Juliet* on a Sunday. Thus educated alone at home by her father in her earliest years, Margaret Fuller was cut off from the feminine subculture of sentimentality and docile language. Instead, under her father's watchful eye and impatient pressure during nightly recitations, she developed a confident language of analysis and debate. Exhausted and exhilarated in turn, the little girl learned to argue like a boy and to value intellectual achievement.

Fuller's biographers tend to discuss the development of her character chiefly in terms of her intellectual relationship with her father. But this was only one part of her formative childhood experiences. Timothy Fuller served in the U.S. House of Representatives, spending as much as six months of every year between 1817 and 1825 in Washington, D.C. Beyond her seventh year, then, Margaret Fuller communicated with her father mostly through letters. Although he continued to supervise her studies by mail, he was not the same commanding presence in her life; indeed, she often pleaded for more frequent letters from him. She spent most of her next eight years with her mother, surrounded by Margarett Crane Fuller's spirituality, country charm, and love of beauty. The importance of this relationship is perhaps most apparent in the nine-year-old's determination to substitute her middle name, Margaret, for her given first name, Sarah.

Often sick with headaches, the exhausted child took refuge from her father's academic demands and severe critiques in her mother's garden. It seemed a true paradise, where "the best hours" of a "lonely childhood" were spent. "Within the house everything was socially utilitarian; my books told of a proud world, but in another temper were the teachings of the little garden. There my thoughts could lie callow in the nest, and only be fed and kept warm, not called to fly or sing before the time," she recalled in her private journal. This nurturing environment required only quiet appreciation, not stressful action. It was unmistakably her mother's world: "I loved to gaze on the roses, the violets, the lilies, the pinks; my mother's hand had planted them, and they bloomed for me. I culled the most beautiful. I looked at them on every side. I kissed them, I pressed them to my bosom with passionate emotions, such as I have never dared express to any human being."[10]

With her mother, Fuller shared a concern for human relationships, a passion for parties and dancing, and a genuine interest in the trivialities of everyday life, for which her father had little patience. She also learned a language and ethic of care and connection from her mother, whose "sweet and gentle spirit" and "tender understanding sympathy" were widely praised. Unlike Timothy Fuller, who rarely mixed approbation with his unrelenting criticism of his daughter, Margarett Crane Fuller preferred not to "appear to be a severe judge, but a judicious *tender* mother" to her children. She acted on her belief that children responded best to open expressions of affection and concern. While Timothy corrected his daughter's letters and returned them to her with admonitions to improve her writing, Margarett inquired closely about her daughter's health and implored her to wear her flannels. As a result, Margaret Fuller "dared to express" herself most playfully, imaginatively, and tenderly with her mother, who also needed her help and care while her father was absent.[11]

Yet Margarett Crane Fuller, who had only an elementary education, could not fully appreciate the enchantment and stimulation that her daughter found in reading. Margaret Fuller often lost—and discovered—herself in books. Trying on the different identities that she encountered in fiction and nonfiction, mythology and history, she tested their possibilities and limitations. The characters in her books were literally role models for the child, as she acted out male and female heroic parts in games with her siblings and in letters to her friends. As she imagined herself inhabiting various situations and identities, her reading helped to shape her own emerging subjectivity.

At a very young age, Fuller learned to love the Romans and Greeks who filled her classical education. The preeminent heroes of her youth (and of her father's republican political vision) were the Romans of the classical republic, men of self-sacrifice and virtuous action. They taught her "what a man can become, not by yielding himself freely to impressions, not by letting nature play freely through him, but by a single thought, an earnest purpose, an indomitable will, by hardihood, self-command, and force of expression." They epitomized "man present in nature, commanding nature too sternly to be inspired by it, standing like the rock amid the sea, or moving like the fire over the land, either impassive, or irresistable; knowing not the soft mediums or fine flights of life, but by the force which he expresses, piercing to the center."[12]

In sharp contrast to these "manly" Roman citizens stood the thinkers and aesthetes of Greece, with whom Fuller also felt a great bond. She learned from the Greek language and mythology that "the law of life in that land was beauty, as in Rome it was stern composure." Here purposeful action, self-sacrifice, and forcefulness were valued less than quiet contemplation, moderation, and gracefulness, for "these Greeks, in an atmosphere of ample grace, could not be impetuous, or stern, but loved moderation as equable life always must, for it is the law of beauty."[13]

Some striking parallels began to form between the child's reading, her parents' gender roles (as far as she perceived them), and her developing sense of self. As the "Roman" side exemplified by her father became her outward identity, the "Greek" side, reflecting her mother's love of beauty and grace, drew inward. "My own world sank deep within, away from the surface of my life," she meditated years later. "But my true life was only the dearer that it was secluded and veiled over by a thick curtain of available intellect, and that coarse, but wearable stuff woven by the ages,— Common Sense."[14]

Pulled between contrasting gender roles and cultural ideals, Fuller felt the opposing parts of her personality to be in conflict from her early youth. She wanted and needed to overcome that dualism, but in an environment of rigid gender boundaries she could not readily find her path. Her private journal recorded her intense inner conflict: "A man's ambition with a woman's heart is an evil lot"; "One should be either private or public. I love best to be a woman; but womanhood is at present too straitly-bounded to give me scope. At hours, I live truly as a woman; at others I should stifle." Neither of her parents could guide her from her isolation and agony to a whole life; her father's assertive intellect and lack of grace were no more attractive alone than her mother's physical weakness and intellectual uncertainty.[15]

To add to his daughter's confusion, when she was thirteen Timothy Fuller began to express his fear that he had educated her too aggressively for her future role. Responding to his wife's traditional concern that "reading so many books and fragments of books enfeebles her mind" and made Margaret "awkward in company," he began to concentrate on his daughter's appearance and deportment. In a strategy certain to fail, he admonished her not to be self-conscious. "Your reluctance to go 'among strangers' cannot too soon be overcome," he wrote her. "With them you have a fair opportunity to *begin the world anew,* to avoid the mistakes and faults, which have deprived you of *some esteem,* among your present acquaintances." Dancing, singing, drawing, and taking piano lessons were added to her other studies, and she was sent to Miss Prescott's Young Ladies' Seminary in rural Groton for a year to quell her rebelliousness and fit her for marriage.[16]

Back in Cambridge in her late teens, Fuller led an active social life. Yet the young Harvard men who were drawn by her quick sympathy, enthusiasm, and intelligence were repelled by her intellectual ambition, sharp wit, and the ironic detachment that masked her insecurity. One of them privately recorded his fascination and perplexity after an afternoon with her: "Never at a loss to explain what to others is inscrutable, never blinded by appearances, with sentiments most noble and generous, with sympathies most wide, with reasoning powers most active and unshackled, standing free from all prejudice, with an understanding that masters the minutest details and an imagination that revels in the widest prospects," she seemed "the most remarkable of women." Still his discomfort remained. "I feel the expansion of her mind, & the decision of her opinions, & my own weakness and wants," he noted candidly. Her brilliant insights left him with "a very decided feeling of mental inferiority"; she never flattered his "vanity." He also realized that she was "not happy" to have "no sphere of action" for her intellectual powers. Not even bookish Cambridge was prepared for such an anomaly.[17]

Fuller's intense consciousness of the division within herself and of her society's disapprobation filled her early conversations and correspondence. "I have had tears for others' woes, and patience for my own,—in short, to climax this journal of many-colored deeds and chances, so well have I played my part, that in the self-same night I was styled by two several persons 'a sprightly young lady,' and 'a Syren'!!' she confided with characteristic self-consciousness and bitter irony to a young female friend in 1830. "Oh rapturous sound! I have reached the goal of my ambition; Earth has nothing fairer or brighter to offer. 'Intelligency' was nothing to it. A 'Supercilious,' 'satirical,' 'affected,' 'pedantic' 'Syren'!!!!" Thus she often stood outside of herself, watching herself perform and others interpret (and limit) her "part" in life. Her society's inability to find a space for young Margaret Fuller left her feeling fragmented, alienated, and alone.[18]

3

Spiritual Crisis and Vision

Margaret Fuller's loneliness and frustration with the social boundaries constricting her identity increased to an unbearable level in the summer of 1831. She felt "a treble weight" pressing down upon her, "the weight of deceived friendship, domestic discontent and bootless love." Many of her female and male friends (including the young man she thought she might love) were marrying and moving away from Boston, leaving her behind both physically and emotionally. In the fall of 1830, her fifteen-year-old brother Eugene entered Harvard College after years of tutoring by his abler older sister, who would never enjoy such an opportunity. Her father expected her to provide similar home schooling to her other five siblings for years to come. Unable to escape her "great burden of family cares" or an unwelcome immersion in "society," she felt "obliged to act my part [at home and in society] as well as I could."[19]

Her sense of desperation and futility deepened at the end of August. Without consulting anyone else's wishes, her father abruptly sold the family house in Cambridge. He wished to emulate his hero, Thomas Jefferson, as well as many members of Boston's commercial and professional elite, and retire to the countryside to farm and write his memoirs. While her mother grieved over the loss of friends, home, and garden, and the family lived temporarily with Timothy Fuller's dictatorial brother in what Margaret Fuller called a "prison," the true constraints of gender roles and the patriarchal family became all too clear to her. Not only would she never attend college, but she would soon be out of reach of the libraries, museums, concerts, and other sources of intellectual stimulation of the city.[20]

In her search for release from her constant migraines and isolation, for a world in which she could reconcile her emotional and aesthetic needs with her intellectual strengths, Fuller developed a singular spiritual vision. She did not plan or prepare for conversion, as was customary in New England. Rather, her spirituality emerged from a searing sense of alienation, an existential crisis, which peaked in November 1831.

It was Thanksgiving day, and I was obliged to go to church, or exceedingly displease my father. I almost always suffered much in church from a feeling of disunion with the hearers and dissent from the preacher; but today, more than ever before, the services jarred upon me from their grateful and joyful tone. I was wearied out with mental conflicts, and in a mood of most childish, child-like sadness. I felt within myself great power, and generosity, and tenderness; but it seemed to me as if they were all unrecognized, and as if it was impossible that they should be used in life. I was only one-and-twenty; the past was worthless, the future hopeless; yet I could not remember ever voluntarily to have done a wrong thing, and my aspiration seemed very high. . . . Today all seemed to have reached its height. It seemed as if I could never return to a world in which I had no place, — to the mockery of humanities. I could not act a part, nor seem to live any longer.[21]

From the depths of her depression that afternoon, Fuller experienced an epiphanic moment that focused her divided personality into one concentrated beam of energy. Characteristically, she found her release from social censure and division in nature, as she wandered alone in a deserted winter field that was transformed from a mirror of her tormented being into a "garden of God" still grander than that of her mother.

I paused beside a little stream, which I had envied in the merry fullness of its spring life. It was shrunken, voiceless, choked with withered leaves. I marvelled that it did not quite lose itself in the earth. There was no stay for me, and I went on and on, till I came to where the trees were thick about a little pool, dark and silent. I sat down there. I did not think; all was dark, and cold, and still. Suddenly the sun shone out with that transparent sweetness, like the last smile of a dying lover, which it will use when it has been unkind all a cold autumn day. And, even then, passed into my thought a beam from its true sun, from its native sphere, which has never since departed from me.[22]

Significantly, Fuller's epiphany brought insight into the limitations placed upon the individual's freedom to act. At the core of her mystical vision lay the hope of transcending the divided self. "I saw how long it must be before the soul can learn to act under these limitations of time and space, and human nature; but I saw, also, that it MUST do it, — that it must make all this false true, — and sow new and immortal plants in the garden of God, before it could return again," she wrote. "I saw there was no self; that selfishness was all folly, and the result of circumstance; that it was only because I thought self real that I suffered; that I had only to live in the idea of the ALL, and all was mine. This truth came to me, and I received it unhesitatingly; so that I was for that hour taken up into God."[23]

Fuller's dream of wholeness lasted well beyond this mystical moment of divine union. From this hour of crisis and faith, beyond church, doctrine, and the strictures of male ministers, she gradually developed a life-affirming, sustaining vision. "Since that day, I have never been more completely engaged in self; but the statue has been emerging, though slowly, from the block," she noted. "Others may not see the promise even of its pure symmetry, but I do, and am learning to be patient. I shall be all human yet; and then the hour will come to leave humanity, and live always in the pure ray." The radical upheaval in her sense of herself and her relationship with others freed her to envision a harmonious, whole personality. In future years, when she periodically felt herself playing "a part" dictated by others, her evolving spiritual vision of symmetry and wholeness would lift her out of crisis.[24]

The hallmark of Fuller's developing spirituality was its concept of an underlying unity that gave meaning and value to a multiplicity of forms. This concept involved a complex refutation of cosmic and social dualism. "A single thought transfuses every form; / The sunny day is changed into the storm, / For light is dark, hard soft, and cold is warm," she wrote. Rejecting the division of the world into good and evil, Fuller affirmed the reality of evil only to claim it as a force for good. Against the influential arguments of some contemporary liberal theologians and philosophers that one should never recognize evil and "that to imagine it possible to fall was to *begin* to fall," she countered that she "believed evil to be a good in the grand scheme of things. . . . In one word, she would not accept the world— for she felt within herself the power to reject it—did she not believe evil working in it for good! Man had gained more than he lost by his fall."[25]

Her unfolding spiritual vision also challenged the prevailing social construction of gender roles on very similar grounds. The division of humanity into strict gender spheres, Fuller believed, was ultimately unnatural, a partition of God's true essence. In poetic form (which she found most congenial for spiritual meditation) she protested, "There are [those] who separate the eternal light / In forms of man and woman, day and night; / They cannot bear that God be essence quite." She found the idea of God as Father too narrow and limiting. Her God was androgynous, possessing both masculine and feminine qualities. Such a deity demanded the full development of human potential in all its multiplicity.[26]

Another important aspect of Fuller's spirituality, and one with which she wrestled throughout her life, was her unshakable belief in the power of divine intuition. Derived in part from her epiphany and in part from her extremely rich dream life, her belief in her own intuition and her fascination with the occult seemed to many intellectuals a capitulation of the intellect. "It was soon evident that there was somewhat a little pagan about her," a male friend noted. "She had a taste for gems, ciphers, talismans, omens, coincidences and birth-days." This "fancy" seemed paradoxical in one whose intellectual and logical powers were so formidable. Yet Fuller's belief in intuition was consonant with her sense of the universe as a perpetually changing mystery, never to be completely deciphered or reduced to rational explanation.[27]

Fuller associated this mystical sense of intuition, or divine madness, with a feminine principle. In doing so, she placed herself and other women in a position close to the secret qualities of divine wisdom and vitality existing in the cosmos. She thus elevated the devalued feminine "underworld" of intuitive spirituality over the valorized masculine world of temporal power. Leila, one of Fuller's quasi-autobiographical figures, embodied this "overflow of the infinite" and functioned as a creative source for women. "And men called Leila mad, because they felt she made them so," she wrote. "Leila, with wild hair scattered to the wind, bare and often bleeding feet, opiates and divining rods in each over-full hand, walked amid the habitations of mortals as a Genius, visited their consciences as a Demon."[28] Certainly this assertion of superior female genius was vital to Fuller at certain moments, desperate as she sometimes was to locate a natural or divine source of creative power for women. Yet this was also a dangerous assertion, for it tended to reinforce the traditional association of femininity with irrationality.

However deeply she plunged for strength into this mystical underworld, Fuller remained strictly conscious of the importance of human relationships and history. As she reflected, "I can pray, I can act, I can learn, I can constantly immerse myself in the Divine Beauty. But I also need to love my fellow-men, and to meet the responsive glance of my spiritual kindred." For her, only the development of the individual and relationships among men and women could begin to realize the divine on earth. Her conviction of the primacy of this life worked against any desire for absorption in mystical unity with the divine. "No! we cannot leave society while one clod remains unpervaded by divine life," she insisted. "We cannot live and grow in consecrated earth, alone. Let us rather learn to stand up like the Holy Father, and with extended arms bless the whole world."[29]

Her desire to develop the immortal spirit in the mortal, material sphere — the affirmation of the historical world imbued with the divine essence — pulled Fuller away from simplistic solutions. "I am deeply homesick, yet where is that home?" she wondered. "If not on earth, why should we look to heaven? I would fain truly live wherever I must abide, [and bear] with full energy on my lot, whatever it is. . . . If I cannot make this spot of ground yield me corn and roses, famine must be my lot forever and ever surely." Thus Fuller resolved to continue her search for full human development on her "spot of ground." She would draw strength from her spiritual vision of creative female power and an androgynous deity.[30]

4

Inside and Outside Transcendentalism

In her twenties, fortified by her unfolding spiritual vision, Margaret Fuller developed close ties with a group of radical young ministers and intellectuals around Boston. Known as the Transcendentalists, these young men were trying to find meaning for their lives as they lost faith in Unitarianism, a recent liberal movement within the Congregational Church that had dominated New England since the Puritan settlement. They repudiated as "corpse-cold" their elders' formal, rational understanding of Christianity, yet they were also uncomfortable with contemporary evangelical Christianity's emphasis on scriptural revelation, emotional enthusiasm, and supernatural intervention. Denouncing those ministers of any sect who "presume to interfere in the communion of the soul with God, and limit the universal bounty of Heaven," the Transcendentalists called into question all traditional authorities. In their place, Ralph Waldo Emerson, Henry David Thoreau, George Ripley, Bronson Alcott, and the other young rebels sought divinity within themselves and nature.[31]

Their search led some of the most influential Transcendentalists to the contemporary German philosophical concept of *Bildung* or self-culture. Unfolding and cultivating the nobler elements of the self, they believed, would reveal the natural divinity of the human soul. To discover God and spiritual perfection, each person had only to look inward, to clear away the "error, vice and disease" of his "superficial or individual nature," and to learn to follow the deeper, purer laws of human nature. In their view, divine spirituality so pervaded the natural world that to know nature and one's own soul was to know God. Thus the true purpose of education or self-culture was to "sink what is individual or personal in us, to stimulate what is torpid of the human nature, and so to swell the individual to the outline of this Universal Man and bring out his original and majestic proportions."[32]

Paradoxically, then, the Transcendentalists hoped to rise above selfishness, isolation, and alienation through solitude and self-culture. In dedicating themselves to the inner life and exemplifying for others a divine, natural "law of growth," they expected to transform the social world. "Build, therefore, your own world," Emerson advised the readers of his first book. "As fast as you conform your life to the pure idea in your mind, that will unfold its great proportions. A correspondent revolution in things will attend the influx of the spirit." The self-reliant pursuit of individual growth and moral perfection, he concluded, would create new men and a new world.[33]

A common dissatisfaction with the existing world drew Fuller to the Transcendentalists. Of course, many of them shared her distrust of traditional religious institutions, authorities, and forms. In the most famous case, Emerson resigned as pastor of Boston's Second Unitarian Church in 1832 (four years before he met Fuller) because he felt that the ritual of communion no longer served his own or his congregation's spiritual needs; for him, it symbolized Christianity's historical "exaggeration of the personal, the positive, the ritual" and its neglect of the "doctrine of the soul." Several other ministers in the group suffered similar, if less public, crises of vocation and faith.[34]

Most of these young men also shared Fuller's frustration with the materialism and social fragmentation of busy nineteenth-century New England. Social relations and religious life alike were being poisoned, they feared, by an obsession with materialism and a mindless conformity. Theirs was a spiritual and cultural rebellion based on the value of the individual and the life of the mind. For a time, they encouraged Fuller's pursuit of individual development and provided her with a much-needed intellectual community.

This community sustained Fuller during her exile on the family's new farm in Groton, Massachusetts, where she shared the hated drudgery of farmwork with her mother, taught her younger brothers and sister in a home school, helped her father organize his papers, and studied German literature and philosophy whenever she could. Her new friends were even more important to her after her father's sudden death from cholera in October 1835. The family was left impoverished and dependent on Timothy Fuller's parsimonious brothers. As the oldest child, Margaret Fuller devoted herself once more to the physical and emotional care of her family and now resolved to support herself and to aid her family financially as well. In this situation, she felt the constraints of gender boundaries in a new way. In a society that offered middle-class women few employment opportunities—"we women have no profession except marriage, mantua-making and school-keeping," as she put it—she had to earn money. She also fervently hoped to keep her mind and spirit alive.[35]

It was not only her "worldliness" and limited opportunities that set Fuller apart from the other Transcendentalists, many of whom lived on professional incomes or inherited wealth. Although most of them deeply admired Fuller and enjoyed her company, few embraced her vision of the creative power of women. Treating her as a remarkable exception, most continued to hold a conventional view of gender spheres. "Marriage unites the severed halves and joins characters which are complements to each other," Emerson declared in a public lecture in 1838. "Man represents Intellect whose object is Truth, Woman Love whose object is goodness. Man loves Reality, woman order; man power, woman grace. Man goes abroad into the world and works and acquires. Woman stays at home to make the house beautiful."[36]

Behind this view lay the traditional belief that woman's nature was determined by biology. "I find them all victims of their temperament," Emerson wrote. "Nature's end of maternity, — maternity for twenty years, — was of so supreme importance, that it was to be secured at all events, even to the sacrifice of the highest beauty." Morally bracing as these sacrifices might be, the unexamined assumption was that few would desire such a destiny. Without self-consciousness, Emerson announced the birth of a friend's daughter with the casual comment "Though no son, yet a sacred event." (To which Fuller responded, "I do believe, O Waldo, most unteachable of men, that you are at heart a sinner on this point. I entreat you to seek light in prayer upon it.") The Transcendentalists' plans for the self-culture of "Universal Man" rarely included women. Despite their sincere admiration for Margaret Fuller, most of these maverick intellectuals were unable to transcend the gender constructions of their culture.[37]

Thus Margaret Fuller took her special place among the New England Transcendentalists. Situated often at the center of the group by virtue of her intelligence, spirit, and love of learning, she never quite lost the perspective of the periphery. She remained at once inside and outside of the privileged circle. Her complex double consciousness infused her developing thought with a productive tension and flexibility. It enabled her to question and redefine the central ideas of Transcendentalism, even as she participated in their creation. Keenly aware of the greater educational and professional opportunities enjoyed by the male Transcendentalists, she stood ready to contribute to, but also to criticize and enlarge, their vision of humanity.

Her unusual position allowed Fuller to experiment with her own ideas about the Transcendentalists' shared, central goal of self-culture. Rooted in her vision of an androgynous deity as well as in her personal understanding of the destructiveness of gender boundaries, her notion of self-culture involved the careful cultivation of all aspects of divinity—or true humanity—within every person. She considered those qualities or capacities labeled masculine (such as intelligence or critical judgment) and those called feminine (such as spirituality or empathy) equally necessary to complete humanity. Both intellect and affect should be developed as fully as possible within each individual, male or female, she held, and women's self-culture was as important and divine as that of men. Her teaching, literary criticism, and friendships in these years all reflected her effort to achieve harmony and wholeness by joining empathy with critical judgment, freedom with discipline, and beauty with power.

Since she considered either marriage or "mantua-making" personally impossible, Fuller began to teach school to earn her living after her father's death. Never content with material benefits alone, however, she also developed a pedagogy of self-culture for her young charges. She began as an assistant at Bronson Alcott's experimental Temple School in Boston in December 1836. While teaching Latin, French, and Italian, she observed Alcott's unusual teaching methods: inspired by some Swiss educational reformers' application of the concept of *Bildung,* Alcott substituted for traditional recitations more open Socratic conversations with the children, in hope of freeing their innate wisdom. Fuller, trained by her father in classical recitation, initially distrusted Alcott's method. She noted in her journal that there was "something in his philosophy which revolts either my common-sense or my prejudices, I cannot be sure which."[38]

Despite her continued dissatisfaction with the lack of discipline in the school, Fuller began to appreciate and modify Alcott's pedagogy. She embraced the idea of free discussion sufficiently to intervene in Alcott's teaching when she believed that he was leading the children too strongly "into an allegorical interpretation . . . when their own minds did not tend towards it." She also defended him against virulent, conservative attacks for allowing the children to air their views of the Gospel and human sexuality, although she wondered at his impracticality in publishing these unorthodox views. In her own teaching, she wished to achieve a finer balance between freedom and discipline. When she left the Temple School (which had only eleven students remaining following the withering public attacks on Alcott) without her promised salary in April, Fuller had developed the foundations of her pedagogy of self-culture.[39]

In June, Fuller moved to the Greene Street School in Providence, Rhode Island, where she taught for eighteen months. In charge of sixty girls and boys of "various ages and unequal training," she worked hard to be both "generous" and "just," to draw out her students' thoughts while correcting their errors. As she confided in a letter to Emerson, she depended principally on dialogue with her students to develop "activity of mind, accuracy in processes, constant looking for principles, and search after the good and beautiful." Through challenging class dialogues she hoped to emulate Alcott's "attempts to teach the uses of language and cultivate the imagination in dealing with young persons who have had no faculties exercised except the memory and the common, practical understanding," without encouraging the deplorable "impatience of labor" that she detected in Alcott's students. In her classes in rhetoric, poetry, history, natural history, Latin, French, and ethics, she also tried to teach intellectual independence and self-discipline.[40]

Fuller's attempts to foster active learning seemed revolutionary to her charges. The girls, who were excluded from participation in the school's public recitations, were surprised to learn that "it must not be our object to come and hear her talk," for "she could not teach us so, *we* must talk and let her understand our minds." Still more startling to them was her pronouncement that she never wished "a lesson learned by heart" in her classroom. "A lesson is as far as possible from being learned by *heart* when it is said to be, it is only learned by *body*," she explained. "I wish *you* to get your lessons by *mind*." She asked them to "*think* as well as *study*, and *talk* as well as *recite*." By example as well as precept, she encouraged her students to question everything, including their textbooks. Her two fundamental classroom rules were "Let nothing pass from you in reading or conversation that you do not understand, without trying to find out" its meaning and "Let not your age or shame of being thought ignorant prevent you from asking questions about things and words you do not understand." She demanded a great deal of her students and of herself.[41]

Alternately empathetic and critical, Fuller inspired more students than she frightened. The older girls were particularly appreciative of her efforts. "She is everything to me, — my teacher, my counsellor, my guide, my friend, my pillar on which I lean for support when disheartened and discouraged," one confided and many agreed. Especially important to these girls were the examples that Fuller provided of learned, accomplished women and her insistence that each of her students speak her mind and plan her future, contrary to prevailing gender conventions. One student noted in her school journal, "It makes me proud when I hear such things as this [an account of a female sculptor] for it shows what our sex is capable of doing and encourages us to go on improving and doing all we can to show that we are not entirely incapable of intellectual cultivation as some think." As another reported, this was precisely the lesson that their teacher intended them to learn: "She spoke upon what woman

A. Bronson Alcott's School of Human Culture. Drawing by Francis Graeter, the Temple School's drawing master, late 1830s. As a teaching assistant at Alcott's experimental Temple School in Boston in 1836–1837, Fuller began to develop her pedagogy of self-culture.

The Greene Street School of Providence, Rhode Island. While teaching at the Greene Street School in 1837–1838, Fuller fostered active learning and intellectual independence in her male and female students, challenging prevailing gender conventions.

could do — said she should like to see a woman everything she might be, in intellect and character." Fuller's pedagogy of self-culture thus challenged gender expectations in content as well as in process.[42]

The main problem with teaching, Fuller decided in the spring of 1838, was that it absorbed all of her time and energy. She found that she could not write: "What grieves me too is to find or fear my theory a cheat — I cannot serve two masters, and I fear all the hope of being a worldling and a literary existence also must be resigned — Isolation is necessary to me as to others. Yet I keep on 'fulfilling all my duties' . . . except to myself." In a lighter vein she noted, "I am as ill placed as regards a chance to think as a haberdasher's prentice or the President of Harvard University."[43]

This situation compounded Fuller's central anxiety: could she, a private woman, create a public role for herself through her writing? She was not certain whether she could write well enough to satisfy herself or a serious audience, or even whether any audience would take her writing seriously, but she knew that she could never succeed as an author in the interstices of schoolteaching. When she left the Greene Street School to return to Boston in December 1838, she dedicated herself to writing literary criticism. She hoped that she would be able to support herself, at least for a time, by the pen.

In her literary criticism as in her teaching, Fuller tried to apply her theory of self-culture as harmonious, androgynous development, by fusing empathy and critical judgment. The prevailing mode of literary criticism measured all works against an external (often moral rather than aesthetic) standard, and pronounced them acceptable or lacking in these terms. In her reviews and a theoretical essay called "A Short Essay on Critics," Fuller developed a radically different approach. She attempted to enter into the spirit of each work before her, to understand its central vision and potential value. Then she would judge, sometimes quite severely, the descriptive power, formal skill, energy, weight, and breadth of vision of the work and decide on its overall success in realizing its promise. Combining empathy and criticism, explication and judgment, her approach attempted to balance intrinsic and extrinsic aesthetic standards.

Most innovative was Fuller's refusal to dictate her readers' responses. She did not wish to become "an infallible adviser" about "what books are not worth reading, or what must be thought of them when read." "Wo[e] to that coterie where some critic sits despotic, intrenched behind the infallible 'We,' " she wrote, for such a "dictatorship in the reviewers" could only yield an "indolent acquiescence" in their readers. Rather, she invited her readers to engage seriously with the books under review. In her most daring and original literary criticism, she juxtaposed multiple critical perspectives on a work by portraying two or more characters in dialogue over its worth and then refused to resolve their differences. Individual readers might find value in different texts, or even discover different values in the same text, she suggested. Her criticism sought to open a conversation between reviewer and reader that would stimulate various readers to study each work for all that it could teach them about the world and their own souls.[44]

Fuller's most ardent literary criticism was written in defense of Goethe. Johann Wolfgang von Goethe (1749–1832) was Germany's most influential, prolific, and powerful modern writer. Playwright, novelist, and poet, he moved between romantic and classical forms with ease. In his old age, Goethe remarked that all of his art traced his inner development; each work formed a part of a single, long confession. Nature and individuality were at the center of that confession, in which neither Christianity nor social and political engagement figured. The pantheism and themes of sexual license and adultery in his literature, as well as widespread rumors of a long extramarital affair and illegitimate children in his personal life, led many of those Americans who knew his work to dismiss it summarily as dangerous and immoral.

Fuller was determined to counter this judgment. Not only had Goethe's work been crucial to her own intellectual and spiritual development, but, she was convinced, he was one of the world's greatest writers. When she began to teach herself German in 1831, she consumed six of his works within three months. From him she learned the doctrine of self-culture in its original form. While laboriously translating several of his works into English, she had been trying to collect material to write his biography, only to be frustrated by her inability to travel to Europe. Although she had heard some of the rumors about his personal life and deplored his use of a young female friend as a "tool" for his artistic growth and "a puppet show for his private entertainment," Fuller could not imagine a literary canon without the work of Goethe.[45]

In her reviews of Goethe's work, Fuller attempted to change the terms of the discussion. She decided that the popular objections to Goethe could be summarized in four simple statements: "He is not a Christian; He is not an Idealist; He is not a Democrat; He is not Schiller." Without disputing the accuracy of any of these judgments, and while admitting that she also had "looked in vain for the holy and heroic elements" in his work, she boldly insisted that these and all other external moral standards imposed by critics entirely missed the mark. "Most men, in judging another man, ask, Did he live up to our standard?" she wrote. "But to me, it seems desirable to ask rather, Did he live up to his own?"[46]

Her alternative approach was based on empathy and aesthetic judgment, as she tried to comprehend Goethe's own standard of self-culture and found him largely successful in reaching it. She praised his power as a writer, as an observer of nature and humanity, and as "a mind which has known how to reconcile individuality of character with universality of thought; a mind which, whatever be its faults, ruled and relied on itself alone; a nature which knew its law, and revolved on its proper axis, unrepenting, never bustling, always active, never stagnant, always calm." Her conviction that his art was important to her own and many other readers' self-culture added weight to her affirmation. She argued that such writing could not be immoral, and she challenged her readers to "draw their moral for themselves."[47]

Many of Fuller's literary reviews and essays were published in the Transcendentalists' journal, the *Dial,* which began publication in July 1840. In October 1839, Fuller agreed to serve as the *Dial*'s first editor. For the next two years, she shaped the journal's editorial policy along lines consonant with her theory of literary criticism and self-culture. She contrasted her broad editorial goal "to let all kinds of people have freedom to say their say, for better, for worse," with Emerson's narrower aim "to make a good periodical and represent your own tastes," as she put the journal into his hands in 1842. Her *Dial* tried "to afford an avenue for what of free and calm thought might be originated among us" and to stimulate each reader "to think for himself, to think more deeply and more nobly by letting [him] see how some minds are kept alive by a wise self-trust."[48]

Her preference for freedom of expression for contributors and her empathy with "all kinds of people" did not signal an end to discipline or critical editorial judgment. While she welcomed a variety of views, Fuller required vigorous writing, accurate information, and individuality of character in the pieces she accepted. She rejected or demanded revisions in contributions which she found insufficiently original, accomplished, or clear, even when they came from Henry David Thoreau or Ralph Waldo Emerson. Meanwhile, she coaxed poetry and essays from lesser known figures, including several female friends. In her editing as in her teaching, Fuller sought to balance freedom and discipline, empathy and judgment, as she quietly overturned conventional gender expectations of superior male creativity.

Throughout these years, Fuller pondered the meaning and value of friendship. In her middle-class circle, lifelong, intimate, emotionally charged, same-sex friendships were quite common. Female friends, like male friends, often confided their love for one another, missed each other deeply during separations, and shared the same bed when together, without raising doubts in themselves or anyone else about their heterosexuality. While at Harvard College in the early 1820s, for example, Ralph Waldo Emerson wrote to a college classmate, "Malcom, I love thee more than women love / And pure and warm and equal is the feeling / Which binds us and our destinies forever / But there are seasons in the change of times / When strong excitement kindles up the light / Of ancient memories."[49]

Fuller enjoyed close friendships with several women in this period, and she celebrated the equality of female friendship in an essay for the *Dial* entitled "Bettine Brentano and Her Friend Günderode." In an age that considered gender divisions stark and immutable, such relationships often seemed more natural, innocent, and simple than friendships between men and women. Fuller shared this conviction to some degree, noting in her private journal that love between women or men "is regulated by the same law as that of love between persons of different sexes, only it is purely intellectual and spiritual, unprofaned by any mixture of lower instincts, undisturbed by any need of consulting temporal interests, its law is the desire of the spirit to realize a whole which makes it seek in another being for what it finds not in itself." It was, she thought, "the same love that we shall feel when we are angels."[50]

Yet some of Fuller's female friendships defied any such simple characterization. Her long, close relationship with Caroline Sturgis and her shorter but even more intense relationship with Anna Barker were both marked at times by a possessiveness, erotic longing, testing, and suffering more typical of male-female romantic love of the period. Barker's engagement in 1840 plunged Fuller into despondency. Far from angelic, Fuller's friendships with women sometimes strained conventional limits in ways she could not acknowledge to herself. They could cause her great pain. More often than not, however, she found in them the support and encouragement she needed to think and to write.

While Fuller valued her female friends highly, she also sought a new level of intimate friendship with several men, including Ralph Waldo Emerson. This wish was often expressed during her extended visits at his and his wife Lidian's home in Concord. She treasured their friendship and revered Emerson's keen intellect, but she felt that he held back too much of himself. In both respects, he seems to have taken the place of Timothy Fuller in her life. Now, however, she was emboldened to protest the limits of the relationship. As Emerson worked on an essay called "Friendship" in 1840, Fuller pressed him to deepen and widen his imaginative exploration. "Mr. E. scarce knows the instincts," she contended in her journal. "And uses them rather for rejection than reception where he uses them at all. In friendship with R. W. E., I cannot hope to feel that I am his or he mine." With a particularly damning commercial metaphor, she concluded, "His friendship is only strong preference and he weighs and balances, buys and sells you and himself all the time." Her sense of his commercialism may have been related to Emerson's open practice of mining his correspondence and conversations with friends to write his public lectures and essays. He found Fuller quite useful in stimulating and shaping his thoughts and texts in this period; she wanted something more.[51]

Emerson was flattered, perplexed, and irritated by Fuller's pressure. Interpreting and dismissing her demands on him as an overreaction to the loss she felt at the impending marriage of two of her most beloved friends in October 1840, he did little to ease her pain. He answered her calls for greater empathetic connection with a rejection of any commitment that would bind his freedom. They lived on different planes and met as "foreign states," he told her in one letter. In another, he insisted, "There is a difference in our constitution. We use a different rhetoric. It seems as if we had been born and bred in different nations." In his private journal, he puzzled over "the barriers of difference" between them: "You would have me love you. What shall I love? Your body? The supposition disgusts you. What you have thought and said? Well, whilst you were thinking and saying them, but not now. I see no possibility of loving any thing but what now is, and is becoming; your courage, your enterprize, your budding affection, your opening thought, your prayer, I can love, — but what else?"[52]

In her response to Emerson, Fuller articulated the theory of friendship that she had been developing and practicing with her female and male friends for years. She interpreted his insistence on their difference, his utter refusal to empathize with her, as a failure of imagination and faith. "In me I did not think you saw the purity, the singleness, into which, I have faith that all this darting motion, and restless flame shall yet be attempered and subdued," she informed him. "I felt that you did not for me the highest office of friendship, by offering me the clue of the labyrinth of my own being. Yet I thought you appreciated the fearlessness which shrinks from no truth in myself and others, and trusted me, believing that I knew the path for myself."[53]

Again and again, Fuller emphasized Emerson's lack of vision (a quality that he prized highly in himself and others). "If you have not seen this stair on which God has been so untiringly leading me to himself, you have indeed been wholly ignorant of me," she argued. "Then indeed, when my soul, in its childish agony of prayer, stretched out its arms to you as a father, did you not see what was meant by this crying for the moon; this sullen rejection of playthings which had become unmeaning?" His desire to deify his friends and permit them no weakness or "childish agony" was "very noble but not enough for our manifold nature," she thought. While he believed "that we must love most the most beauteous," she felt "a deeper tenderness and even a higher hope" for her friends in moments of crisis and failure than "in the greatest perfection they ever attained." He closed his eyes to pain; she saw potential greatness in it.[54]

Friends, Fuller thought, trusted and cared for one another as parents did for children. As "ministering angels," they also guided each other toward full self-realization, "seeing the perfect through the imperfect" and "making it come there." Her sense of the inestimable value of personal intimacy clashed strongly with Emerson's calculation of its high cost. "Almost all people descend to meet," he wrote in 1840. "All association must be a compromise, and, what is worst, the very flower and aroma of the flower of each of the beautiful natures disappears as they approach each other. What a perpetual disappointment is actual society, even of the vir-

Ralph Waldo Emerson. Steel engraving by Stephen Alonzo Scheff, after Samuel Worcester Rowse. Their long, intense friendship nourished the intellectual development of both Fuller and Emerson, although not always along similar lines. Emerson claimed that Fuller's conversation was the most brilliant and stimulating of the period.

tuous and gifted!" She could not understand his periodic reluctance to "study [his friends'] visions, lest [he] lose [his] own." For Fuller, true friends "not only know themselves more, but *are* more for having met, and regions of their being, which would else have laid sealed in cold obstruction, burst into leaf and bloom and song."[55]

Empathy, or a willingness to enter into the other's spirit, was the first step in the sort of relationship that Fuller envisioned, for each person's "labyrinth of . . . being" was individual and distinct. One had to sense it through instinct, intuition, and sympathy. Critical judgment was then needed to discern when a friend was straying from his or her own path to divinity. Fuller did not seek uncritical sympathy from her intimate friends, nor did she give it; she never hesitated to correct what she perceived as a serious misstep in a friend's development, and she hoped that her friends would do the same for her. "I did not well understand what you felt, but I am willing to admit that what you said of my 'over-great impetuosity' is just," she told one steady correspondent. "You will, perhaps, feel it more and more. It may at times hide my better self. When it does, speak, I entreat, as harshly as you feel. Let me be always sure I know the worst. I believe you will be thus just, thus true, for we are both servants of Truth." Only by joining empathy and judgment, the emotional and the rational, she thought, could one perform the "highest office of friendship," to discover, nurture, guide, and love a friend's individuality or soul.[56]

Several prominent Transcendentalists attested to Fuller's success in realizing her own vision of friendship. One of her closest male friends, the Unitarian minister James Freeman Clarke, claimed that she had revealed "the worth and meaning of Life" to him. "Whatever we owe to those who give us confidence in ourselves, who make us believe we *are* something distinct and can do something special, who arouse our individual consciousness by an intelligent sympathy with tendencies and feelings we ourselves only half understand—all this I owe to you," he declared. "You gave me to myself." Another Unitarian minister, William Henry Channing, relied on her during a crisis of faith. He believed that she had "done more to unfold my buried nature than any friend." Ednah Dow Cheney described Fuller's "wonderful influence" on her female friends in remarkably similar terms: "She opened the book of life and helped us to read it for ourselves."[57]

On more than one occasion, Emerson himself quietly paid tribute to Fuller's unusual capacity for friendship. Although critical of her impatience, her carelessness, and her affinity for gossip, he craved her sociability, insight, and provocation. In March 1843, after a long separation from her, he borrowed her own words to reflect in his journal, "Beside her friendship, all other friendships seem trade, and by the firmness with which she treads her upward path, all mortals are convinced that another road exists than that which their feet know." She was, he concluded, an "inspirer of courage, the secret friend of all nobleness, the patient waiter for the realization of character, forgiver of injuries, gracefully waiving aside folly, and elevating lowness, — in her presence all were apprised of their fettered estate and longed for liberation, of ugliness and longed for their beauty; of meanness, and panted for grandeur."[58]

Despite their appreciation of her extraordinary friendship, however, very few of Fuller's friends were able to reciprocate in kind. As Emerson acknowledged sadly, "You have a right to expect great activity great demonstration and large intellectual contributions from your friends, and tho' you do not say it you receive nothing. As well be related to mutes as to uncommunicating egoists." While he undoubtedly exaggerated here, he correctly sensed her disappointment that the Transcendentalists generally failed to embrace her ideal of friendship or to meet her emotional and intellectual needs. In private, she mourned her "isolation" in the midst of her friends: "No one loves me. But I love many a good deal, and see some way into their eventual beauty." At times she believed "that I was always to return to myself, to be my own priest, pupil, parent, child, husband, and wife." Such complete self-reliance often seemed chilling to Fuller. She continued to yearn for intimate friends who could see and sympathize with her special path, even if she had not yet discovered it herself.[59]

In expecting both empathy and judgment from her friends, Fuller asked them to ignore the customary association of empathy with women and judgment with men. Artificial gender boundaries had to be crossed fearlessly, she believed, to assist a friend in her or his quest for wholeness and self-culture. One had to be mother and father alike to one's friends. On several levels, then, Fuller's conception of friendship mirrored the central ideas of her pedagogy and literary criticism. In each of these areas, she acted "a 'foe' in [the] friend," subtly pushing the Transcendentalists toward broader formulations of self-culture and humanity.[60]

Fuller's most explicit challenge to conventional attitudes came in her articulation of the unjust limitations on the development of women in her own society. Her ever clearer perception of the dichotomy between the autonomy of men and the dependence of women in society grew only in part out of her childhood and adolescent experiences. Besides teaching young girls various academic subjects that they could not incorporate into their adult lives (a faint echo of her own situation), she had begun tutoring women who left their domestic duties for a few hours of instruction each week to learn some of what their husbands had learned in school. With her greater immersion in society, her sense of being a creature apart, uniquely situated and not made for this earth, fell away to a more universal analysis of patriarchy and gender.

Gradually Fuller realized that women's isolation in a devalued domestic sphere was a common experience in middle-class American society and that these women's inner strength palsied for lack of self-expression and community support. "Woman is the flower and man is the bee," she wrote. "She sighs out melodious fragrance, and invites the winged laborer. He drains her cup, and carries off the honey. She dies on the stalk; he returns to the hive, well fed, and praised as an active member of the community." Fuller's rising gender consciousness thus summoned the Transcendentalists to broaden their vision of a community of autonomous individuals, and to begin at home.[61]

Fuller did not limit herself to theoretical statements on this subject. As her concern for the women around her grew, she determined to build a community for them. She established a Conversation Club for women in November 1839 in Boston and continued the highly successful experiment until she left New England in 1844. Forming in some respects the female parallel to the largely male Transcendental Club (which met about thirty times between 1836 and 1840 to consider broad philosophical and cultural developments and controversies), Fuller's Conversations invited women to discuss "What were we born to do? How shall we do it?" and other large questions "which so few ever propose to themselves 'till their best years are gone by." She envisioned a cooperative effort, in which "well-educated and thinking women" might "state their doubts and difficulties with hope of gaining aid from the experience or aspirations of others" and learn together how to build "the life of thought upon the life of action."[62]

The first thirteen-week Conversation series attracted twenty-five women; more than two hundred women attended one or more of the series that Fuller offered each fall and spring for five years. Most were the wives, fiancées, daughters, or sisters of the Transcendentalists and local dignitaries. Frequently in attendance were Eliza Quincy (married to Josiah Quincy, the president of Harvard), Eliza Farrar (the wife of Harvard's Professor John Farrar), Mary Channing (the Reverend William Ellery Channing's daughter), Mary Peabody (engaged to Horace Mann), Sophia Peabody (engaged to Nathaniel Hawthorne), Maria White (engaged to James Russell Lowell), Lidian Emerson, Sophia Ripley, and Lydia Cabot Parker (all married to prominent Transcendentalists), as well as Sarah Clarke (the sister of James Freeman Clarke), Elizabeth Hoar, Elizabeth Peabody, Lydia Maria Child and various other Boston abolitionists, and some of Fuller's old friends and former students. The fees that Fuller charged to lead the Conversations allowed her to support herself and assist her family for most of this period.

The Conversations drew upon Fuller's pedagogy of self-culture as well as her sense of the artificiality and harmfulness of gender conventions. She hoped that open discussion of philosophical and social issues would lead women to explore their hidden resources and develop their own voices. Women needed, she argued, to "lay aside the shelter of vague generalities, the cant of coterie criticism and the delicate disdains of *good society* and fearless meet the light although it flow from the sun of truth." She invited the women who attended to shed their feminine socialization and to think of themselves first as intelligent human beings. The relative failure of her third series of Conversations in 1841, the only set open to men, confirmed her belief that the presence of men inhibited the women's free expression, growth, and self-realization.[63]

Fuller's goals were thus spiritual and social as well as intellectual. Her first series in 1839–1840 introduced the question of the range and depth of women's spiritual and intellectual power; this was the implicit or explicit subject of most of the series. She often opened the two-hour sessions with examples from mythology and history of female power and creativity. She wanted no silent observers in the group and insisted that "those who do not talk will not derive the same advantages with those who openly state their impressions and consent to learn by blundering as is the destiny of Man here below." In learning to speak their minds and to respect themselves and each other, she believed, women could aspire to realize their divine potential. Their deep wisdom and divine intuition could emerge as purpose and activity, as they collectively claimed a power to re-create themselves and the world. In the process, some central gender conventions and expectations would be overturned and exposed as artificial and meaningless. In this context, self-culture would also bring social transformation.[64]

Fuller saw herself as "truly a teacher and a guide" in these Conversations. She did not wish to dominate the sessions. "My wish has been more & more to purify my own conscience when near them, give clear views of the aims of this life, show them where the magazines of knowledge lie, & leave the rest to themselves & the Spirit who must teach & help them to self-impulse," she reflected. Renowned for her ready sympathy, wit, and brilliance in private conversation, she drew out the democratic and feminist implications of a form that (unlike a lecture) shared authority among many speakers. She was flexible and nurturing, but also a conscience and force for change, as she encouraged wide participation, connected ideas, demanded clarity and precision of expression, and "repelled the sentimentalism that took away woman's moral power of performing stern duty." No doubt she was also a role model for many.[65]

The participants in the Conversations generally admired Fuller's "courage, ability, self-possession and grace" and welcomed her interventions. "Though she spoke rudely searching words and told you startling truths, though she broke down your little shams and defenses, you felt exhilarated by the compliment of being found out, or even that she had cared to find you out," a frequent participant explained. If the Conversations never quite fulfilled Fuller's own need for intellectual stimulation—never drove her "home for ammunition; never put [her] to any expense; never truly called [her] out"—they did place her firmly in the center of a circle of supportive female friends. For Fuller, this was an unusually secure position from which to broaden and develop the Transcendentalists' vision. "Our last meeting yesterday was beautiful," she wrote in 1844. "How noble has been my experience of such relations for six years now, and with so many, and so various minds! Life *is* worth living—is it not?"[66]

In some respects, Fuller's Conversation Club resembled the many popular reform societies that appeared in the wake of the period's widespread evangelical revivals. Women took a leading role in the Benevolent Empire, as the great network of these societies was called. They attempted to awaken their contemporaries to various pressing social problems, to eradicate sin and corruption, and to prepare the way for the millennium. In the process, these middle-class women could incidentally increase their social power, barred though they were from formal positions in political, economic, or religious institutions. Building upon the widely acclaimed moral influence of virtuous women, these female reformers left their firesides for the streets, all in the name of restoring social order.

Fuller's Conversations shared the Benevolent Empire's emphasis on individual responsibility rather than structural change and thus appeared similarly to support the middle-class social order. Yet Fuller went further than most popular reformers of her day in seeking to empower women for their own sake rather than for some external end (such as abolishing slavery, redeeming drunkards, ending prostitution, or promoting bran diets). She openly advocated liberation for women, not the restoration of social order. In this way, she stood apart from the general reform movement, even as she guided her Conversations to more explicitly social and political topics. Her social goal, linked to her Transcendental spiritual vision of full self-development for all people, was potentially far more subversive and radical than most. As Elizabeth Cady Stanton, who participated in one of Fuller's winter series, insisted decades later, the Conversations were "in reality a vindication of woman's right to think."[67]

The concerns and material of her Conversations increasingly shaped Fuller's writing. Here, too, she moved between mythology and history, aesthetic and social issues, as she experimented with different forms and voices, searching for those in which she would not "palsy" as a woman artist. She contributed a variety of literary pieces and social criticism to the *Dial*. Often these informed each other, as her social criticism drew out the feminist implications of her mystical meditations on female creativity and spiritual power. Beauty and intelligence came together to make the power of women "secret, radiant, profound ever, and never to be known," she rhapsodized in "The Magnolia of Lake Pontchartrain." "All the secret powers are 'Mothers.' There is but one paternal power."[68]

This feminist perspective, developed in Fuller's teaching, literary criticism, friendships, and Conversations over the years, was most clearly articulated in her long essay of 1843, "The Great Lawsuit: Man *versus* Men; Woman *versus* Women." Expanded and published in 1845 as *Woman in the Nineteenth Century*, this would be her most important and famous book and one of the most significant achievements of the Transcendentalists. It would also be Fuller's valedictory address to Transcendentalism and New England.

5

Turning "All to Muse"

Before undertaking the revision and expansion of "The Great Lawsuit," Margaret Fuller took a long-anticipated and well-deserved vacation. In the summer of 1843 she toured the Great Lakes, Illinois, and the Wisconsin Territory by steamboat and covered wagon with friends. Beginning at Niagara Falls, she went as far north as Mackinac Island, as far west as Milwaukee, and as far south as Pawpaw, Illinois. It was the greatest distance she had ever traveled, and she relished the opportunity to explore the West. Schooled in Jeffersonian philosophy by her father, she expected to be moved and inspired by natural wonders and the frontier spirit.

Yet Fuller was not at all prepared for the intensity or character of her reaction to western society. "When I have been in the country, its beauty has filled me with rapture, but among *men* oh, how lonely!" she wrote from Chicago to a friend. "I have earnestly wished to see things as they are, and to appreciate the great influences which are at work here at their just value. But they seem to me to tend so exclusively to bring the riches out of the earth; should that task ever have a long period *exclusively to itself?*" She was "silenced by these people" who appeared to her to be "all life and no thought," content with a "merely instinctive existence." Despite ample "good will," she found that her powers of empathy and judgment operated quite unexpectedly during the trip. She was drawn to the perspective of the isolated, hardworking, homesick women she encountered and critical of the materialism and utilitarianism of their husbands.[69]

Upon her return to Boston in the fall, Fuller decided to write a book about her journey. Travel books by men and women sold very well at the time and she clearly hoped to profit from a popular genre. She also wished to transform it. Rather than chronicling the physical details of her trip, she would trace her inner journey of discovery. "I have not been particularly anxious to give the geography of the scene," she commented, professing not even to know how many miles she had traveled. "What I got from the journey was the poetic impression of the country at large; it is all I have aimed to communicate." She wanted her readers to understand her experience empathetically and then to analyze its roots. To complete her own analysis, she obtained unprecedented permission to conduct research in the library of Harvard College. There she worked "day after day, under the covert gaze of the undergraduates who had never before looked upon a woman reading within those sacred precincts." In this inhospitable atmosphere, *Summer on the Lakes, in 1843* was born.[70]

The book opened with Fuller in the role of the eager, middle-class American tourist, whose expectations had been shaped by her culture. "I knew where to look for everything, and everything looked as I thought it would," she noted with "a quiet satisfaction." Stopping first at Niagara Falls, she gazed obediently at this great natural wonder, prepared to experience inspiration. Her culture's standard images of awe and "undefined dread" filled her imagination: "For continually upon my mind came, unsought and unwelcome, images, such as never haunted it before, of naked savages stealing behind me with uplifted tomahawks; again and again this illusion recurred, and even after I had thought it over, and tried to shake it off, I could not help starting and looking behind me." At the beginning of her inner and outer journey, this image reveals, she saw herself as the civilized insider at once threatened and riveted by the "savages" who inhabited the West. She felt powerless to escape her culture's images and expectations.[71]

Almost immediately, Fuller's posture shifted. She had seen too many descriptions and reproductions of the Falls to thrill to their sublimity; their commercialization had made them appear old and tired. Moreover, as she tried to recapture that lost sense of innocence, an unknown American robbed her of it forever. While she was seated in her favorite spot, "a man came to take his first look. He walked close up to the fall, and, after looking at it a moment, with an air as if thinking how he could best appropriate it to his own use, he spat into it." With that contemptuous gesture, he simultaneously claimed the place as his own and deprived Fuller of a more passive, aesthetic enjoyment of it.[72]

In that instant, Fuller moved a considerable distance from cultural insider to outsider. Her phantom of the savage Indian dispelled, she was increasingly ready to empathize with the dispossessed and to criticize those who would exploit people and despoil nature in the name of utility or progress. It grieved her to hear the "immigrants who were to be the fathers of a new race" all talking "not of what they should do, but of what they should get in the new scene. It was to them a prospect, not of the unfolding nobler energies, but of more ease, and larger accumulation." She searched the frontier in vain for men of true vision and balance:

"When will this country have such a man? It is what she needs; no thin Idealist, no coarse Realist, but a man whose eye reads the heavens while his feet step firmly on the ground, and his hands are strong and dexterous for the use of human implements." Rather, she found that the American settlers' preoccupation with utility and material progress corrupted all that they touched and destroyed America's chance to create spiritual and social progress in its westward expansion.[73]

That a man dispossessed a woman of her enjoyment of nature in the book's dramatic opening gesture was no accident. Primed by her personal experiences and her Conversation Clubs, Fuller was acutely aware of the stultifying effect of conventional gender relations. She had hoped to find both frontier men and women liberated from their artificial gender spheres. She desperately wanted to believe in the "power uncommon characters will always exert of breaking down the barriers custom has erected round them." She learned instead that the American settlers had carried their gender definitions with them as they moved west, profoundly inappropriate as those definitions were to their new situation. Still girls were educated to be decorative rather than strong and able; still men were ruinously unappreciative of the aesthetic beauty that surrounded them; still the intellectual and spiritual power of women withered under rigid gender conventions.[74]

Perhaps recalling her mother's misery at leaving her home in Cambridge for rural Groton, Fuller sympathized deeply with the frontier women who had reluctantly followed their husbands westward only to suffer isolation and deprivation. These women seemed to become virtual captives in their new homes: trapped by codes of domesticity and inadequate educations, they were unable to escape their endless domestic duties even long enough to enjoy the beauty of the prairie. Fuller's attention to their experiences, as well as her unusual decision to insert a quasi-autobiographical fiction into the heart of the book, attested to her empathy. The story of Mariana, whose intelligence and spirit were tragically suppressed first by the conformist pressures of a girls' school and then in an unequal marriage, demonstrated Fuller's ability to imagine herself in the place of the women she encountered and to analyze their situation in terms of "the defect in the position of woman."[75]

Feeling the pain of frontier women and analyzing the gender constructions that entrapped them led Fuller to wonder who else might be suffering in this patriarchal society. Gradually, *Summer on the Lakes* began to consider the experiences of Indians, whom Fuller found huddled in encampments on the lakes, wandering homeless in Milwaukee, and gathered at Mackinac Island to collect their annual payment from the government. Dispossessed of their land, they seemed impoverished spiritually and materially; at times they were reduced to begging or performing for their subsistence. She observed that white men hated the Indians with an intensity reserved for those whom they knew they had wronged. Moreover, even those white women who struggled futilely against the dirt of the frontier, Fuller noted with bitter irony, loathed these "hapless owners of the soil" for "their dirt, their tawny skins, and the vices the whites have taught them."[76]

Fuller tried to resist those "inherited prejudices" that pulled her and her contemporaries to interpret the Indians' degradation as a natural consequence of their lack of "civilization." Applying the principles of her literary criticism to her encounter with those her peers considered most "savage," she decided that the Indian too must be met with a "sympathizing spirit" and judged "by his own standard." Even in their oppressed state and in the hopelessly distorted accounts of white historians and traders, she caught "a glimpse of what was great in Indian life and Indian character," including heroism, nobility, self-sacrifice, virtue, and faith.[77]

Particularly as she conversed with Indian women who invariably seemed gentle, courteous, dignified, and weary, Fuller's heart and mind went out to them. Her sympathy further complicated her analysis. Unable entirely to resist "inherited prejudices," she thought these women more subjugated in their society than white women were in hers. She saw no promise of equality in their apparently unrelieved drudgery, as they did the work of white men in addition to that of white women, all under the most squalid conditions and extreme poverty. Try as she might, she simply could not assess gender relations among the Indians by their "own standard."

Unlike most of her predecessors and contemporaries, however, Fuller did not use this judgment against Indian gender relations to establish the superiority of American civilization. Rather, she began to explore the analogies between the social positions of Indians and white women. "Has the Indian, has the white woman, as noble a feeling of life and its uses, as religious a self-respect, as worthy a field of thought and action, as man?" she asked in terms that recalled her own adolescent crisis. "If not, the white woman, the Indian woman, occupies an inferior position to that of man." Deep were the "sorrows of unequal relations," wherever they were found.[78]

Ultimately Fuller rebuked American missionaries, politicians, and citizens for their hypocrisy in preaching civilization to those they exploited. She warned with apocalyptic fervor, "Yet let every man look to himself how far this blood shall be required at his hands." Without much hope of redemption, she demanded that American statesmen "save us from sinning still more deeply" against the Indians and that "every man and every woman, in their private dealings with the subjugated race, avoid all share in embittering, by insult or unfeeling prejudice, the captivity of Israel." Fuller had journeyed far from her initial fear of "savage" Indians, although her fatalism about their eventual extinction tempered the radicalism of her critique. Still convinced of the inevitability of American expansion westward, she was less sanguine about its results. The problems of American expansion now seemed much more complex and intractable to her and the dream of progress much more remote.[79]

Following the publication of her first book in May 1844, Fuller turned to the promised revision of "The Great Lawsuit." Once again, deep anxieties about her ability to create and fill a public role as a serious woman author surfaced as she prepared to write; now they were augmented by her fear of public censure for addressing political topics forbidden to women. There was also personal pain involved in analyzing, directly and at length, "the defect in the position of woman." Family pressures and disappointing friendships continued to weigh heavily upon her, causing her to reflect in her private journal that "life begins to press with her iron glove."[80]

Yet Fuller worked through her pain. She determined to "turn all to Muse," to use her own suffering to further her understanding of the harm of conventional gender divisions. Turning often to poetry to explore and express these insights, she composed more than thirty long, complex poems during the summer and fall of 1844. This poetry wrestled with her private demons and invoked a heterodox group of goddesses, including Leila, Diana, Hecate, the Sphynx, Isis, and the Virgin Mother. Fuller seems to have summoned these powerful female figures for inspiration, drawing on their undeniable creativity to recover her balance, strength, and positive spiritual vision.[81]

Fuller's success in turning "all to Muse" was apparent in her next book—her second in eight months. In a sense, *Woman in the Nineteenth Century* can be read as the optimistic, visionary counterpart to *Summer on the Lakes*. While the latter had concluded bleakly that America's westward expansion had not produced the individual freedom, spiritual progress, or social harmony of the Jeffersonian dream, Fuller's new book attempted to chart a different course toward harmonious social relations and full individual development. Significantly, her new hopes for American progress centered on the liberation of women and men from the constraints of prevailing gender categories.

Rooted in Fuller's searing experience of the divided self, *Woman in the*

Nineteenth Century reflected her thirst for harmony and wholeness. The book depicted a disunified and fragmented world and humankind's capacity to change that world. Yet, as her earlier, preferred title in the *Dial* indicated, she did not intend to catalog women's grievances against male tyranny. She refused to portray women as the oppressed victims of a patriarchal society. Rather, she "aimed to show that no age was left entirely without a witness to the equality of the sexes in function, duty and hope." Further, she claimed that men and women alike suffered impoverished lives in contemporary American society, because women's full development was thwarted. "I believe that the development of the one cannot be effected without that of the other," she explained, for man and woman were "the two halves of one thought." Fuller's feminism took shape as a call for human solidarity and mutual development.[82]

This broad feminist vision was far from quietistic or passive. As she had over the years in her Conversations, teaching, and friendships, Fuller boldly contested widely held, essentialist notions of gender differences. Persistence, courage, and creativity were not exclusively men's traits, she argued, nor were nurturance and self-sacrifice purely those of women. Nature "sends women to battle, and sets Hercules spinning; she enables women to bear immense burdens, cold, and frost; she enables the man, who feels maternal love, to nourish his infant like a mother." There was no doubt in her mind that presently nature "will make a female Newton, and a male Syren."[83]

Fuller theorized that within all human beings, as within the androgynous deity of her spiritual vision, both "feminine" and "masculine" qualities existed. Societies divided that which nature had joined. "It is no more the order of nature that it ["Femality"] should be incarnated pure in any form, than that the masculine energy should exist unmingled with it in any form," she declared. "Male and female represent the two sides of the great radical dualism. But, in fact, they are perpetually passing into one another. Fluid hardens to solid, solid rushes to fluid. There is no wholly masculine man, no purely feminine woman." Unable to escape her culture's division of the universe into "masculine" and "feminine" characteristics, she subverted it by insisting upon the natural permeability of the gendered "great radical dualism." In this passage and throughout her book, Fuller dared to redefine human character for nineteenth-century America.[84]

Alluding to ancient mythology, Fuller called the two basic elements of human character coexisting within woman "Minerva" and the "Muse." The Muse was "electrical in movement, intuitive in function, spiritual in tendency," the "unimpeded clearness of the intuitive powers which a perfectly truthful adherence to every admonition of the higher instincts would bring to a finely organized human being. It may appear as prophecy or as poesy." As she had since her own epiphany, Fuller thought women to be "especially capable" of this mystical, creative "sight of the world of causes, this approximation to the region of primitive motions." Far from passive or submissive (two characteristics of the "true woman" in the conventional view), the Muse provided women with a "magnetic or electric" source of creativity and power.[85]

Ever present within women, too, was the "masculine" energy of Minerva. Minerva was the source of "intellectual power" and "practical reason." Less poetic or prophetic than the Muse, this element in women's character inspired logical reasoning and forceful prose. It was as natural to woman as the Muse. "The growth of man[kind] is two-fold, masculine and feminine," she explained. "As far as these two methods can be distinguished, they are so as Energy and Harmony. Power and Beauty. Intellect and Love. Or by some such rude classification, for we have not language primitive and pure enough to express such ideas with precision." Destabilizing the "rude" (and perhaps ultimately indistinguishable) categories of gender difference even as she reinscribed them, Fuller claimed the "masculine" qualities of energy, power, and intellect for women as Minerva.[86]

If only these complementary elements were allowed to develop freely and fully within each individual man and woman, Fuller held, the frustrations of the divided self would evaporate. Conflicts within and between individuals would cease: "There cannot be a doubt that, if these two developments were in perfect harmony, they would correspond to and fulfil one another, like hemispheres, or the tenor and bass in music." Even those men who continued to display predominantly "masculine" qualities and those women in whom "feminine" characteristics prevailed would perceive "the law of their common being" as they reached their individual "true proportions." With "a clearer recognition of truth and justice," both commonalities and differences could be celebrated. "There would be unison in variety, congeniality in difference." Social harmony would replace gender domination, strife, and contention. The divine will would be done.[87]

In a powerful central image, Fuller envisioned a new kind of marriage. Decrying traditional hierarchical notions of wedlock, much as she had rejected the hierarchical relationship between God and the Church on which marriage was based, she hoped for a marital relationship free of unequal power. Marriage, she believed, should be a celebration of two individuals' relationship with the deity and with each other. Their union should be a "pilgrimage towards a common shrine," in which the pilgrims would "assist each other" according to their own strengths. They should care for and nurture each other and share their intellectual insights and joys, "for how sad it would be on such a journey to have a companion to whom you could not communicate thoughts and aspirations as they sprang to life; who would have no feeling for the prospects that open, more and more glorious as we advance; who would never see the flowers that may be gathered by the most industrious traveller."[88]

Although she provided a few examples of such marriages from history and literature, Fuller looked mainly to the future. "I have in my eye a youth and a maiden whom I look to as the nucleus of such a class. They are both in early youth, both as yet uncontaminated, both aspiring, without rashness, both thoughtful, both capable of deep affection, both of strong nature and sweet feelings, both capable of large mental development," she wrote. "They reside in different regions of earth, but their place in the soul is the same. To them I look as, perhaps, the harbingers and leaders of a new era, for never yet have I known minds so truly virgin, without narrowness or ignorance." They were also notably without gender spheres or divided souls.[89]

The world might not yet be ready for "Los Exaltados" and "Las Exaltadas," she acknowledged, "but the world would not sneer always, for from them would issue a virtue by which it would, at last, be exalted too." Individual growth and virtue would eventually transform such social institutions as marriage, which would in turn foster greater individual development. Thus the "undulated course" of history would create an irresistible, and perhaps unending, upward spiral of human progress. In Fuller's millennial vision, human beings would ultimately realize and accept their shared androgyny and begin to thrive in marital harmony.[90]

Marriages marked by equality and mutual respect between the partners might transform the world, but such a "union is only possible to those who are units." At present, Fuller argued, women were not regarded as independent units. Defined in law and society as daughters, sisters, wives, and mothers — always in relation to men — they could not enter any new union freely: "That her hand may be given with dignity, she must be able to stand alone." The depth of Fuller's cultural critique was evident in her contention that "it is not amended institutions, it is not improved education, it is not another selection of individuals for union, that can meliorate the sad result, but the *basis* of the union must be changed." Hers was a vision of basic, structural change.[91]

Fuller saw few signs of such fundamental change around her. She found even the recent expansion of educational opportunities for girls "sullied by the usual selfishness" and narrowness of vision. "So much is said of women being better educated, that they may become better companions and mothers *for men*," she complained. "But a being of infinite scope must not be treated with an exclusive view to any one relation. . . . The intellect, no more than the sense of hearing, is to be cultivated merely that she may be a more valuable companion to man, but because the Power who gave a power, by its mere existence, signifies that it must be brought out towards perfection."[92]

To escape the dominant belief "that woman was made *for man*," Fuller thought, would require an intellectual revolution. Women would have to "lay aside all thought . . . of being taught and led by men" and "retire within themselves" to break the "habit of dependence on others." They had to learn to recognize themselves as "possessors of and possessed by immortal souls" that deserved cultivation and expression for their own sake. Above all, women should become "self-centred," devoted to the recovery of their long-suppressed subjectivity: "What woman needs is not as a woman to act or rule, but as a nature to grow, as an intellect to discern, as a soul to live freely and unimpeded, to unfold such powers as were given her when we left our common home." Convinced that "men, as at present instructed, will not help this work, because they also are under the slavery of habit," Fuller concluded that a period of celibacy, in which women attended to their own self-culture, might be a necessary prelude to marital harmony in the future.[93]

If *Woman in the Nineteenth Century* was generally positive in tone, then, it was not free of the marks of Fuller's prolonged personal struggle against social limitations. The argument was punctuated by sharp observations about present social injustices, as well as various calls for practical action and some specific reforms. "We would have every arbitrary barrier thrown down. We would have every path laid open to woman as freely as to man," she declared. In one of the most celebrated (or notorious) phrases of the book, Fuller called for the opening of all employment opportunities to women: "But if you ask me what offices they may fill, I reply—any. I do not care what case you put; let them be sea-captains, if you will." She also vigorously inveighed against American slavery, the annexation of Texas and an imperialist foreign policy, prostitution and the double standard, and the denial of property and voting rights to women—even as she argued that no institutional or political reform could succeed without accompanying deep, moral, internal reform.[94]

Many American reformers of the 1840s embraced the views of the French utopian socialist Charles Fourier, who advocated sweeping institutional reforms to achieve social change. He called for the creation of communities in which the members would each do the kind of work that most attracted them and freely release their passions of all sorts; by the calculations of this former mathematician, a community of 1,620 carefully chosen people would allow every taste to be satisfied. Fuller was particularly impressed by Fourier's inclusion of women in his scheme of "attractive industry" and by his desire to eliminate patriarchal marriages. Yet she worried that, in his stress on physical living and working arrangements, he neglected the crucial area of self-culture. She believed that the insights of Fourier and Goethe were both necessary to achieve full humanity and harmony:

> Fourier says, As the institutions, so the men! All follies are excusable and natural under bad institutions.
> Goethe thinks, As the man, so the institutions! There is no excuse for ignorance and folly. A man can grow in any place, if he will.
> Ay! but Goethe, bad institutions are prison walls and impure air that make him stupid, so that he does not will.
> And thou, Fourier, do not expect to change mankind at once, or even "in three generations" by arrangement of groups and series, or flourish of trumpets for attractive industry. If these attempts are made by unready men, they will fail.
> Yet we prize the theory of Fourier no less than the profound suggestion of Goethe. Both are educating the age to a clearer consciousness of what man needs, what man can be, and better life must ensue.[95]

Characteristically, Fuller attempted to hold opposing views in equipoise, as different sides of a single truth. If she seemed to emphasize Minerva over the Muse to correct current imbalances in women's lives, she hoped that this would not overshadow her vision of harmonious balance for the future. "It is, therefore, only in the present crisis that the preference is given to Minerva. The power of continence must establish the legitimacy of freedom," she proclaimed. "Grant her, then, for a while, the armor and the javelin. Let her put from her the press of other minds and meditate in virgin loneliness. The same idea shall re-appear in due time as Muse, or Ceres, the all-kindly patient Earth-Spirit." For the moment, then, the development of women seemed to require more concentration on reason than emotion, on intelligence than intuition. Someday each woman would find her own individual balance.[96]

Perhaps most remarkable in a book written so quickly, the literary style and structure of *Woman in the Nineteenth Century* itself reflected Fuller's theory of harmonizing "Minerva" and the "Muse." As a result,

the book was harshly criticized by some literary critics as diffuse and mer-
curial. Part of the book was written as a forum for Minerva. In these sections, the narrator raised popular arguments and then rebutted them with
her impressive knowledge of history and contemporary European and
American events. She skillfully debated representative American husbands and "traders," who feared that the empowerment of women would
disrupt established domestic and commercial relations. To the suggestion by reformers that women "be publicly represented by women," she
imagined—and then answered point by point—a series of objections
from the opposition:

> ["]That can never be necessary,["] cry the other side. ["]All men are
> privately influenced by women; each has his wife, sister, or female
> friends, and is too much biased by these relations to fail of representing
> their interests, and, if this is not enough, let them propose and enforce
> their wishes with the pen. The beauty of home would be destroyed, the
> delicacy of the sex be violated, the dignity of halls of legislation degraded
> by an attempt to introduce them there. Such duties are inconsistent with
> those of a mother["]; and then we have ludicrous pictures of ladies in
> hysterics at the polls, and senate chambers filled with cradles.
>   But if, in reply, we admit as truth that woman seems destined by na-
> ture rather for the inner circle, we must add that the arrangements of
> civilized life have not been, as yet, such as to secure it to her. Her circle,
> if the duller, is not the quieter. If kept from "excitement," she is not from
> drudgery. Not only the Indian squaw carries the burdens of the camp,
> but the favorites of Louis the Fourteenth accompany him in his jour-
> neys, and the washerwoman stands at her tub and carries home her
> work at all seasons, and in all states of health. Those who think the
> physical circumstances of woman would make a part in the affairs of
> national government unsuitable, are by no means those who think it
> impossible for the negresses to endure field work, even during preg-
> nancy, or the sempstresses to go through their killing labors.[97]

The exquisite irony, incisive logic, and well-developed political consciousness in such mock debates all recalled the voice of Timothy Fuller,
the lawyer and politician. So too did the narrator's invocation of the
promise of equality in the Declaration of Independence in order to demand
the logical extension of "the liberty of law" to American women. At various points, the prosecutorial narrator called as witnesses to the strength
and intellectual equality of women Isabella of Spain and Elizabeth I of England, the French authors Germaine de Staël and George Sand, the French
revolutionary Manon Roland, the radical American abolitionist Abby Kelley, and the English scientist Mary Somerville, among others.[98]
    Fuller also testified herself, thinly disguised as the model female in-

tellectual Miranda, whose father had "addressed her not as a plaything, but as a living mind." When questioned by the narrator, Miranda observed that the education that had been granted her as an extraordinary favor should be every woman's right. She refused to endorse the conservative position that the restraints on women "were insuperable only to those who think them so, or who noisily strive to break them." Noting that "men never, in any extreme of despair, wished to be women," she insisted that the cultural barriers to women's "self-dependence" and "self-respect" were deeply "rooted" in men's vanity and structural inequalities of power. Women, she declared, must think their way through these serious impediments together and "learn self-help."[99]

Acting as a good attorney, the narrator drew forth Miranda's radical convictions through skillful, pointed questioning. Without appearing to lead the witness, she directed the testimony to support her general argument. Indeed, many parts of the book are marked by a similar clarity and precision of expression. They advance the central argument rapidly, directly, and effectively through political allusions, debate and cross-examination, and historical examples. Writing these sections in the voice of Minerva, Fuller employed a hortatory style and maintained an instrumental, even aggressive relationship to the text.

At other times, however, Fuller's narrative voice was conversational, prophetic, and exuberant. Her references here were to Greek, Indian, Egyptian, and Native American mythology and to European and American literature; the emphasis was not on social realities but on the imaginative creation and re-creation of humanity. Her words now were sensuous and mystical, written in the language of the Muse:

> Thou, Lord of Day! didst leave us to-night so calmly glorious, not dismayed that cold winter is coming, not postponing thy beneficence to the fruitful summer! Thou didst smile on thy day's work when it was done, and adorn thy down-going as thy up-rising, for thou art loyal, and it is thy nature to give life, if thou canst, and shine at all events!
>
> I stand in the sunny noon of life. Objects no longer glitter in the dews of morning, neither are yet softened by the shadows of evening. Every spot is seen, every chasm revealed. Climbing the dusty hill, some fair effigies that once stood for symbols of human destiny have been broken; those I still have with me, show defects in this broad light. Yet enough is left, even by experience, to point distinctly to the glories of that destiny; faint, but not to be mistaken streaks of the future day. I can say with the bard, "Though many have suffered shipwreck, still beat noble hearts."[100]

The profusion of natural imagery, the prophetic tone, and the intimate form of address to God in such passages are all reminiscent of

Fuller's epiphanal moment at age twenty-one, her childhood experiences of bliss in her mother's garden, and perhaps Margarett Crane's own soft voice. Fuller also turned to the Muse's favorite form of expression, poetry, at moments of high emotion and spiritual vision throughout the book:

> Those, who initiated are,
> Declare,
> As the hours
> Usher in varying hopes and powers;
> It changes its face,
> It changes its age,
> Now a young beaming Grace,
> Now Nestorian Sage:
> . . . .
> What it teaches native seems,
> Its new lore our ancient dreams;
> Incense rises from the ground,
> Music flows around;
> Firm rest the feet below, clear gaze the eyes above,
> When Truth to point the way through Life assumes the wand of
>   Love;
> But, if she cast aside the robe of green,
> Winter's silver sheen,
> White, pure as light,
> Makes gentle shroud as worthy weed as bridal robe had been.[101]

Thus the Muse periodically interrupted the logical flow of Minerva's argument for full human development, both to reinforce it from another side of human experience and to infuse the text with poetic beauty and prophetic hope. As it crossed between history and literature, politics and mythology, prose and poetry, and "masculine" and "feminine" voices, *Woman in the Nineteenth Century* challenged the solidity and permanence of all cultural boundaries. Luxuriating in multiple modes of being and expression, Fuller demonstrated her social vision of the "undulated course" of human progress in the aesthetics of her most complex and successful book. Small wonder that, upon completing it, she told a friend, "I felt a delightful glow as if I had put a good deal of my true life in it, as if, suppose I went away now, the measure of my foot-print would be left on the earth."[102]

6

New York and Europe

Her attempts to harmonize aesthetic and social concerns in her writing won Fuller the attention and admiration of Horace Greeley, the owner and editor of the progressive Whig *New-York Daily Tribune*. He offered her a position as a journalist and literary editor and critic on his newspaper. Established in 1841, the *Tribune* was already the third largest and most influential paper in New York City. Fuller accepted Greeley's offer of a generous (man's) salary and room and board with his family and moved to New York with mingled hope and trepidation in December 1844. Almost four times the size of Boston, New York in the 1840s was the nation's largest city and one of the fastest growing cities in the world. It was also the site of rising anti-immigrant sentiment, working-class riots, and slums that rivaled Europe's worst for filth and viciousness.

As one of the first female members of the working press and the first woman to serve on the editorial staff of a leading American newspaper, Fuller was excited about her expanding world and audience. "I like the position; it is so central, and affords a far more various view of life than any I ever before was in," she reported soon after her arrival. Learning about a number of social reforms championed by Greeley—and inventing some of her own—represented a further opportunity to build "the life of thought upon the life of action," her central goal for the women of her Boston Conversations. Moreover, she was clearly contributing to a democratic movement of considerable force. "The Newspaper promises to become daily of more importance, and if the increase of size be managed with equal discretion, to draw within itself the substance of all other literature of the day," she decided. Her column appeared regularly on the front page of a newspaper with more than twenty-eight thousand readers.[103]

During her twenty months as literary editor of the *Tribune,* Fuller published 250 articles with a byline (her work was marked with a star rather than her name) as well as many unsigned translations and brief reviews. Her column covered a wide range of social and cultural issues: she wrote

Margaret Fuller in July 1846. Daguerreotype copy by Southworth and Hawes made in the early 1850s of a daguerreotype by John Plumbe. This is the only surviving photograph of Margaret Fuller.

with new insight and urgency about prison conditions at Sing Sing, the mistreatment of Irish immigrants, slavery, prostitution, and the poverty of New York's slums. She also introduced and reviewed a wide variety of new American and European literature, translating and commenting on works in several languages. Whatever her subject, she urged Americans to read their literature and social institutions carefully and critically, to "learn from all the nations," and to build understanding across class, gender, and racial lines by deliberately adopting the perspectives of those differently situated in society.[104]

Fuller's literary criticism continued to take risks and to set new standards. She promoted the work of the young, unknown American authors Edgar Allan Poe, Herman Melville, and Nathaniel Hawthorne and introduced Americans to the English poetry of Elizabeth Barrett, Robert Browning, and Alfred Tennyson. Open to various sorts of literature and still attempting to judge each by its own standard, she also praised the popular American writers Lydia Sigourney, Caroline Kirkland, and Anna Mowat. They, too, had achieved excellence, she thought, although of a different kind.

Fearlessly, Fuller championed the work of the French novelist George Sand, who was generally excoriated by American critics for smoking, wearing masculine attire, and disregarding her marriage vows. "It is her works and not her private life that we are considering," Fuller reminded recalcitrant readers. "Of her works we have means of judging—of herself not; but among those who have passed unblamed through the walks of life, we have not often found a nobleness of purpose and feeling, a sincere religious hope to be compared with the spirit that breathes through the pages" of Sand's "serene" portrait of an independent woman.[105]

At the same time, Fuller dared to suggest that the celebrated American poet Henry Wadsworth Longfellow was overrated and that the prominent British author Thomas Carlyle was mistaken in his increasingly conservative historical judgments. Emerson she hailed as a spiritual "father of the country," while criticizing his obscure style and detachment. "We [think] this friend raised himself too early to the perpendicular and did not lie along the ground long enough to hear the secret whispers of our parent life," she concluded. "We could wish he might be thrown by conflicts on the lap of mother earth, to see if he would not rise again with added powers." Hers was an independent, bold, and influential critical voice.[106]

In preparing her columns on New York City's hospitals, prisons, almshouses, and insane asylums, Fuller followed her customary method. The Muse and Minerva both played a part, as she attempted first to

empathize with the people she interviewed in these institutions and then
to analyze their situations critically. As in her earlier writing, she frequently approached broad social issues through an initial focus on the
condition and concerns of women. Her keen consciousness of the inequalities of power in gender relations gradually broadened to include
analyses of class and race relations in America.

Fuller's journalistic investigations openly broached subjects that
middle-class women were socially proscribed from discussing even in private. She often reached startlingly unconventional conclusions. The prostitutes who filled New York's prisons for women had seen no other alternative to a life of poverty and abuse, she declared in an indictment of
gender and class relations alike. Class boundaries as well as the sexual
double standard had dictated their choice. Moreover, the institutions designed by the middle class for the poor served only to deepen their dependence and poverty, since they offered no education or vocational
training and failed to grapple with the underlying causes of criminality.
With almshouses that did not educate and prisons that did not rehabili-
tate, she concluded, the United States perpetuated its class system.

Fuller reserved her sharpest criticism for American slavery and race
relations. *Woman in the Nineteenth Century* had taken the Declaration of
Independence as America's central founding document and built a case
for women's equality and "liberty of law" upon it. In the *Tribune,* Fuller
extended her reading of this text to reveal the fundamental contradiction
between its promise of universal freedom and equality and the perpetu-
ation of slavery and racial injustice in the United States. On the anniver-
sary of the emancipation of slaves in the British West Indies, she noted
that even imperialistic England was "entitled to cry Shame to us." American slavery was the "most shameful deed . . . that ever disgraced a nation," she declared, "because the most contrary to consciousness of right.
Other nations have done wickedly, but we have surpassed them all in
trampling under foot the principles that had been assumed as the basis
of our national existence, and our willingness to forfeit our honor in the
face of the world."[107]

In a powerful parable, Fuller imagined a group of men arguing about
how to replant a blighted forest in their country. Just as they had decided
to reject a basket of black butternuts in favor of white English walnuts,
a mysteriously compelling stranger "of a darker complexion" appeared
among them. He carried a banner that read "PEACE AND GOOD WILL TO
MEN." Cracking open a few of the nuts, he showed the "planters" that the
butternuts were sound and the walnuts rotten inside. He advised the men
to "plant them together, lest none or few of the walnuts be sound." Mix-

ing the white and the black would allow all that could to grow and thrive. A new, healthier forest would be created.[108]

Still the men hesitated. Should they trust this beautiful stranger? Unlocking the political meaning of the parable, the Christ figure announced with profound irony, "I came hither . . . an uninvited guest, because I read sculptured above the door—'All men born Free and Equal,' and in this dwelling hoped to find myself at home." To dismiss him, he implied, was to distrust their own best thoughts and words and to reject the original promise of their country. His hopes were shattered as he learned that the planters associated the color black with evil and thus justified slavery and racial discrimination. In desperation, the dark stranger "put his hand to his brow and cried in a voice of the most penetrating pathos, 'Have I been so long among ye and ye have not known me?' " and vanished from their sight. His banner "was left trailing in the dust."[109]

This article's title, "What Fits a Man to Be a Voter? Is It to Be White Within, or White Without?," made clear that Fuller's criticism was not directed solely at the South and slavery. So did her denunciation of the decision of the citizens of New Bedford, Massachusetts, to exclude blacks from membership in the town's lyceum (a public lecture series) and to confine them to "a particular part of the house" during public lectures. In a brief and trenchant notice, she applauded those lecturers who had "declined addressing an audience whose test of merit, or right to the privileges of a citizen consists not in intelligence or good character, but the color of the skin."[110]

Similarly, Fuller warmly recommended the *Narrative of the Life of Frederick Douglass, an American Slave, Written by Himself* as "an excellent piece of writing, and on that score to be prized as a specimen of the powers of the Black Race, which Prejudice persists in disputing." She wished that "every one may read his book and see what a mind might have been stifled in bondage, — what a man may be subjected to the insults of spendthrift dandies, — or the blows of mercenary brutes, in whom there is no whiteness except of the skin, no humanity except in the outward form, and of whom the Avenger will not fail yet to demand — 'Where is thy brother?' "[111]

These articles expressed more than a horror of slavery. Each also addressed the deeper, more intractable problem of American racism and the construction of racial categories in the North and the South. To judge, categorize, and limit people by their biological characteristics, Fuller knew from experience and prolonged gender analysis, severely constrained the development of individuals and of humanity as a whole. Freeing America's slaves, then, was a necessary but not a sufficient measure. If the United States did not allow the full growth and contributions of free African Americans, her parable and other articles suggested, America would be the weaker—much as it was for stifling the development of women. Thus Fuller's empathetic stance and gender analysis were embedded in her journalistic critique of class and racial injustices in America.

Greeley was well pleased with Fuller's social vision and especially with her increasingly direct, terse, and economical writing style. "Good judges have confirmed my own opinion, that, while her essays in the *Dial* are more elaborate and ambitious, her reviews in the *Tribune* are far better adapted to win the favor and sway the judgment of the great majority of readers," he announced.[112] In short, he believed that he had taught her to work hard and to write well. Fuller herself was less confident about the latter. Pressed by daily deadlines as well as the fast pace of public issues, she had to sacrifice her experiments with different literary styles and modes of expression. In her writing, the Muse gave way to Minerva.

Criticized by some of her old friends in New England for abandoning *belles lettres* for journalism, Fuller defended herself uneasily. "They think I ought to produce something excellent, while I am content for the present to aid in the great work of mutual education in this way. I never regarded literature merely as a collection of exquisite products, but as a means of mutual interpretation," she reminded a sympathetic correspondent. "Feeling that many are reached and in some degree aided, the thoughts of every day seem worth writing down, though in a form that does not inspire me. . . . All the signs of life appear to me at least superficially, and, as I have had a good deal of *the depths*, an abode of some length in *the shallows* may do me no harm."[113] Her language, defensive tone, and note of self-sacrifice all indicate Fuller's lingering insecurity and internal conflict over the compromises that journalism demanded of her.

So, too, did her eager search for the Muse in New York's literary salons, concerts, and art galleries—and in her intense, troubled relationship with James Nathan. In her letters to this German-Jewish businessman (whom she met secretly around the city in the spring of 1845), Fuller assumed an uncharacteristically submissive voice. "I hear you with awe assert power over me and feel it to be true. It causes awe, but not dread, such as I felt sometime since at the approach of this mysterious power, for I feel deep confidence in my friend and know that he will lead me on in a spirit of holy love," she told him. "I have deep mystic feelings in myself and intimations from elsewhere." The effect of their relationship, she noticed, was to make her "so passive, waiting," that she neglected to ask any important questions. "You must tell me things, and I will forget myself; that is always the best way," she concluded.[114]

A year before, Fuller had recorded in one of her most poignant journal entries her yearning for a friend and lover: "With the intellect I always have—always shall overcome, but that is not the half of the work. The life, the life, O my God! shall the life never be sweet?" Now that longing led her to place "deep confidence" in a false friend and to tolerate a new version of the divided self. Working in a male journalistic world by day and posing as a "true woman" by night, she wore masks and played parts in both worlds. The personal and intellectual integration toward which she had aspired for years had perhaps never been further away.[115]

Increasingly disheartened by the irreconcilable paradoxes of her life, Fuller leapt at the chance to escape the exciting confusion of New York City, that "great city struggling up through the love of money." In August 1846, she departed for Europe with two new friends, the wealthy New England reformers Marcus and Rebecca Spring, who offered to pay her travel expenses if she would tutor their twelve-year-old son during the trip. She also agreed to serve as a foreign correspondent for the *Tribune* (another first for women in journalism). Although she believed that, at age thirty-six, she was too old to learn in Europe what she might have a decade earlier, Fuller still "cried for joy" at the opportunity so long denied her.[116]

The visitor in Europe was treated with a respect and admiration that the resident of America rarely received. Known for *Woman in the Nineteenth Century* and armed with letters of introduction from notable Americans, Fuller was graciously accepted into prominent intellectual circles in London and Paris. The British author Thomas Carlyle, the English poet William Wordsworth, and the French novelist George Sand all welcomed her into their homes. Fuller wrote home appreciatively: "I find myself much in my element in European society. It does not, indeed, come up to my ideal; but so many of the encumbrances are cleared away that used to weary me in America, that I can enjoy a freer play of faculty, and feel, if not like a bird in the air, at least as easy as a fish in water."[117]

She was not an uncritical guest. Unlike many American tourists, Fuller went from Europe's art galleries and salons to its coal mines, prisons, slums, and factories; she saw the unemployment, famine, social unrest, and government corruption that filled Europe in the mid-1840s. She lamented the degradation of the poor and the heedlessness of the rich and powerful. The *Tribune* carried her accounts of "persons, especially women, dressed in dirty, wretched tatters, worse than none, and with an expression of listless, unexpecting woe upon their faces, far more tragic than the inscription over the gate of Dante's *Inferno*,"[118] as well as her dire warnings to those "who have eyes and see not, ears and hear not, the convulsions and sobs of injured Humanity!"[119] Yet she also admired the model, experimental schools and *crèches* (child care centers for working mothers) that she visited. Above all, she felt free to discuss social and aesthetic problems with her European hosts and the *Tribune*'s readers. Her columns and letters recorded a renewed sense of unity and purpose. Fuller met two men in London and Paris who came very close to her idea of intimate friends. Giuseppe Mazzini, exiled from his native Genoa for his revolutionary activities in 1830–1831 and selflessly dedicated to the cause of a free and united Italy, seemed to embody her youthful ideal of the virtuous Roman citizen; yet he was also "beauteous and pure music" to her soul. The Polish patriot and poet Adam Mickiewicz was the man she "had long wished to see, with the intellect and passions in due proportion for a full and healthy human being, with a soul constantly inspiring." Unlike her highly rational father or the temperate and cautious Emerson, Mazzini and Mickiewicz were men with intense political commitments and deep personal friendships. Fuller found their spiritually based republican nationalism as inspiring as their acceptance of her zeal and intellect. She felt that she had finally found her spiritual and intellectual guides.[120]

Moreover, their warm reception echoed again and again when Fuller arrived in Italy in the spring of 1847. Her willingness to carry forbidden, uncensored letters from Mazzini to his supporters and relatives opened many doors for her. She was immediately welcomed into the extended community of Italian patriots and revolutionaries. "I made many and ardent friends, of all ranks, from the very highest to the lowest," she informed her mother. "The Italians sympathize with my character and understand my organization, as no other people ever did; they admire the ready eloquence of my nature, and highly prize my intelligent sympathy (such as they do not find often in foreigners) with their sufferings in the past and hopes for the future." To another correspondent, she wrote simply and joyfully, "Italy receives me as a long-lost child and I feel myself at home here."[121]

In Italy, then, Fuller launched her final attempt to achieve the harmony and wholeness of being that she had envisioned on that solitary Thanksgiving Day in New England so long before. But now she was not alone. She bound her private quest to that of the Italian people, as they strove for national unification and independence from foreign rule. Since 1815, most of Italy's small states had been ruled despotically by a variety of princes and dukes under the influence of Austria. In 1847, foreign influence was still strong throughout Italy. In the north, Austrian troops occupied Lombardy and Venetia, the regions directly under Austrian rule; the duchies of Tuscany, Parma, and Modena, as well as the Papal States in central Italy, were tightly bound to Catholic Austria. In the south, a Spanish Bourbon (also tied to Austria) held the thrones of Naples and

Sicily. Everywhere Austria used its influence to stifle dissent and suppress democratic reforms that threatened its imperial power.

Fuller saw the effects of this foreign and internal oppression as she toured Genoa, Naples, Rome, Florence, Bologna, Ravenna, and Venice with the Springs. She learned of Italy's misery still more fully after parting from her friends in July 1847. While they went on to visit Germany and Austria and then to return home, she spent the summer alone in Milan, the principal city in Lombardy. There she met men and women who had been physically tortured, condemned to death, imprisoned, or stripped of their possessions by Austrian authorities and who were passionately committed to the cause of Italian independence and unification. They won her sympathy, admiration, and understanding. Yet she did not remain in Milan. Prepared by her classical education and Mazzini's political vision to find the heart of Italy in Rome, she was drawn particularly strongly to that city and returned there to reside in October 1847.

In the early months of 1848, Fuller watched the opening acts of the Italian revolution through the eyes of rejoicing Romans. As Naples, Sicily, Venice, Modena, Parma, and Milan all erupted in local revolts, she informed the *Tribune*'s readers, Roman "men were seen dancing" and "women weeping with joy along the street." Pope Pius IX, who ruled Rome politically as well as spiritually, had begun the wave of reform when he came to power in 1846 by granting amnesty to political prisoners and relaxing restrictions on freedom of speech and of the press. Now he seemed willing to support the Italian fight for independence from Austrian imperial rule. Roman "youth rushed to enroll themselves in regiments to go to the frontier." They went in search of freedom and social justice, Fuller believed. She urged Americans to learn from Europeans "the real meaning of the words FRATERNITY, EQUALITY," and to "learn to reverence, learn to guard, the true aristocracy of a nation, the only really noble — the LABORING CLASSES." For Fuller, the political excitement in Rome was palpable. This seemed to be the place and time she had "always dreamed of, and for long secretly hoped to see."[122]

Rome also held other attractions for Fuller. Soon after her arrival, she met and fell in love with Giovanni Angelo Ossoli, a Roman nobleman turned republican, who was ten years her junior. There is no surviving record of their marriage. To be legally recognized at the time in Rome, marriages had to be consecrated in the Catholic Church. Theirs would have required a rare papal dispensation, since Ossoli was a Catholic and Fuller a Protestant. They may have been married in a private, civil ceremony on April 4, 1848; their correspondence suggests obliquely that the date held special meaning for them. In any case, such a ceremony would not have legitimized their union in the eyes of Roman authorities. Fearing the disapproval of their families and friends, they kept their relationship secret for more than a year.[123]

There is no doubt, however, about the strength and endurance of their commitment to each other or of its importance to Margaret Fuller. "My life at Rome is thus far all I hoped," she wrote to her mother, without revealing the cause. "I have not been so well since I was a child, nor so happy ever as during the last six weeks." In her relationship with Ossoli she suppressed less of herself than ever before; their correspondence mingled political news with vows of love and mutual support. He was willing—as no man in America had been—to accept her as both an intelligent and a passionate woman. She, in turn, cherished his gentleness and loyalty. Their love affirmed the ideal of "two halves of one thought" in which she had believed so long on faith alone.[124]

Fuller worked on her newspaper columns in Rome until well into an unexpected pregnancy. She was filled with dread, first that she would lose the baby because of her age, next that she would not survive childbirth, and then that she would not be able to continue to support herself. These were not unfounded fears in the mid-nineteenth century. At the end of May 1848, she reluctantly left Rome for the quieter, safer mountains to the northeast to bear her child. Ossoli remained with his civic guard unit in Rome and visited her as often as he could. They were together on September 5, when their son Angelo Eugenio Filippo was born.

Fuller cherished the moments she spent with her infant. Yet she also chafed at her forced isolation during and after her pregnancy. While Ossoli continued his revolutionary activities unabated, she suffered "six months of seclusion." Fearing notoriety and ostracism for herself and the destruction of Ossoli's chances to come into his inheritance if his family learned of Angelo's birth, she could not simply take her baby to Rome with her. A new form of the divided self appeared in her life, as motherhood and political engagement pulled her in opposite directions. Minerva and the Muse began to battle on new ground. An old solution occurred to her: unable to participate for a time in the Italian revolution, she began to write its history. Once again, her writing seemed to be her best hope of realizing her dream of autonomy and harmony.[125]

With great anguish, Fuller left her infant son in the care of a wet nurse in the mountain town of Rieti in November 1848 and rejoined Ossoli in Rome. There the popular mood had turned bitter when the pope, increasingly wary of internal reform and frightened by Austria's defeat of revolutionary Milan over the summer, had disavowed the war against Austria and withdrawn his support for the independence movement. Re-

Piazza del Popolo in Rome. In squares such as this "Plaza of the People" Fuller witnessed the dramatic events of the Roman Revolution.

publicans in Rome wanted the pope to renounce his temporal power. As Austrian troops advanced toward Rome in November, Fuller witnessed the rising fury of the Roman people turn to violence. She chronicled the assassination of the papal prime minister, a popular attack on a papal palace, and the pope's flight from the city (all in November) and then the establishment of an independent Roman Republic with Giuseppe Mazzini at its head in February 1849.

Fuller's dispatches to the *Tribune* did not attempt to disguise her deep, personal involvement with the revolutionary cause in Rome. Of the pope's hasty departure she wrote jubilantly, "No more of him! His day is over." The proclamation of the republic by Rome's new, democratically elected constituent assembly made her want to join the crowds in shouting, *"Viva la Republica! viva Italia!"* She could not understand the apathy or disapproval of other Americans in Rome. "The imposing grandeur of the spectacle to me gave new force to the thought that already swelled my heart;

Giovanni Angelo Ossoli in the late 1840s.

my nerves thrilled," she told the newspaper public. To her mother she added, "Oh Rome, *my* country, city of the soul!"[126]

Fuller's and Rome's celebration was short-lived. On June 3, 1849, the young Roman Republic was besieged and bombarded by French troops. The French Republic, itself established by revolution in 1848 but in desperate need of support from French Catholics, had pledged to restore the pope to political power in Rome. Volunteering as a nurse and director of a Roman hospital and writing impassioned, graphic accounts of Rome's suffering for the *Tribune,* Fuller also worried about Ossoli, still active in Rome's civic guard, and Angelino, possibly in danger in Rieti. She was "the Mater Dolorosa," mourning the dead and wounded children of Rome as she waited every day "in the burning sun . . . in the crowd, for letters" about her baby, and barely sleeping at night, "consumed as by nightly fever" with "anxiety and anguish." She constantly seemed "to hear him call." Fuller and Ossoli escaped to Rieti in July, as the Roman Republic fell.[127]

Deep anguish was apparent in Fuller's desperate cry to her American readers to *"do something"* as individuals and citizens of the world. "Do you owe no tithe to Heaven for the privileges it had showered on you, for whose achievement so many here suffer and perish daily?" she asked them. "Deserve to retain them, by helping your fellow-men to acquire them." Americans with empathy and judgment enough to recognize a divine effort should send money, encouragement, and acknowledgments of the revolutionary leaders throughout Europe before it was too late. "Friends, countrymen, and lovers of virtue, lovers of freedom, lovers of truth!—be on the alert," she implored them. "Rest not supine in your easier lives, but remember 'Mankind is one, / And beats with one great heart.' " By summer's end, the republic of Venice had fallen to the Austrian army. The Italian revolution was over.[128]

Fuller's last two dispatches to the *Tribune,* written after the fall of Rome and the failure of the revolution throughout Italy, were unrepentant and contemptuous of the forces of reaction. Filled with descriptions of French hypocrisy, Austrian cruelty, and Italian suffering and bravery, they also prophesied the ultimate triumph of freedom, democracy, and social justice in Europe. "Probably many pairs of eyes close sealed before, were thus opened in a direction that may lead to the redress of the frightful social ills of Europe, by a peaceful though radical revolution instead of bloody conflict," she wrote in November 1849. "The Kings may find their thrones rather crumbling than tumbling; the priests may see the consecration wafer turn into bread to sustain the perishing millions even in their astonished hands. God grant it."[129]

At some moments, Fuller envisioned a peaceful, socialist revolution overtaking Europe. At others, her language and imagery were violent, even apocalyptic. "The seeds for a vast harvest of hatreds and contempts are sown over every inch of Roman ground, nor can that malignant growth be extirpated, till the wishes of Heaven shall waft a fire that will burn down all, root and branch, and prepare the earth for an entirely new culture. The next revolution, here and elsewhere, will be radical," her final

Margaret Fuller during the siege of Rome. Portrait by Thomas Hicks.

dispatch from Italy proclaimed. "Do you laugh, Roman Cardinal, as you shut the prison-door on [the] woman weeping for her son martyred in the cause of his country? Do you laugh, Austrian officer, as you drill the Hungarian and Lombard youth to tremble at your baton? Soon you, all of you, shall 'believe and tremble.' "[130]

Fuller's life with her reunited family in subdued Florence that autumn and winter seemed almost idyllic after the months of suffering, separation, and war. "Casting aside the past and the future," she wrote to a friend from Rome, "I have enjoyed many bright and peaceful hours this winter. My little baby flourishes in my care; his laughing eyes, his stammered words and capricious caresses afford me the first unalloyed quiet joy I have ever known." Despite her fear of losing the precious "liberty of single life" upon "entering on the jog-trot of domestic life," she enjoyed living with Ossoli. Yet a sense of sadness and loss pervaded their "simple, natural life at home," for "without tie to the public, we gave up the peculiar beauty of our lives." The "peculiar beauty" of Fuller's life in Italy had been the confluence of "the life of thought" and "the life of action." Her spirit and intelligence had both been intensely engaged in her personal identification with a public cause. Now in the isolation of a private, domestic world, a source of her energy was gone.[131]

Even as Fuller recovered her health, worked on her history of the Italian revolution, conversed with her many curious visitors, and played with her family, she was filled with a dark foreboding. Growing upon her ever since the fall of Rome, and especially as she contemplated the necessity of returning to America, was a sense of personal doom. Several of her letters from Florence were consciously letters of farewell. To her mother she wrote in May 1850, "For me, I long so very much to see you, should any thing hinder it on earth again (and I say it merely because there seems somewhat more of danger on sea than on land) think of your daughter as one who always wished at least to do her duty, and who always cherished you according as her mind opened to discover excellence." Fuller's visions of death were often peaceful ones—except for her nightmares of dying at sea.[132]

She had much to worry her in 1850. Ossoli's conservative family, appalled by his revolutionary politics and his relationship with the foreign, Protestant Fuller, had cut him off financially. Although he was learning to sculpt in Florence, it was clear that Fuller would have to provide most of the financial support for her family. There seemed to be no way to accomplish this in Europe among the many destitute, exiled revolutionaries. She saw no alternative to a speedy return to the United States, although her closest friends in New York and New England advised against it. As Emerson noted in his journal, "The timorous said, What shall we do? how shall she be received, now that she brings a husband and child home?" With considerable courage, Fuller prepared herself for the "social inquisition" she expected from those "timorous" friends who were shocked by her love for a man "of no intellectual culture," concerned about her marital status, and generally unprepared for the risks and passions of her life in Italy.[133]

The ship carrying Fuller and her family to the United States in the summer of 1850 never arrived. Caught in a hurricane, it was shipwrecked off the coast of New York on July 19. Fuller, Ossoli, and their son were all drowned within sight of the shore. During the twelve hours that the waves tore at the broken ship, survivors said, Fuller clung to two-year-old Angelino, singing to him to calm his terror. She steadily refused to swim to shore alone. She would not be separated from Ossoli or her son, even to save her life.

7

Conclusion:
Margaret Fuller's Legacy

Margaret Fuller believed in July 1850 that she carried with her two vital pieces of her legacy, her son and her last book. Before she died she saw them both swept into the sea. We will never know if either could have realized her dreams or how she might have responded to the new situation she would have faced at home. Now we can only hope to recover her legacy by reading the text of her life and works, as they illuminate each other. We must resist the temptation to view her "partially" or to privilege one part of her rich life over the rest. We must take seriously her protest against a widespread tendency to locate her essential self in one or another of her works or quasi-autobiographical figures. "People seem to think that not more than one phase of character can be shown in one life," she cautioned. We must try to see her whole at last.[134]

Only thus can we move beyond Bronson Alcott's distant (and distancing) awe of Fuller: "Imperial creature that she was, and, alike in ideal excellencies and bearing, mythological!" She was both more and less than this; she was Minerva and the Muse in intensely human form. Throughout her short life, she struggled, often with great pain, to join together spirit and intellect, empathy and judgment, freedom and discipline, thought and action, individualism and social consciousness. She was one of the early Republic's most effective prophets of self-culture, an architect of middle-class subjectivity. Yet her desire for self-realization also led her to contest prevailing gender constructions, to confront the injustices of race and class relations, and to raise basic questions about the nature of identity itself. The tensions and paradoxes shaped her life and her vision.[135]

Fuller expected her legacy to be read in her life as much as in her work. "What concerns me now is, that my life be a beautiful, powerful, in a word, a complete life in its kind," she concluded in *Woman in the Nineteenth Century*. "Had I but one more moment to live I must wish the same." She might well have been content to have others remember her as she described a female friend: "So womanly, so manly, so childlike, so human!" Whether or not she ever achieved this plenitude of being, she never lost sight of her vision of individual and social harmony. In her lifelong quest for complete humanity, Margaret Fuller posed a compelling, complex, and unforgettable challenge to her own and succeeding generations.[136]

NOTES

CHAPTER 1

[1]Henry James, *William Wetmore Story and His Friends,* 2 vols. (Boston, 1903), 1:127–28.
[2]Ralph Waldo Emerson to Thomas Carlyle, July 31, 1846, *The Correspondence of Emerson and Carlyle,* ed. Joseph Slater (New York, 1964), 407, 403–4; Ralph Waldo Emerson, in *Memoirs of Margaret Fuller Ossoli,* ed. R. W. Emerson, W. H. Channing, and J. F. Clarke, 2 vols. (Boston, 1852), 1:215 (cited hereafter as *Memoirs*). The *Memoirs* contains selections from Fuller's letters and journals, as well as the editors' (and others') judgments and comments about her. Some of the selections were accurately reproduced, but others were heavily edited and the original manuscripts defaced; some of the original sources were destroyed or lost. The selections in the first volume are generally more reliable than those in the second. Indispensable but sometimes untrustworthy as a guide to Fuller's ideas, the *Memoirs* clearly reveals the three editors' views of her life and thought.
[3]A. Bronson Alcott, Journal, July 15, 1851, *The Journals of Bronson Alcott,* ed. Odell Shepard, 2 vols. (Port Washington, N.Y., 1966), 1:252; Elizabeth Cady Stanton, Susan B. Anthony, and Matilda Joslyn Gage, eds., *History of Woman Suffrage,* 2 vols. (New York, 1881), 1:dedication, 801.
[4]Nathaniel Hawthorne, "The French and Italian Notebooks," April 3, 1858, *The Centenary Edition of the Works of Nathaniel Hawthorne,* ed. William L. Charvat et al., 20 vols. to date (Columbus, Ohio, 1962–), 14:156–57; [Orestes A. Brownson], *Brownson's Quarterly Review* 6 (October 1844): 546–47; Edgar Allan Poe, "The Literati of New York City, No. IV. Sarah Margaret Fuller," *Godey's Magazine and Lady's Book* 33 (August 1846), 72–75; Samuel Gray Ward, in *The Journals and Miscellaneous Notebooks of Ralph Waldo Emerson,* ed. William H. Gilman et al., 16 vols. (Cambridge, Mass., 1960–82), 11:488 (cited hereafter as *Journals of Emerson*).
[5]Margaret Fuller to [?], [ca. Winter] 1829–1830, *The Letters of Margaret Fuller,* ed. Robert N. Hudspeth, 6 vols. (Ithaca, 1983–94), 1:159 (cited hereafter as *Letters*).

CHAPTER 2

[6]Timothy Dwight, *Travels in New-England and New York,* modern critical edition, ed. Barbara Miller Solomon, 4 vols. (New Haven, 1821; Cambridge, Mass., 1969), 1:366.
[7]Joseph Richardson, *Sermon on the Duty and Dignity of Woman, Delivered April 22, 1832* (Hingham, Mass., 1833), 14–15.
[8]Margaret Fuller, in *Memoirs,* 1:12, 14; Diary of Timothy Fuller, November 15, 1804, Fuller Manuscripts and Works, fMS Am 1086, Houghton Library, Harvard University, 2:6 (cited hereafter as Fuller Manuscripts).
[9]Margaret Fuller, in *Memoirs,* 1:12–13.
[10]Ibid., 23–24; Margaret Fuller, Journal, [ca. August 1838], Fuller Manuscripts, 9:264.
[11]Eliza Rotch Farrar to Margaret Fuller, July 25, [1843], Fuller Manuscripts, 17:41; Margarett Crane Fuller to Timothy Fuller, December 17, 1820, Fuller Manuscripts, 6:102. Timothy Fuller's letters to Margaret Fuller are in Fuller Manuscripts, 5:1–47; Margarett Crane Fuller's letters to Margaret Fuller are in Fuller Manuscripts, 8:183–223.
[12]Margaret Fuller, in *Memoirs,* 1:18–19.
[13]Ibid., 22.
[14]Ibid., 18.
[15]Ibid., 229; Margaret Fuller to [?], n.d., *Letters,* 6:143–44.
[16]Margarett Crane Fuller to Timothy Fuller, February 18 and 22, 1818, Fuller Manuscripts, 6:16, 20; Timothy Fuller to Margaret Fuller, [ca. 1823], Fuller Manuscripts, 5:16.
[17]James Freeman Clarke, "Journal of People and Things," September 12, 1831, James

Freeman Clarke Collection, bMS Am 1569.2(9), Houghton Library, Harvard University; James Freeman Clarke, "Journal of the Understanding," December 11, 1832, James Freeman Clarke Collection, bMS Am 1569.2(8).

[18] Margaret Fuller to Almira P. Barlow, November 19, 1830, *Letters,* 1:171.

CHAPTER 3

[19] Margaret Fuller to Jane F. Tuckerman, October 21, 1838, *Letters,* 1:347. Bracketed material has been added by the author.

[20] Margaret Fuller to James F. Clarke, May 3, 1833, *Letters,* 6:200.

[21] Margaret Fuller, in *Memoirs,* 1:139–40.

[22] Ibid., 140–41.

[23] Ibid., 141.

[24] Ibid., 142. Fuller had another transformative mystical experience in the autumn of 1840, as she struggled to accept the impending marriage of Samuel Gray Ward (whom she had known and loved for several years) and Anna Barker (one of her closest female friends). In a powerful echo of her first spiritual crisis, in 1831, a sense of desolation drove her toward isolation and renunciation. She also emerged from this crisis renewed, convinced that "all has been revealed, all foreshown yet I know it not. Experiment has given place to certainty, pride to obedience, thought to love, and truth is lost in beauty." See Margaret Fuller to Caroline Sturgis, September 26, 1840, *Letters,* 2:158.

[25] Margaret Fuller, "The One in All," *Life Without and Life Within,* ed. Arthur B. Fuller (Boston, 1860), 391; Ralph Waldo Emerson, cited in Caroline W. Healey, *Margaret and Her Friends, or Ten Conversations with Margaret Fuller upon the Mythology of the Greeks . . . Beginning March 1, 1841* (Boston, 1895), 118; Margaret Fuller, ibid., 113–14.

[26] Margaret Fuller, "One in All," 390. See also Margaret Fuller to Frederic H. Hedge, February 1, 1835, *Letters,* 1:222–24, in which Fuller explained, "I have no confidence in God as a Father" (224).

[27] Ralph Waldo Emerson, in *Memoirs,* 1:219.

[28] [Margaret Fuller], "Leila," *Dial* 1 (April 1841): 462, 466.

[29] Margaret Fuller to William H. Channing, n.d., *Letters,* 6:99; Margaret Fuller, in *Memoirs,* 2:107.

[30] Margaret Fuller to William H. Channing, August 16, 1843, *Letters,* 3:142.

CHAPTER 4

[31] Ralph Waldo Emerson, Journal, 1846, *Journals of Emerson,* 9:381; George Ripley, *The Latest Form of Infidelity Examined* (Boston, 1839), in *The Transcendentalists: An Anthology,* ed. Perry Miller (Cambridge, Mass., 1950), 220. The group, loosely associated in clubs and friendships in the 1830s and 1840s, was derisively named the Transcendentalists by its enemies, who believed adherents to be (at once) vague, incomprehensible, heretical, dangerous, and disconnected from reality. The young intellectuals resisted the name, in large part because they treasured their individuality and philosophical differences. Their most famous publications were Ralph Waldo Emerson's *Nature* (1836) and "The Divinity School Address" (1838) and Henry David Thoreau's *Civil Disobedience* (1849) and *Walden* (1854).

[32] Ralph Waldo Emerson, Introductory to "The Philosophy of History," *The Early Lectures of Ralph Waldo Emerson,* ed. Stephen E. Whicher, Robert E. Spiller, and Wallace E. Williams, 3 vols. (Cambridge, Mass., 1959–1972), 2:12.

[33] S. Margaret Fuller, *Woman in the Nineteenth Century* (New York, 1845), 162; Ralph Waldo Emerson, *Nature* (1836), in *The Collected Works of Ralph Waldo Emerson,* ed. Alfred R. Ferguson et al., 5 vols. to date (Cambridge, Mass., 1971–), 1:45 (cited hereafter as *Collected Works of Emerson*).

[34] Ralph Waldo Emerson, "The Divinity School Address" (1838), *Collected Works of Emerson,* 1:82.

[35] Margaret Fuller to George T. Davis, February 1, 1836, *Letters*, 6:279.

[36] Ralph Waldo Emerson, "Love," *Early Lectures of Emerson*, 3:62. In a journal entry of August 28, 1842, Fuller noted, "Waldo [Emerson] must not shake me in my worldliness"; see "Margaret Fuller's 1842 Journal: At Concord with the Emersons," ed. Joel Myerson, *Harvard Library Bulletin* 21 (1973): 320–40, quotation 329.

[37] Ralph Waldo Emerson, Journal, 1851, *Journals of Emerson*, 11:445; Ralph Waldo Emerson to Margaret Fuller, April 29, 1843, *The Letters of Ralph Waldo Emerson*, ed. Ralph L. Rusk, 8 vols. (New York, 1939), 3:170 (cited hereafter as *Letters of Emerson*); Margaret Fuller to Ralph Waldo Emerson, May 9, [1843], *Letters*, 3:124.

[38] Margaret Fuller, "Memoranda of Interviews, Conversations and Public Discourses," Fuller Manuscripts, Box 3.

[39] Margaret Fuller, in Madelon Bedell, *The Alcotts: Biography of a Family* (New York, 1980), 128.

[40] Margaret Fuller, in *Memoirs*, 1:177; Margaret Fuller to M. W. A., S. F. H., E. M., M. M., M. D. M., and M. D. A., n.d., *Letters*, 6:93; Margaret Fuller to [Ralph Waldo Emerson?], July 3, 1837, *Letters*, 1:288; Margaret Fuller to A. Bronson Alcott, June 27, 1837, *Letters*, 1:287.

[41] Mary Ware Allen to her parents, December 20, 1837, and January 18, 1838, in Harriet Hall Johnson (Allen's daughter), "Margaret Fuller as Known by Her Scholars," *Christian Register*, April 21, 1910, 426–29, quotations 427; Ann Brown, Journal, March 15, 1838, in "Margaret Fuller as a Teacher in Providence: The School Journal of Ann Brown," ed. Laraine Fergenson, *Studies in the American Renaissance* (1991): 59–118, quotation 83. Another student, Anna Gale, recorded several occasions on which Fuller questioned or contradicted the assigned textbook; portions of her journal are reproduced in Edward A. Hoyt and Loriman S. Brigham, "Glimpses of Margaret Fuller: The Green Street School and Florence," *New England Quarterly* 29 (1956): 87–98.

[42] Unidentified classmate to Mary Ware Allen, October 28, 1838, in Johnson, "Fuller as Known by Her Scholars," 428; Evelina Metcalf, Journal, May 7, 1838, Department of Special Collections, Thomas Cooper Library, University of South Carolina; Mary Ware Allen, *Greene Street School Journal*, no. 1, 77, in Judith Strong Albert, "Margaret Fuller and Mary Ware Allen: 'In Youth an Insatiate Student'—a Certain Kind of Friendship," *Thoreau Quarterly Journal* 12 (July 1980): 9–22, quotation 13.

[43] Margaret Fuller to Ralph Waldo Emerson, March 1, 1838, *Letters*, 1:327; Margaret Fuller to Frederic Henry Hedge, April 6, 1837, *Letters*, 1:266.

[44] [Margaret Fuller], "A Short Essay on Critics," *Dial*, July 1840, 5–11, quotations 8.

[45] Fuller published a critique of Goethe's hierarchical, utilitarian friendship in "Bettine Brentano and Her Friend Günderode," *Dial*, January 1842, 313–57, quotation 316. The more searing indictment was made privately in Margaret Fuller to William H. Channing, February 19, 1841, *Letters*, 2:202.

[46] S. M. Fuller, *Conversations with Goethe in the Last Years of His Life, Translated from the German of Eckermann* (Boston, 1839), xii, xxi; [Margaret Fuller], "Menzel's View of Goethe," *Dial*, January 1841, 340–47, quotation 344. See also [Margaret Fuller], "Goethe," *Dial*, July 1841, 1–41. Friedrich von Schiller (1759–1805), a German dramatist and poet, was known and admired in America for his indictments of tyranny and his idealistic faith in moral progress. He was considered as moral as Goethe was immoral. Ironically, Schiller and Goethe were close friends from their first meeeting in 1794 until Schiller's early death in 1805.

[47] Fuller, *Conversations with Goethe*, xx, xiv.

[48] Margaret Fuller to Ralph Waldo Emerson, April 9, 1842, *Letters*, 3:58; Margaret Fuller to William H. Channing, March 22, 1840, *Letters*, 2:126.

[49] Ralph Waldo Emerson, Journal, [1821?], *Journals of Emerson*, 1:292.

[50] Margaret Fuller, Journal, [October 1842], in "Margaret Fuller's Journal for October 1842," ed. Robert D. Habich, *Harvard Library Bulletin* 33 (1985), 280–91, quotations 286–87.

[51] Margaret Fuller, Journal Fragment, January 22, [1840?], Emerson Family Papers, Os 735Z 1840.1.22, Houghton Library, Harvard University, printed in *Letters*, 2:161 n.

[52] Ralph Waldo Emerson to Margaret Fuller, September 25, 1840, *Letters of Emerson*,

2:336–37; Ralph Waldo Emerson to Margaret Fuller, October 24, 1840, *Letters of Emerson,* 2:352; Ralph Waldo Emerson, Journal, 1840, *Journals of Emerson* 7:400. Many scholars have adopted Emerson's view of Fuller's demands on him as a confused attempt to sublimate her sexual drives after the engagement of Samuel Gray Ward and Anna Barker. There is no doubt that Fuller experienced their marriage as a betrayal of trust; for more on her reaction, see note 24. Nonetheless, her thoughtful, sustained critique of Emerson's ideal of friendship demands more serious consideration.

[53] Margaret Fuller to Ralph Waldo Emerson, September 29, 1840, *Letters,* 2:159–60.

[54] Ibid.; Margaret Fuller to William H. Channing, [July? 1841?], *Letters,* 2:214; Margaret Fuller to Ralph Waldo Emerson, [October 1841?], *Letters,* 2:235.

[55] Margaret Fuller to William H. Channing, [July? 1841?], *Letters,* 2:214; Ralph Waldo Emerson, "Friendship" (1841), *Collected Works of Emerson,* 2:117, 126; Margaret Fuller, in *Memoirs,* 1:37.

[56] Margaret Fuller to William H. Channing, n.d., *Letters,* 6:96.

[57] James Freeman Clarke to Margaret Fuller, March 1, 1838, *The Letters of James Freeman Clarke to Margaret Fuller,* ed. John Wesley Thomas (Hamburg, Germany, 1957), 129; *Memoir of William Henry Channing,* ed. O. B. Frothingham (Cambridge, Mass., 1886), 181; *Reminiscences of Ednah Dow Cheney* (Boston, 1902), 205.

[58] Ralph Waldo Emerson, Journal, 1843, *Journals of Emerson,* 8:368.

[59] Ralph Waldo Emerson to Margaret Fuller, [October 2, 1840?], *Letters of Emerson,* 2:342; Margaret Fuller, Journal, [ca. Fall 1839], 120, Margaret Fuller Ossoli Collection, Boston Public Library; Margaret Fuller to [?], n.d., *Letters,* 6:134. By 1842, convinced that he could not change without being untrue to himself, Fuller had decided to accept Emerson's friendship on his own terms. She "thought it was the only way, to take him for what he is, as he wishes to be taken," she told his wife, Lidian, in early September. Upon leaving the Emersons' home later that month, she noted in her journal, "Farewell, dearest friend, there has been dissonance between us, and may be again, for we do not fully meet, and to me you are too much and too little by turns, yet thanks be to the Parent of Souls, that gave us to be born into the same age and the same country and to meet with so much of nobleness and sweetness as we do, and I think constantly with more and more." See Margaret Fuller, Journal, [September 2 and 25] 1842, "Margaret Fuller's 1842 Journal: At Concord with the Emersons," ed. Joel Myerson, *Harvard Library Bulletin* 21 (1973): 320–40, quotations 332 and 340.

[60] Margaret Fuller to Ralph Waldo Emerson, September 29, 1840, *Letters,* 2:160.

[61] Margaret Fuller, *Life Without and Life Within,* 349.

[62] Margaret Fuller to [Sophia Ripley?], August 27, 1839, *Letters,* 2:86–87. Fuller was usually the only woman invited to meetings of the Transcendental Club and attended at least eight of the thirty recorded meetings; see Joel Myerson, "A Calendar of Transcendental Club Meetings," *American Literature* 44 (1972): 197–207.

[63] Margaret Fuller to [Sophia Ripley?], August 27, 1839, *Letters,* 2:87–88.

[64] Ibid., 88.

[65] Margaret Fuller to [?], [Autumn? 1839?], *Letters,* 2:97; Margaret Fuller, Journal, [July] 25, 1844, " 'The Impulses of Human Nature': Margaret Fuller's Journal from June through October 1844," ed. Martha L. Berg and Alice de V. Perry, *Proceedings of the Massachusetts Historical Society* 102 (1990): 38–126, quotation 94; [Elizabeth Palmer Peabody], "Journal of Margaret Fuller's 'Conversations,' " Elizabeth Palmer Peabody Papers, American Antiquarian Society, in "Margaret Fuller's Boston Conversations: The 1839–1840 Series," ed. Nancy Craig Simmons, *Studies in the American Renaissance* (1994), 195–226, quotation 215.

[66] Sarah A. Clarke to James Freeman Clarke, November 17, 1839, in Thomas Wentworth Higginson, *Margaret Fuller Ossoli* (Boston, 1884), 117; Margaret Fuller to [?], [Autumn? 1839?], *Letters,* 2:97; Margaret Fuller to Elizabeth Hoar, [April? 1844?], *Letters,* 3:185.

[67] Elizabeth Cady Stanton, in *History of Woman Suffrage,* 1:801.

[68] Margaret Fuller to [?], n.d., *Letters,* 6:144; [Margaret Fuller], "The Magnolia of Lake Pontchartrain," *Dial,* January 1841, 299–305, quotation 304.

CHAPTER 5

[69] Margaret Fuller to William H. Channing, August 16, 1843, *Letters* 3:141; Margaret Fuller to Ralph Waldo Emerson, August 17, 1843, *Letters* 3:143.

[70] S. M. Fuller, *Summer on the Lakes, in 1843* (Boston, 1844), 67; Higginson, *Margaret Fuller Ossoli*, 194.

[71] Fuller, *Summer on the Lakes*, 4–5.

[72] Ibid., 6.

[73] Ibid., 18, 103.

[74] Ibid., 181.

[75] Ibid., 102.

[76] Ibid., 183.

[77] Ibid., 235, 233.

[78] Ibid., 182, 205.

[79] Ibid., 235–36.

[80] Ibid., 102; Margaret Fuller, Journal, [July 5, 1844], " 'The Impulses of Human Nature': Margaret Fuller's Journal from June through October 1844," 78. Among her new family woes were her brothers' difficulties at Harvard and work, her inability to find a situation for her emotionally disturbed youngest brother, and her sister's desperately unhappy marriage.

[81] Fuller, Journal, [July 8, 1844], ibid., 80. Diana was the Roman goddess of the moon and the hunt; Hecate was a Greek goddess of magic and the underworld; in Greek mythology, the Sphynx was a winged monster with a lion's body and a woman's head who puzzled men with her riddles; and Isis was a powerful Egyptian fertility goddess. Leila, a creation of Fuller's, fused the attributes of all of these figures. Diana, Isis, and the Virgin Mother, popularly associated with both fertility and virginity (in the sense of belonging to no man), symbolized female creative power and independence.

[82] Fuller, *Woman in the Nineteenth Century*, 157, vi.

[83] Ibid., 103.

[84] Ibid.

[85] Ibid., 102, 104.

[86] Ibid., 154–55. Fuller's use of the typology of human character in ancient mythology dated back to her Conversations of 1839, which focused on Greek mythology as "a complete expression of the cultivation of a nation" and defined Minerva as the "type" of "Intellectual Power, Practical Reason." See [Peabody], "Margaret Fuller's Boston Conversations: The 1839–1840 Series," 204; Ralph Waldo Emerson, in *Memoirs*, 1:333.

[87] Fuller, *Woman in the Nineteenth Century*, 155–56, 44.

[88] Ibid., 69.

[89] Ibid., 141.

[90] Ibid., 141, 155.

[91] Ibid., 106, 161, 183.

[92] Ibid., 84. Thus Fuller implicitly criticized the theory of republican motherhood under which she was raised as well as the relatively conservative stances of the American educational reformer Catharine Beecher (who justified expanding women's educational opportunities in terms of the nation's growing need for schoolteachers) and Sarah Josepha Hale, the influential editor of *Godey's Magazine and Lady's Book* (who supported the education of women but opposed their public participation). Fuller's position was closer to that of the English author Mary Wollstonecraft, whose controversial *Vindication of the Rights of Woman* (1792) demanded education for women as a fundamental natural right.

[93] Fuller, *Woman in the Nineteenth Century*, 25, 107, 108, 105, 45, 162, 27, 107.

[94] Ibid., 26, 159. In formulating her list of social injustices and particular reforms, Fuller drew upon, modified, and extended the feminist insights of the English authors Mary Wollstonecraft, Anna Jameson (who dared to discuss the plight of prostitutes sympathetically in her *Winter Studies and Summer Rambles in Canada* [1838]), and Harriet Martineau

(whose contentious *Society in America* [1837] was highly critical of America's undemocratic treatment of its slaves and women), as well as the Americans Catharine Maria Sedgwick (whose sentimental novels and domestic advice books cautiously explored women's problems inside and outside of marriage) and Lydia Maria Child (who joined other radical female abolitionists in comparing the injustices suffered by American women and slaves). Of these pioneering studies, only Wollstonecraft's *Vindication* approaches *Woman in the Nineteenth Century* in boldness or scope.

[95] Fuller, *Woman in the Nineteenth Century,* 111–12.

[96] Ibid., 106, 108.

[97] Ibid., 23–24, 18–19.

[98] Ibid., vi.

[99] Ibid., 27–30.

[100] Ibid., 163.

[101] Ibid., 124–25.

[102] Ibid., 155; Margaret Fuller to William H. Channing, November 17, 1844, *Letters,* 3:241. *Woman in the Nineteenth Century* far exceeded the popularity of other Transcendentalist publications: the entire first edition of one thousand copies sold out within two weeks of publication. By contrast, only five hundred copies of Emerson's *Nature* (1836) were sold over seven years.

CHAPTER 6

[103] Margaret Fuller to Samuel Gray Ward, December 29, 1844, *Letters,* 3:256; [Margaret Fuller], "Items of Foreign Gossip," *New-York Daily Tribune,* September 24, 1845, 1. Fuller had first written of her wish for women to build "the life of thought upon the life of action" in 1839, as she initiated her first Conversation in Boston; see Margaret Fuller to [Sophia Ripley?], August 27, 1839, *Letters,* 2:87.

[104] [Margaret Fuller], "French Gayety," *New-York Daily Tribune,* July 9, 1845, 1.

[105] [Margaret Fuller], *New-York Daily Tribune,* June 24, 1846, 1. See Document 28.

[106] [Margaret Fuller], "Emerson's Essays," *New-York Daily Tribune,* December 7, 1844. See Document 27.

[107] [Margaret Fuller], "First of August, 1845," *New-York Daily Tribune,* August 1, 1845, 1.

[108] [Margaret Fuller], "What Fits a Man to Be a Voter? Is It to Be White Within, or White Without?" *New-York Daily Tribune,* March 31, 1846, 1. See Document 32.

[109] Ibid.

[110] [Margaret Fuller], "Lyceum of New-Bedford, Mass.," *New-York Daily Tribune,* December 9, 1845, 1. See Document 31.

[111] [Margaret Fuller], "Narrative of the Life of Frederick Douglass, an American Slave, Written by Himself," *New-York Daily Tribune,* June 10, 1845, 1.

[112] Horace Greeley, in *Memoirs,* 2:158.

[113] Margaret Fuller to James F. Clarke, [August 14, 1845], *Letters,* 6:359.

[114] Margaret Fuller to James Nathan, [May 4?, 1845], *Letters,* 4:95; Margaret Fuller to James Nathan, June 12, 1845, *Letters,* 4:117; Margaret Fuller to James Nathan, May 19, [1845], *Letters,* 4:102. Fuller's letters, which Nathan kept against her will, were first published after his death by his son.

[115] Margaret Fuller, "Fragments of Margaret Fuller's Journal: 1844–1845," Fruitlands Museum Library, Harvard, Mass. Nathan left for Europe in June 1845. After using Fuller's influence to obtain letters of recommendation, he withdrew from their correspondence without explanation. He announced his engagement to another woman in September 1846 and his marriage in November 1846.

[116] [Margaret Fuller], "Cassius M. Clay," *New-York Daily Tribune,* January 14, 1846, 1; Rebecca Spring, "Friendships of Rebecca Buffum Spring," arr. Beatrice Buffum-Spring Borchardt, Raritan Bay Union Collection, New Jersey Historical Society, 6, cited in *"These*

Sad But Glorious Days": Dispatches from Europe, 1846–1850, ed. Larry J. Reynolds and Susan Belasco Smith (New Haven, 1991), 7.

[117]Margaret Fuller to Ralph Waldo Emerson, November 16, 1846, *Letters,* 4:245.

[118]"Abandon all hope, you who enter here."

[119][Margaret Fuller], "Things and Thoughts in Europe, No. VI," November 1846, Paris, *New-York Daily Tribune,* December 23, 1846, 1; [Margaret Fuller], "Things and Thoughts in Europe. No. XIII," n.d., [Naples], *New-York Daily Tribune,* May 29, 1847, 1.

[120]Margaret Fuller to Ralph Waldo Emerson, November 16, 1846, *Letters,* 4:248; Margaret Fuller to Ralph Waldo Emerson, March 15, 1847, *Letters,* 4:261.

[121]Margaret Fuller to Margarett C. Fuller, October 16, 1847, *Letters,* 4:299–300; Margaret Fuller to Elizabeth Hoar, September 1847, *Letters,* 4:293.

[122][Margaret Fuller], "Things and Thoughts in Europe, No. XXIII," March 29, 1848, Rome, *New-York Daily Tribune,* May 4, 1848, 1; Margaret Fuller to William H. Channing, March 29, 1848, *Letters,* 5:58.

[123]On April 4, 1849, Fuller wrote to Ossoli, "How very strange it is that we cannot spend this day together. We must pray to be happier another year." See Margaret Fuller to Giovanni Angelo Ossoli, April 4, 1849, *Letters,* 5:223.

[124]Margaret Fuller to Margarett C. Fuller, December 16, 1847, *Letters,* 4:312; Fuller, *Woman in the Nineteenth Century,* vi.

[125][Margaret Fuller], "Things and Thoughts in Europe. No. XXVI," December 2, 1848, Rome, *New-York Daily Tribune,* January 26, 1849, 1.

[126]Ibid.; [Margaret Fuller], "Things and Thoughts in Europe. No. XXVIII," February 20, 1849, Rome, *New-York Daily Tribune,* April 4, 1849, 1; Margaret Fuller to Margarett C. Fuller, November 16, 1848, *Letters,* 5:147. She repeated the phrase, with darker overtones, in a letter to Ralph Waldo Emerson, June 10, 1849, *Letters,* 5:240.

[127]Margaret Fuller to Ellen Fuller Channing, December 11, 1849, *Letters,* 5:293; Margaret Fuller to Caroline Sturgis Tappan, [ca. December 17, 1849], *Letters,* 5:302. The French army entered the defeated city of Rome on July 3, 1849; Fuller and Ossoli escaped with American passports on July 12.

[128][Margaret Fuller], "Things and Thoughts in Europe. No. XXXIII," July 6, 1849, Rome, *New-York Daily Tribune,* August 11, 1849, 2. See Document 35.

[129][Margaret Fuller], "Things and Thoughts in Europe, No. XXXV," November 15, 1849, Florence, *New-York Daily Tribune,* January 9, 1850, 1.

[130][Margaret Fuller], "Italy," January 6, 1850, Florence, *New-York Daily Tribune,* February 13, 1850, Supplement, 1. See Document 36.

[131]Margaret Fuller to Arthur Hugh Clough, February 16, [1850], *Letters,* 6:64–65; Margaret Fuller to William H. Channing, December 17, 1849, *Letters,* 5:301; Margaret Fuller, in *Memoirs,* 2:311.

[132]Margaret Fuller to Margarett C. Fuller, May 14, 1850, *Letters,* 6:86–87.

[133]Ralph Waldo Emerson, Journal, 1850, *Journals of Emerson,* 11:256; Margaret Fuller to Emelyn Story, November 30, 1849, *Letters,* 5:285; Margaret Fuller to Costanza Arconati Visconti, [August 1849], *Letters,* 5:250.

CHAPTER 7

[134]Margaret Fuller to William H. Channing, [June? 1844], *Letters,* 3:199.

[135]A. Bronson Alcott, Journal, October 18, 1851, *Journals of Bronson Alcott,* 1:255. Emerson gave a remarkably similar private assessment of Fuller in 1843: "She rose before me at times into heroical & godlike regions, and I could remember no superior woman, but thought of Ceres, Minerva, Proserpine, and the august ideal forms of the Foreworld." See Ralph Waldo Emerson, Journal, 1843, *Journals of Emerson,* 8:368–69.

[136]Fuller, *Woman in the Nineteenth Century,* 163; Margaret Fuller to Jane F. Tuckerman, September 21, 1838, *Letters,* 1:341.

PART TWO

The Documents

8

Early Letters
and "Autobiographical Sketch"

Unpublished during Margaret Fuller's lifetime, this first set of documents reveals the many sides of her early development. She faithfully corresponded with dozens of people throughout her life. The letters printed here are but a small sample from the three volumes that she wrote during her years in New England. They shed light upon Fuller's relationship with her parents and her unusual education (Documents 1–4), her social life (5), her spiritual crisis and unfolding vision (6–7), her philosophy of teaching (8–9), her hopes for the Dial *(10–11), her theory of friendship (12–14), and her experiences in leading the Conversation Club for women in Boston between 1839 and 1844 (15–17). These letters form an interesting comparison with the last selection (Document 18), from Fuller's unfinished "Autobiographical Sketch." Written in 1840 and published after her death in* The Memoirs of Margaret Fuller Ossoli, *the "Autobiographical Sketch" can be read as Fuller's first sustained attempt to understand the positive and negative implications of her childhood and education for her emerging sense of self.*

1

To Timothy Fuller

Cambridge. 16 January 1820

My dear father.

I received your letter of the 29th about a week ago. I should have written to you much sooner but have been very busy. I begin to be anxious about my letter of the 28th which you do not mention having received in

---

The Letters of Margaret Fuller, ed. Robert N. Hudspeth, 6 vols. (Ithaca, 1983–1994), 1:93–95.

any of your letters. If it has not miscarried it reached you a fortnight ago. Your letter to me was dated the day after mine was written but you do not mention it in any of your letters to Mamma.

I attend a school which is kept by Aunt Abigail for *Eugene* and *myself* and my *cousins* which with writing and singing schools and my lessons to Uncle Elisha takes up most of my time—[1] . . .

You will let me read Zeluco? will you not and no conditions.[2] Have you been to the theatre this winter? Have they any oratorios at Washington?—I am writing a new tale called The young satirist. You must expect the remainder of this page to be filled with a series of unconnected intelligence My beautiful pen now makes a large mark I will write no farther. 17th January 1820

Yesterday I threw by my pen for the reason mentioned above. Have you read Hesitation yet.[3] I knew you would (though you are no novel reader) to see if they were rightly delineated for I am possessed of the greatest blessing of life a good and kind father. Oh I can never repay you for all the love you have shown me But I will do all I can

We have had a dreadful snowstorm today. I never look around the room and behold all the comforts with which Heaven has blessed me without thinking of those *wretched* creatures who are wandering in all the snow without food or shelter. I am too young No I am not. In nine years a great part of my life I can remember but two good actions done those more out of se[l]fishness than charity. There is a poor woman of the name of Wentworth in Boston she would willingly procure a subsistence but has not the means. My dear father a dollar would be a great sum to this poor woman. You remember the handsome dollar that I know your generosity would have bestowed on [me] when I had finished my Deserted Village[4] I shall finish it well and desire nothing but the pleasure of giving it to her. My dear father send it to me immediately I am going into town

---

[1]While her father was away in Washington, D.C., Margaret Fuller recited her Latin and Greek lessons to Elisha Fuller, her father's brother. Aunt Abigail was her mother's sister, Abigail Crane.

[2]In a letter of December 25, 1819, Fuller had begged her father's permission to read John Moore's *Zeluco: Various Views of Human Nature Taken from Life and Manners, Foreign and Domestic* (London, 1789). See Margaret Fuller to Timothy Fuller, December 25, 1819, *Letters*, 1:90–91.

[3]Fuller had told her father that she was reading a "moral-novel" called *Hesitation* (ibid.). This was *Hesitation: or, To Marry, or Not to Marry?* (London, 1819). Timothy Fuller responded on January 25, 1820, that he wanted her to "acquire a taste for books of higher order than tales and novels." See Timothy Fuller to Margaret Fuller, January 25, 1820, Fuller Manuscripts, 5:4.

[4]Fuller was translating the English poet Oliver Goldsmith's poem "The Deserted Village" (1770) into Latin.

this week I have a thousand things to say but neither time or paper to say them in. Farewel my dear Father I am Your affectionate daughter

MARGARET FULLER

P S I do not like Sarah, call me Margaret alone, pray do![5]

[5] In his reply of January 25, 1820, Timothy Fuller ignored his daughter's desire to change her name, but he did grant her permission to give a dollar to the poor woman "and to charge it to me." See Timothy Fuller to Margaret Fuller, January 25, 1820, Fuller Manuscripts, 5:4.

2

To Margarett C. Fuller

Boston. 2d Dec. 1821

Dear Mother

I received today your affectionate letter dated 28th Nov. I should be very much pleased to hear some particulars of the conversation which pleased you so much between Mr Frey and Mr Cushman.[1] I am very sorry for your disappointment at the theatre. It was hardly worth the trouble of dressing oneself. Miss Abba Crane[2] has not as yet done me the favor of writing to me I dare say she will not this winter. Pray if you hear from her tell me how the children do. Tell my dear father that I have not cried once since he went away. I am as happy here as I can be separated from you. I walked out to C P[3] yesterday afternoon. Sophia Williams is better She sent her love to you and intreats you to write to her. She can speak much more distinctly. Poor Mrs Stuart is much better. The Physicians say that she may probably linger on a month. I called on Mrs Mycall and repented of it for she kept me almost an hour to hear good advice.[4] Uncle Thomas is worse.[5] He has a very good nurse.

5th Dec I have for different reasons defered finishing my letter until now. Poor Susan Williams is threatened with a fever. I hope she will not lose all her places, she is a very sweet tempered, amiable girl. I love her

[1] Fellow passengers on the Fullers' journey to Washington, D.C., whom Margarett Crane Fuller had mentioned in a letter of November 28, 1821.
[2] Margaret Fuller's aunt, Abigail Crane.
[3] Cambridgeport, the Fullers' home.
[4] These were all neighbors of the Fuller family.
[5] Thomas Williams, Timothy Fuller's cousin and the father of Margaret Fuller's schoolmate Susan Williams (mentioned in the next paragraph).

The Letters of Margaret Fuller, ed. Robert N. Hudspeth, 6 vols. (Ithaca, 1983–1994), 1:113–14.

very much and I hope that she will not have to go to the foot in all the classes.[6] If she can get well by next Tuesday for the rest of the week is vacation because it is Thanksgiving. Professor Everett[7] will preach for us Thanksgiving day and thus I shall have the opportunity I have long desired of hearing this celebrated preacher. Grandmamma intends to write to papa very soon Tell him I am writing a long composition but it will be three weeks before it is given up. He will not have it till I know what the Dr. says to it. I am next to the head in the second class in E parsing. Perhaps I may get up to the head and so get a medal I have had three medals, but Susan Channing[8] who went into the class three months before I did has been up to the head a long time it has brought her seventeen medals and she has had three medals for composition and one accurate and now she has got the eye of Intelligence because she has made up her twenty one medals but she would not have had it this year if it had not been for that class, if I can get up to the head I shall keep there for I have not made one mistake in that class; indeed I have taken great pain not to, perhaps I may have the eye, before you return which is the highest medal in school. But dear mother I forget, this is probably not as interesting to you as it is to me. Farewell I am your affectionate daughter

SARAH M FULLER

[6]While her parents were away, Fuller (and her cousin Susan) attended the Boston Lyceum for Young Ladies, conducted by Dr. John Park (1775–1852), a graduate of Dartmouth College.
[7]Edward Everett (1794–1865), a brilliant orator, was professor of Greek at Harvard in 1821. He later became a political leader in Massachusetts.
[8]Susan Cleveland Channing was another schoolmate.

3

To Timothy Fuller

Groton [Massachusetts] 14th Feb. 1825.

My dear father,
    Your letter of the 6th inst reached me yesterday accompanied by the Albion. That, dated the 15th, was not received until Thursday, mine, I think, was mailed on Wednesday, consequently I could not acknowledge the receipt of yours. I believe, papa, if you will take the trouble to over-

The Letters of Margaret Fuller, ed. Robert N. Hudspeth, 6 vols. (Ithaca, 1983–1994), 1:148–49.

look my letters, that you will find (though, I confess, my general want of that exactitude necessary to please *men* of *business* may have given you just reason to suspect me) that I *have endeavored* to comply with your wishes in this respect, as far as I know them; the receipt is always mentioned, I fancy though perhaps the dates may not be. I will try to remember in future. I have received six of the following dates the 22d and 27th Dec, 3d 13th and 27th Jan, and one this month already mentioned. . . . I should always, as you have desired send you word how I do, but when I reperuse the letter, these formal notices of my health and well being look *so* egotistical, they remind me so forcibly of the invariable beginning of the little girl's letters with whom I used to go to school "I take this opportunity to inform you that we are all well and hoping that you enjoy the same blessing." Besides, mon cher pere, you do not conform to your own rule; not once this winter have you told me whether you are well, ill, or indifferent. However, if you wish it't is enough, here it comes without any more prosing. *"J'ai un rhume avec une tous qui me génent beaucoup, d' ailleurs, je me trouve asser bien."*[1]

By the emphasis laid on the word slovenliness I see what you think of my letters. I confess that I do not bestow on you that attention that I do on other correspondents, who will I think be more critical and less kind.[2] I have abused your indulgence I own. I must request that you will burn my letters, all that you now have, let this affair of confessions, extenuations and palliations share the common lot; and I will in future assume a *fairer outer* guise at least in my epistles though this matter may not recommend them more highly to your eye, mind's eye I mean. Indeed, I cannot make myself interesting to you; to your strictures on my conduct manners &c however valuable to me I can return nothing but thanks; my delineations of such scenes and characters as I meet with in my retired situation, however much matter of reflection they may afford to me, would not probably interest you, who can contemplate human nature on so much more extensive a scale and under so many diversified forms, neither if I thought my ideas and conclusions would interest you, should I be willing to impart them to the paper which might prove not a sure, though a senseless confidant. I have numberless things to say to you, that I hope will interest you who I know my dear, kind father makes all the views and affairs of his

---

[1]"I have a cold with a cough that inconveniences me a great deal, but other than that I am well enough" (French).

[2]Timothy Fuller's letter of February 6, 1825, offered a detailed critique of his daughter's writing and noted that his own youthful letters were not "in general liable to the charge of slovenliness." See Timothy Fuller to Margaret Fuller, February 6, 1825, Fuller Manuscripts, 5:44.

little daughter his own, and when we all meet again (and I trust that time is not far distant) we shall have a delightful time by our own fireside . . . Your ever affectionate daughter

SARAH M. FULLER.

4

To Susan Prescott[1]

Cambridge, 11 July 1825

Having excused myself from accompanying my honored father to church, which I always do in the afternoon, when possible, I devote to you the hours which Ariosto and Helvetius ask of my eyes, — as, lying on my writing-desk, they put me in mind that they must return this week to their owner.[2]

You keep me to my promise of giving you some sketch of my pursuits. I rise a little before five, walk an hour, and then practise on the piano, till seven, when we breakfast. Next I read French, — Sismondi's Literature of the South of Europe, — till eight, then two or three lectures in Brown's Philosophy.[3] About half-past nine I go to Mr. Perkins's school and study Greek till twelve, when, the school being dismissed, I recite, go home, and practise again till dinner, at two.[4] Sometimes, if the conversation is very agreeable, I lounge for half an hour over the dessert, though rarely so lavish of time. Then, when I can, I read two hours in Italian, but I am often interrupted. At six, I walk, or take a drive. Before going to bed, I play or sing, for half an hour or so, to make all sleepy, and, about eleven, retire to write a little while in my journal, exercises on what I have read, or a series of characteristics which I am filling up according to advice. Thus, you see, I am learning Greek, and making acquaintance with metaphysics, and French and Italian literature.

"How," you will say, "can I believe that my indolent, fanciful, pleasure-

[1]Susan Prescott (1796–1869) conducted the Young Ladies Seminary in Groton, Massachusetts, between 1819 and 1829. Fuller attended the girls' school in 1824–1825.

[2]Prescott had loaned Fuller works by the Italian poet Lodovico Ariosto (1474–1533) and the French *philosophe* Claude Adrien Helvétius (1715–1771).

[3]The Swiss historian Leonard Simonde de Sismondi (1773–1842) published *De la littérature du midi de l'Europe* (1813) in four volumes. Thomas Brown (1778–1820), professor of moral philosophy at Edinburgh, published his *Lectures on the Philosophy of the Human Mind* in 1820.

[4]George William Perkins, an 1824 graduate of Yale College, taught school for a year in Cambridgeport before attending the Yale Divinity School.

The Letters of Margaret Fuller, ed. Robert N. Hudspeth, 6 vols. (Ithaca, 1983–1994), 1:151–52.

loving pupil, perseveres in such a course?" I feel the power of industry growing every day, and, besides the all-powerful motive of ambition, and a new stimulus lately given through a friend. I have learned to believe that nothing, no! not perfection, is unattainable. I am determined on distinction, which formerly I thought to win at an easy rate; but now I see that long years of labor must be given to secure even the "*succes de societe*,"[5]—which, however, shall never content me. I see multitudes of examples of persons of genius, utterly deficient in grace and the power of pleasurable excitement. I wish to combine both. I know the obstacles in my way. I am wanting in that intuitive tact and polish, which nature has bestowed upon some, but which I must acquire. And, on the other hand, my powers of intellect, though sufficient, I suppose, are not well disciplined. Yet all such hindrances may be overcome by an ardent spirit. If I fail, my consolation shall be found in active employment.

[5]Social success (French).

5

To Almira P. Barlow[1]

Cambridge, Nov 19. 1830
Having some reason to flatter myself with present possession of a vacant evening, a vacant heart, head, &c, &c, I think this a suitable occasion to address the apprehensive ear of my amiable Almira. I wish the evening to be free from interruption, expecting the letter to occupy half an hour in the inditing; and the "tenderly playful" reminiscences which cluster round your once-invoked image, four or five additional. A vacant heart and head because, — but oh! it is too tedious to why and wherefore in this style.

My dear Simplicetta, why don't you get well? Really this additional pain in your fascinating ankles is *too* heart-breaking. The Trevetts, Coffins, Breeds &c, are too exciting for you I know.[2] Never before have your *ankles* been excited, even by my overwhelming power. Close your door, I entreat you, against the Lynn population. Rude health would be in much

[1]Almira Cornelia Penniman was one of Fuller's closest childhood friends. She married the minister David Hatch Barlow in 1830.
[2]The Barlows' neighbors in Lynn, Massachusetts.

The Letters of Margaret Fuller, ed. Robert N. Hudspeth, 6 vols. (Ithaca, 1983–1994), 1:170–72.

better keeping with the elegant simplicity of your abode, than these complicated ills. Come and see me; I will *reason* you out of them.

Many things have happened since I echoed your farewell laugh. Elizabeth and I have been fully occupied.[3] She has cried a great deal, fainted a good deal and played the harp most of all. I have neither fertilized the earth with my tears, edified its inhabitants by my delicacy of constitution, nor wakened its echoes to my harmony,—yet some things have I achieved in my own soft feminine style. I hate glare, thou knowest, and have hitherto successfully screened my virtues therefrom. I have made several garments fitted for the wear of American youth; I have written six letters, and received a correspondent number; I have read one book,—a piece of poetry entitled "Two Agonies", by M. A. Browne, (pretty caption, is it not?) and J. J. Knapp's trial;[4] I have given advice twenty times,—I have taken it once; I have gained two friends, and recovered two; I have felt admiration four times,—horror once, and disgust twice; I have been a journey, and shewed my penetration in discovering the beauties of Nature through a thick and never-lifted shroud of rain; I have turned two new leaves in the book of human nature; I have got a new pink bag, (beautiful!) I have imposed on the world time and again, by describing your Lynn life as the perfection of human felicity, and adorning my visit there with all sorts of impossible adventures,—thus at once exhibiting my own rich invention and the credulous ignorance of my auditors (light and dark you know, dear, give life to a picture). I have had tears for others' woes, and patience for my own,—in short, to climax this journal of many-colored deeds and chances, so well have I played my part, that in the self-same night I was styled by two several persons "a sprightly young lady", and "a Syren!!" Oh rapturous sound! I have reached the goal of my ambition; Earth has nothing fairer or brighter to offer. "Intelligency" was nothing to it. A "Supercilious", "satirical", "affected", "pedantic" "Syren"!!!! Can the olla-podrida[5] of human nature present a compound of more varied ingredients, or higher gusto?

Loveliest of created minister's wives! I have egotized as became a friend so interesting as myself, to one so sympathizing as thyself For the present I pause. When, oh when shalt thou gather strength to come and hear the remainder? Let the hour hasten forward. I sigh to laugh with thee. And we *will* laugh, my beloved! as Leila said to Mignoun,[6] in those

---

[3] Elizabeth Randall, another friend of Fuller's youth.
[4] Probably the poetry of Mary Ann Browne (1812–1844) and the transcript of a Salem, Massachusetts, murder trial.
[5] A miscellaneous mixture or stew.
[6] Characters in the German author Johann Wolfgang von Goethe's novel *Wilhelm Meisters Lehrjahre* (Wilhelm Meister's Apprenticeship), one of Fuller's favorite books.

beautiful Persic poems we have so often conned together in more studious hours. "Let fate do her worst &c!" I send thee the candy: six cents and a quarter I did remit to Boston for it, I do assure thee, small as the package may seem. May it visit thy palate with the sweetness of manna! Adieu; say unutterable things from me to Frederic and Josephene, and forget not my regards to Mr Barlow.

P.S. Write soon and let the letter be sentimental. Sentiment now bears unbounded sway in the palace of my heart. But write soon, or the tide may ebb. . . . Faithfully yours,

MARGARET F.

6

To Jane F. Tuckerman[1]

Providence [Rhode Island], October 21. 1838.
I am reminded by what you say, of an era in my own existence; it is seven years bygone. For bitter months a treble weight had been pressing on me; the weight of deceived friendship, domestic discontent, and bootless love. I could not be much alone; a great burden of family cares pressed upon me; I was in the midst of society, and obliged to act my part there as well as I could. It was at the time I took up the study of German, and my progress was like the rebound of a string pressed almost to bursting. My mind being then in the highest state of action, heightened by intellectual appreciation, every pang, and Imagination, by prophetic power, gave to the painful present, all the weight of as painful a future.

At this time I never had any consolation, except in long, solitary walks, and my meditations then were so far aloof from common life that on my return, my fall was like that of the eagle which the sportsman's hand calls bleeding from his lofty flight to stain the earth with his blood.

In such hours we feel so noble, so full of love and bounty that we cannot conceive that any pain should have been needed to teach us. It then seems we are so born for good, that such means of leading us to it were wholly unnecessary. But I have lived to know that the secret of all things

---

[1]Jane Francis Tuckerman (1821?–1856) was one of Fuller's students and later her assistant at the *Dial*.

The Letters of Margaret Fuller, ed. Robert N. Hudspeth, 6 vols. (Ithaca, 1983–1994), 1:347–48.

is pain and that Nature travaileth most painfully with her noblest product. I was not without hours of deep spiritual insight, and consciousness of the inheritance of vast powers. I touched the secret of the universe, and by that touch was invested with talismanic power which has never left me, though it sometimes lies dormant for a long while.

One day lives always in my memory; one chastest, heavenliest day of communion with the soul of things. It was Thanksgiving-Day. I was free to be alone; in the meditative woods, by the choked-up fountain I passed its hours, each of which contained ages of thought and emotion. I saw then how idle were my griefs; that I had acquired *the thought* of each object which had been taken from me, that more extended personal relations would only have given me pleasures which then seemed not worth my care, and which would surely have dimmed my sense of the spiritual meaning of all which had passed. I felt how true it was that nothing in any being which was fit for me, could long be kept from me, and that if separation could be, real intimacy had never been. All the films seemed to drop from my existence, and I was sure that I should never starve in this desert world, but that manna would drop from heaven, if I would but rise with every rising sun to gather it.

In the evening I went into the church-yard; the moon sailed above the rosy clouds. That cresent moon rose above the heavenward-pointing spire. At that hour a vision came upon my soul, whose final scene last month interpreted. The rosy clouds of illusion are all vanished, the moon has waxed to full. May my life be a church, full of devout thoughts, and solemn music. I pray thus, my dearest child: "Our Father, let not the heaviest shower be spared, let not the gardener forbear his knife, till the fair hopeful tree of existence be brought to its fullest blossom and fruit!"

7

To Caroline Sturgis[1]

Jamaica plain [Massachusetts], 26th Septr 1840.
My dear Caroline,
   . . . Of the mighty changes in my spiritual life I do not wish to speak, yet surely you cannot be ignorant of them. All has been revealed, all fore-

---

[1] Caroline Sturgis (1819–1888), the daughter of a wealthy Boston merchant, was Fuller's closest, lifelong female friend. She married William Aspinwall Tappan in 1847.

The Letters of Margaret Fuller, ed. Robert N. Hudspeth, 6 vols. (Ithaca, 1983–1994), 158–59.

shown yet I know it not. Experiment has given place to certainty, pride to obedience, thought to love, and truth is lost in beauty "I am no more below"—I have no words, nor can I now perceive that I shall be able to paint for any one the scenery, nor place in order the history of these great events Yet I have no wish to exclude any one, and of you I almost daily think with love. When we meet you may probably perceive all in me. When we meet you will find me at home. Into that home cold winds may blow, keen lightnings dart their bolts, but I cannot be driven from it more. From that home I look forth and address you sweetly as my friend. Is it not enough?—

8

To A. Bronson Alcott[1]

Providence [Rhode Island] 27th June, 1837.

Dear Sir,

I had flattered myself that you would have been in haste to begin our correspondence since you disappointed me of the expected oppor[tunit]y of conversing with you at the time of the dedication of the school[2]—But since you will neither come nor write my desire to hear from you is so strong that I must do something on my side . . .

I am much pleased with my new haunt as far as the eye is concerned—I believe you have never seen the building—it is in excellent taste and all the arrangements speak of comfort quiet and even elegance. Nothing is wanting to make it look the home of thought except more books, a few casts and a picture or two which will be added in due time. . . . Mr Fuller[3] is in many respects particularly suited to this business. His ready sympathy, his active eye, and pious, tender turn of thought are so adapted to all the practical part; The danger arising from that sort of education which has unfolded there is that he may not be sufficiently systematic and not

---

[1]A. Bronson Alcott (1799–1888), a Transcendentalist and educational reformer, hired (but never paid) Fuller to teach in his Temple School in Boston in the fall of 1836.

[2]Fuller was teaching at the Greene Street School in Providence, Rhode Island, which opened in June 1837.

[3]Hiram Fuller (1814–1880) owned and operated the Greene Street School. He and Margaret Fuller were not related.

The Letters of Margaret Fuller, ed. Robert N. Hudspeth, 6 vols. (Ithaca, 1983–1994), 1:286–87.

observe due gradation and completeness in his plans. However all is tentative that is doing yet and those Powers who have so [favored] him will now, it is to be hoped, turn a [fairer] side to the light—I often think, dear Sir, with pleasure on the roundness (as Mr Emerson perhaps would express it) of your world—There were details in which I thought your plan imperfect, but it only needs to compare pupils who have been treated as many of these have with those who have been under your care to sympathize with your creed that those who would reform the world should begin with the beginning of life—Particularly do I feel the importance of your attempts to teach the uses of language and cultivate the imagination in dealing with young persons who have had no faculties exercised except the memory and the common, practical understanding. In *your* children I found an impatience of labor but a liveliness of mind, in many of *these* with well-disposed hearts, [the] mind has been absolutely torpid. Those who have been under Mr F's care are in far better state than the rest.—

I hope you will write soon and let me know as much of your thoughts and affairs as you can. Please give my regards to Mrs Alcott and believe me always sincerely your friend.

S. M. FULLER.

9

To Ralph Waldo Emerson [?][1]

Providence R I July 3d 1837

. . . I cannot yet say whether I shall stay here, at first I was much disappointed on examining my field of action. It seemed to me that I could not work at all on subjects so unprepared as I found here. However I tried and think I already perceive that it is not in vain. There is room here, if I mistake not, for a great move in the cause of education, but whether it is I who am to help move, I cannot yet tell. I some times think yes, because the plan is becoming so complete in my mind, ways and means are continually occurring to me, and so far as I have tried them, they seem to succeed. I am left almost as much at liberty as if no other person were concerned with

[1]Ralph Waldo Emerson (1803–1882), a prominent American essayist and lecturer, was a leading member of the Transcendentalist circle. Following their first meeting in July 1836, he and Fuller became close friends. The bracketed question mark here (and in Documents 13–16) indicates that the identity of the addressee has been established contextually.

The Letters of Margaret Fuller, ed. Robert N. Hudspeth, 6 vols. (Ithaca, 1983–1994), 1:288–89.

me. The arrangements I have made in the school are satisfactory to me for the present. I am sure I shall do good in the way of clearing the ground either for myself or somebody else. About sixty pupils, I should think, are under my care more or less, and they many of them begin already to attempt to walk in the ways I point but which are unknown indeed to most of them. Activity of mind, accuracy in processes, constant looking for principles, and search after the good and beautiful, "that's the ground I go upon" as Mr S says in Vivian Gray,[2] and many of those who have never studied any thing but words seem much pleased with their new prospects—However I am aware that if there is difficulty, there is charm too to them in all this novelty, and am prepared to see new obstacles constantly rising up. Besides, my own progress in any of those acquirements, wh[ic]h I have most loved will be no wise aided by staying here. I must work years to get ready a hill side for my vineyard. As to Goethe I scarce know how to answer you. I should think after hearing me say so much about him, you wld be aware that I do not consider him from that point of view you wish me to take. I do not go to him as a guide or friend but as a great thinker, who makes me think, a wonderful artist who gratifies my tastes—As far as he had religion or morality, I shld say they were expressed in this poem of his *"Eins und Alles,"*[3] of which I send you a rude translation.

[2] *Vivian Grey* (London, 1826) was the anonymously published first novel of the English author and statesman Benjamin Disraeli (1804–1881). Mr. Septimus Sessions, a very minor character in the long novel, punctuates his remarks with the phrase, "that's the ground I stand upon."

[3] "One and All" (German). Written in October 1821, the poem claims that an individual must surrender his or her "being" to join the "World Soul."

10

To Frederic H. Hedge[1]

Jamaica Plain [Massachusetts]. 10th March 1840
Henry, I adjure you, in the name of all the Genii, Muses, Pegasus, Apollo, Pollio, Apollyon, ("and must I mention"—) to send me something good for this journal[2] before the 1st May. All mortals, my friend, are slack and

[1] Frederic Henry Hedge (1805–1890) was a Transcendentalist, a Unitarian minister, and a serious student of German philosophy and theology.
[2] The *Dial*, the Transcendentalists' journal.

The Letters of Margaret Fuller, ed. Robert N. Hudspeth, 6 vols. (Ithaca, 1983–1994), 2:124–25.

bare; they wait to see whether Hotspur wins, before they levy aid for as good a plan as ever was laid.[3] I know you are plagued and it is hard to write, just so is it with me, for I also am a father. But you can help, and become a godfather! if you like, and let it be nobly, for if the first number justify not the magazine, it will not find justification; so write, my friend, write, and paint not for me fine plans on the clouds to be achieved at some future time, as others do who have had many years to be thinking of immortality.

I could make a number myself with the help Mr. E. will give, but the Public, I trow, is too astute a donkey not to look sad at *that*.

[3]William Shakespeare, *I Henry IV,* 2.3.16–18.

11

To William H. Channing[1]

Jamaica Plain [Massachusetts], 22d March, 1840
My dear friend,

. . . A perfectly free organ[2] is to be offered for the expression of individual thought and character. There are no party measures to be carried, no particular standard to be set up. A fair calm tone, a recognition of universal principles will, I hope pervade the essays in every form I hope there will neither be a spirit of dogmatism nor of compromise. That this periodical will not aim at leading public opinion, but at stimulating each man to think for himself, to think more deeply and more nobly by letting them see how some minds are kept alive by a wise self-trust. I am not sanguine as to the amount of talent which will be brought to bear on this publication. I find all concerned rather indifferent, and see no great promise for the present. I am sure we cannot show high culture, and I doubt about vigorous thought. But I hope we shall show free action as far as it goes and a high aim. It were much if a periodical could be kept open to accomplish no outward object, but merely to afford an avenue

[1]William Henry Channing (1810–1884) was a Unitarian minister, a socialist and reformer, and one of Fuller's closest friends.
[2]The *Dial*.

The Letters of Margaret Fuller, ed. Robert N. Hudspeth, 6 vols. (Ithaca, 1983–1994), 2:125–27.

for what of free and calm thought might be originated among us by the wants of individual minds. . . .

S. MARGARET FULLER.

12

To Ralph Waldo Emerson

29 Sept 1840

I have felt the impossibility of meeting far more than you; so much, that, if you ever know me well, you will feel that the fact of my abiding by you thus far, affords a strong proof that we are to be much to one another. How often have I left you despairing and forlorn. How often have I said, this light will never understand my fire; this clear eye will never discern the law by which I am filling my circle; this simple force will never interpret my need of manifold being.

Dear friend on one point misunderstand me less. I do not love power other than every vigorous nature delights to feel itself living. To violate the sanctity of relations, I am as far from it as you can be. I make no claim. I have no wish which is not dictated by a feeling of truth. Could I lead the highest Angel captive by a look, that look I would not give, unless prompted by true love. I am no usurper. I ask only mine own inheritance. If it be found that I have mistaken its boundaries, I will give up the choicest vineyard, the fairest flower-garden, to its lawful owner.

In me I did not think you saw the purity, the singleness, into which, I have faith that all this darting motion, and restless flame shall yet be attempered and subdued. I felt that you did not for me the highest office of friendship, by offering me the clue of the labyrinth of my own being. Yet I thought you appreciated the fearlessness which shrinks from no truth in myself and others, and trusted me, believing that I knew the path for myself. O it must be that you have felt the worth of that truth which has never hesitated to infringe our relation, or aught else, rather than not vindicate itself. If you have not seen this stair on which God has been so untiringly leading me to himself, you have indeed been wholly ignorant

---

The Letters of Margaret Fuller, ed. Robert N. Hudspeth, 6 vols. (Ithaca, 1983–1994), 2:159–61.

of me. Then indeed, when my soul, in its childish agony of prayer, stretched out its arms to you as a father, did you not see what was meant by this crying for the moon; this sullen rejection of playthings which had become unmeaning? Did you then say 'I know not what this means; perhaps this will trouble me; the time will come when I shall hide my eyes from this mood;'—then you are not the friend I seek. But did not you ask for a "foe" in your friend? Did not you ask for a "large formidable nature"? But a beautiful foe, I am not yet, to you. Shall I ever be? I know not. My life is now prayer. Through me sweetest harmonies are momently breathing. Shall they not make me beautiful,—Nay, beauty! Shall not all vehemence, all eccentricity, be purged by these streams of divine light? I have, in these hours, but one pain; the sense of the infinite exhausts and exalts: it cannot therefore possess me wholly; else, were I also one wave of gentlest force. Again I shall cease to melt and flow; again I shall seek and pierce and rend asunder.

But oh, I am now full of such sweet certainty, never never more can it be utterly shaken. All things have I given up to the central power, myself, you also; yet, I cannot forbear adding, dear friend. I am now so at home, I know not how again to wander and grope, seeking my place in another Soul. I need to be recognized. After this, I shall be claimed, rather than claim, yet if I speak of facts, it must be as I see them.

To L. my love.[1] In her, I have always recognized the saintly element. *That,* better than a bible in my hand, shows that it cannot be to me wholly alien. Yet am I no saint, no anything, but a great soul born to know all, before it can return to the creative fount. . . .

---

[1]Lidian Jackson Emerson (1802–1892), Ralph Waldo Emerson's second wife, often welcomed Fuller (and many other guests) into her home for extended visits.

13

To William H. Channing [?]

[n.d.]

I would have my friends tender of me, not because I am frail, but because I am capable of strength;—patient, because they see in me a principle that must, at last, harmonize all the exuberance of my character. I did

---

not well understand what you felt, but I am willing to admit that what you said of my "over-great impetuosity" is just. You will, perhaps, feel it more and more. It may at times hide my better self. When it does, speak, I entreat, as harshly as you feel. Let me be always sure I know the worst. I believe you will be thus just, thus true, for we are both servants of Truth.

14

To William H. Channing [?]

25 August 1842 Concord [Massachusetts]
Beneath this roof of peace, beneficence, and intellectual activity, I find just the alternation of repose and satisfying pleasure that I need.
Do not find fault with the hermits and scholars. The true text is:—

> "Mine own Telemachus
> He does his work—I mine."[1]

All do the work, whether they will or no; but he is "mine own Telemachus" who does it in the spirit of religion, never believing that the last results can be arrested in any one measure or set of measures, listening always to the voice of the Spirit,—and who does this more than [Emerson]?[2]

After the first excitement of intimacy with him,—when I was made so happy by his high tendency, absolute purity, the freedom and infinite graces of an intellect cultivated much beyond any I had known,—came with me the questioning season. I was greatly disappointed in my relation to him. I was, indeed, always called on to be worthy,— this benefit was sure in our friendship. But I found no intelligence of my best self; far less was it revealed to me in new modes; for not only did he seem to want the living faith which enables one to discharge this holiest office of a

---

[1] From "Ulysses" by the English poet laureate Alfred, Lord Tennyson (1809–1892): "Most blameless is he, centred in the sphere / Of common duties, decent not to fail / In offices of tenderness, and pay / Meet adoration to my household gods / When I am gone. He works his work, I mine." According to Greek legend, Telemachus was the son of Odysseus and Penelope. He contrived with his father to slay his mother's suitors. Telemachus was educated in his father's absence by Mentor, his trusted counselor and guide.
[2] Ralph Waldo Emerson, at whose home in Concord Fuller was staying.

The Letters of Margaret Fuller, ed. Robert N. Hudspeth, 6 vols. (Ithaca, 1983–1994), 3:90–92.

friend, but he absolutely distrusted me in every region of my life with which he was unacquainted. The same trait I detected in his relations with others. He had faith in the Universal, but not in the Individual Man; he met men, not as a brother, but as a critic. Philosophy appeared to chill instead of exalting the poet.

But now I am better acquainted with him. His "accept" is true; the "I shall learn," with which he answers every accusation, is no less true. No one can feel his limitations, in fact, more than he, though he always speaks confidently from his present knowledge as all he has yet, and never qualifies or explains. He feels himself "shut up in a crystal cell," from which only "a great love or a great task could release me," and hardly expects either from what remains in this life. But I already see so well how these limitations have fitted him for his peculiar work, that I can no longer quarrel with them; while from his eyes looks out the angel that must sooner or later break every chain. Leave him in his cell affirming absolute truth; protesting against humanity, if so he appears to do; the calm observer of the courses of things. Surely, "he keeps true to this thought, which is the great matter." He has already paid his debt to his time; how much more he will give we cannot know; but already I feel how invaluable is a cool mind, like his, amid the warring elements around us. As I look at him more by his own law, I understand him better; and as I understand him better, differences melt away. My inmost heart blesses the fate that gave me birth in the same clime and time, and that has drawn me into such a close bond with him as, it is my hopeful faith, will never be broken, but from sphere to sphere ever more hallowed.

What did you mean by saying I had imbibed much of his way of thought? I do indeed feel his life stealing gradually into mine; and I sometimes think that my work would have been more simple, and my unfolding to a temporal activity more rapid and easy, if we had never met. But when I look forward to eternal growth, I am always aware that I am far larger and deeper for him. His influence has been to me that of lofty assurance and sweet serenity. He says, I come to him as the European to the Hindoo, or the gay Trouvére[3] to the Puritan in his steeple hat. Of course this implies that our meeting is partial. I present to him the many forms of nature and solicit with music; he melts them all into spirit and reproves performance with prayer. When I am with God alone, I adore in silence. With nature I am filled and grow only. With most men I bring words of now past life, and do actions suggested by the wants of their natures rather than my own. But he stops me from doing anything, and makes me think.

[3] *Trouvères* were minstrels in medieval France.

15

To Sophia Ripley [?][1]

Jamaica Plain [Massachusetts], 27th August, 1839

My dear friend,

I find it more difficult to give on paper a complete outline of my plan for the proposed conversations than I expected. There is so much to say that I cannot make any statement satisfactory to myself within such limits as would be convenient for your purpose. As no one will wish to take the trouble of reading a long manuscript, I shall rather suggest than tell what I wish to do, and defer a full explanation to the first meeting. I wish you to use this communication according to your own judgment; if it seems to you too meagre to give any notion of the plan, lay it aside and interpret for me to whomsoever it may concern.

The advantages of such a weekly meeting might be great enough to repay the trouble of attendance if they consisted only in supplying a point of union to well-educated and thinking women in a city which, with great pretensions to mental refinement, boasts at present nothing of the kind and where I have heard many of mature age wish for some such means of stimulus and cheer, and these people for a place where they could state their doubts and difficulties with hope of gaining aid from the experience or aspirations of others. And if my office were only to suggest topics which would lead to conversation of a better order than is usual at social meetings and to turn back the current when digressing into personalities or commonplaces so that—what is invaluable in the experience of each might be brought to bear upon all. I should think the object not unworthy of an effort. But my own ambition goes much farther. Thus to pass in review the departments of thought and knowledge and endeavor to place them in due relation to one another in our minds. To systematize thought and give a precision in which our sex are so deficient, chiefly, I think because they have so few inducements to test and classify what they receive. To ascertain what pursuits are best suited to us in our time and state of society, and how we may make best use of our means for building up the life of thought upon the life of action.

---

[1]Sophia Dana Ripley (1803–1861), a frequent participant in Fuller's Conversations, was married to the social reformer George Ripley (1802–1880). In 1841 they founded the experimental community of Brook Farm, which Fuller often visited.

The Letters of Margaret Fuller, ed. Robert N. Hudspeth, 6 vols. (Ithaca, 1983–1994), 2:86–89.

Could a circle be assembled in earnest desirous to answer the great questions. What were we born to do? How shall we do it? which so few ever propose to themselves 'till their best years are gone by. I should think the undertaking a noble one, and if my resources should prove sufficient to make me its moving spring, I should be willing to give it a large portion of those coming years which will as I hope be my best. I look upon it with no blind enthusiasm, nor unlimited faith, but with a confidence that I have attained a distinct perception of means which if there are persons competent to direct them, can supply a great want and promote really[?] high objects. So far as I have tried them yet they have met with success so much beyond my hopes, that my faith will not be easily shaken, or my earnestness chilled.

Should I however be disappointed in Boston I could hardly hope that such a plan could be brought to bear upon general society in any other city of the U.S. But I do not fear if a good beginning can be had, I am confident that twenty persons cannot be brought together for better motives than those of vanity or pedantry to talk upon such subjects as we propose without finding in themselves great deficiencies which they will be very desirous to supply. Should the enterprize fail, it will be either from incompetence in me or that sort of vanity in others which wears the garb of modesty. On the first of these points I need not speak. I can scarcely have felt the wants of others so much without feeling my own still more deeply. And from the depth of my feeling and the earnestness it gave such power as I have thus far exerted has come. Of course those who propose to meet me feel a confidence in me. And should they be disappointed I shall regret it not solely or most on my own account, I have not given my gage without weighing my capacity to sustain defeat. For the other I know it is very hard to lay aside the shelter of vague generalities, the cant of coterie criticism and the delicate disdains of *good society* and fearless meet the light although it flow from the sun of truth. Yet, as without such generous courage nothing can be done, or learned I cannot but hope to see many capable of it. Willing that others should think their sayings crude, shallow or tasteless if by such unpleasant means they may secure real health and vigor which may enable them to see their friends undefended by rouge or candlelight.

Since I saw you I have been told that several persons are desirous to join, if only they need not talk. I am so sure that the success of the whole depends on conversation being general that I do not wish any one to join who does not intend, *if possible,* to take an active part. No one will be forced, but those who do not talk will not derive the same advantages with those who openly state their impressions and consent to learn by blundering as is the destiny of Man here below. And general silence or side talks would paralyze me. I should feel coarse and misplaced if I were to be haranguing too much. In former instances I have been able to make it easy and even pleasant to twenty five out of thirty to bear their part, to question, to define, to state and examine their opinions. If I could not do as much now I should consider myself unsuccessful and should withdraw. But I should expect communication to be effected by degrees and to do a great deal myself at the first meetings. . . .

I do not wish at present to pledge myself to any course of subjects. Except generally that they will be such as literature and the arts present in endless profusion. Should a class be brought together, I should wish first to ascertain our common ground and in a few meetings should see whether it be practicable to follow up the design in my mind which would look as yet too grand on paper. Let us see whether there will be any organ and if so note down the music to which it may give breath.

I believe I have said as much as any one will wish to read. I am ready to answer any questions which may be proposed Meanwhile [I] will add nothing more here except always yours truly

S. M. FULLER.

16

To [?]

[Autumn? 1839?]
The circle I meet interests me. So even devoutly thoughtful seems their spirit, that, from the very first I took my proper place, and never had the feeling I dreaded, of display, of a paid Corinne.[1] I feel as I would, truly a teacher and a guide. All are intelligent; five or six have talent. But I am never driven home for ammunition; never put to any expense; never truly called out. What I have is always enough; though I feel how superficially I am treating my subject.

---

[1]Fuller refers to the heroine of the novel *Corinne* (1807), by the French author Anne Louise Germaine (1766–1817), baronne de Staël-Holstein (popularly known as Mme. de Staël). Corinne was an *improvisatrice,* a wild and unpredictable female improviser or genius.

The Letters of Margaret Fuller, ed. Robert N. Hudspeth, 6 vols. (Ithaca, 1983–1994), 2:97.

17

To Elizabeth Hoar[1]

[April? 1844?]

I send you 3 papers written for my class, two by S. Clarke, one by Marianne Jackson.[2] Our last meeting yesterday was beautiful; how noble has been my experience of such relations for six years now, and with so many, and so various minds! Life *is* worth living—is it not?

[1]Elizabeth Sherman Hoar (1814–1878) was engaged to Charles Emerson (Ralph Waldo Emerson's younger brother) when he died in 1836. She then lived with the Emerson family and became one of Fuller's close friends.

[2]Sarah Clarke (1808–1896), the sister of Fuller's friend James Freeman Clarke (1810–1888), was an accomplished artist who toured the Great Lakes with Fuller in the summer of 1843. Marianne Jackson (1820–1846) was another friend who participated in Fuller's Conversations.

The Letters of Margaret Fuller, ed. Robert N. Hudspeth, 6 vols. (Ithaca, 1983–1994), 3:185–87.

18

Autobiographical Sketch

Parents

My father was a lawyer and a politician. He was a man largely endowed with that sagacious energy, which the state of New England society, for the last half century, has been so well fitted to develop. His father was a clergyman, settled as pastor in Princeton, Massachusetts, within the bounds of whose parish-farm was Wachuset. His means were small, and the great object of his ambition was to send his sons to college. As a boy, my father was taught to think only of preparing himself for Harvard University, and when there of preparing himself for the profession of Law. As a Lawyer, again, the ends constantly presented were to work for distinction in the community, and for the means of supporting a family. To

Memoirs of Margaret Fuller Ossoli, ed. R. W. Emerson, W. H. Channing, and J. F. Clarke, 2 vols. (Boston, 1852), 1:11–24.

be an honored citizen, and to have a home on earth, were made the great aims of existence. To open the deeper fountains of the soul, to regard life here as the prophetic entrance to immortality, to develop his spirit to perfection, motives like these had never been suggested to him, either by fellow-beings or by outward circumstances. The result was a character, in its social aspect, of quite the common sort. A good son and brother, a kind neighbor, an active man of business in all these outward relations he was but one of a class, which surrounding conditions have made the majority among us. In the more delicate and individual relations, he never approached but two mortals, my mother and myself.

His love for my mother was the green spot on which he stood apart from the common-places of a mere breadwinning, bread-bestowing existence. She was one of those fair and flower-like natures, which sometimes spring up even beside the most dusty highways of life—a creature not to be shaped into a merely useful instrument, but bound by one law with the blue sky, the dew, and the frolic birds. Of all persons whom I have known, she had in her most of the angelic,—of that spontaneous love for every living thing, for man, and beast, and tree, which restores the golden age.

Death in the House

My earliest recollection is of a death,—the death of a sister, two years younger than myself. Probably there is a sense of childish endearments, such as belong to this tie, mingled with that of loss, of wonder, and mystery; but these last are prominent in memory. I remember coming home and meeting our nursery-maid, her face streaming with tears. That strange sight of tears made an indelible impression. I realize how little I was of stature, in that I looked up to this weeping face;—and it has often seemed since, that—full-grown for the life of this earth, I have looked up just so, at times of threatening, of doubt, and distress, and that just so has some being of the next higher order of existences looked down, aware of a law unknown to me, and tenderly commiserating the pain I must endure in emerging from my ignorance.

She took me by the hand and led me into a still and dark chamber,— then drew aside the curtain and showed me my sister. I see yet that beauty of death! The highest achievements of sculpture are only the reminder of its severe sweetness. Then I remember the house all still and dark,—the people in their black clothes and dreary faces,—the scent of the newly-made coffin,—my being set up in a chair and detained by a gentle hand to hear the clergyman,—the carriages slowly going, the procession slowly doling out their steps to the grave. But I have no remembrance of what I have since been told I did,—insisting, with loud cries, that they should not put the body in the ground. I suppose that my emotion was spent at the time, and so there was nothing to fix that moment in my memory.

I did not then, nor do I now, find any beauty in these ceremonies. What had they to do with the sweet playful child? Her life and death were alike beautiful, but all this sad parade was not. Thus my first experience of life was one of death. She who would have been the companion of my life was severed from me, and I was left alone. This has made a vast difference in my lot. Her character, if that fair face promised right, would have been soft, graceful and lively; it would have tempered mine to a gentler and more gradual course.

Overwork

My father,—all of whose feelings were now concentred on me,—instructed me himself. The effect of this was so far good that, not passing through the hands of many ignorant and weak persons as so many do at preparatory schools, I was put at once under discipline of considerable severity, and, at the same time, had a more than ordinarily high standard presented to me. My father was a man of business, even in literature; he had been a high scholar at college, and was warmly attached to all he had learned there, both from the pleasure he had derived in the exercise of his faculties and the associated memories of success and good repute. He was, beside, well read in French literature, and in English, a Queen Anne's man.[1] He hoped to make me the heir of all he knew, and of as much more as the income of his profession enabled him to give me means of acquiring. At the very beginning, he made one great mistake, more common, it is to be hoped, in the last generation, than the warnings of physiologists will permit it to be with the next. He thought to gain time, by bringing forward the intellect as early as possible. Thus I had tasks given me, as many and various as the hours would allow, and on subjects beyond my age; with the additional disadvantage of reciting to him in the evening, after he returned from his office. As he was subject to many interruptions, I was often kept up till very late; and as he was a severe teacher, both from his habits of mind and his ambition for me, my feel-

[1] An admirer of the literature written during the reign of Queen Anne of England, 1702–1714.

ings were kept on the stretch till the recitations were over. Thus frequently, I was sent to bed several hours too late, with nerves unnaturally stimulated. The consequence was a premature development of the brain, that made me a "youthful prodigy" by day, and by night a victim of spectral illusions, nightmare, and somnambulism, which at the time prevented the harmonious development of my bodily powers and checked my growth, while, later, they induced continual headache, weakness and nervous affections, of all kinds. As these again re-acted on the brain, giving undue force to every thought and every feeling, there was finally produced a state of being both too active and too intense, which wasted my constitution, and will bring me,—even although I have learned to understand and regulate my now morbid temperament,—to a premature grave.

No one understood this subject of health then. No one knew why this child, already kept up so late, was still unwilling to retire. My aunts cried out upon the "spoiled child, the most unreasonable child that ever was,—if brother could but open his eyes to see it,—who was never willing to go to bed." They did not know that, so soon as the light was taken away, she seemed to see colossal faces advancing slowly towards her, the eyes dilating, and each feature swelling loathsomely as they came, till at last, when they were about to close upon her, she started up with a shriek which drove them away, but only to return when she lay down again. They did not know that, when at last she went to sleep, it was to dream of horses trampling over her, and to awake once more in fright, or, as she had just read in her Virgil, of being among trees that dripped with blood, where she walked and walked and could not get out, while the blood became a pool and plashed over her feet, and rose higher and higher, till soon she dreamed it would reach her lips. No wonder the child arose and walked in her sleep, moaning all over the house, till once, when they heard her, and came and waked her, and she told what she had dreamed, her father sharply bid her "leave off thinking of such nonsense, or she would be crazy,"—never knowing that he was himself the cause of all these horrors of the night. Often she dreamed of following to the grave the body of her mother, as she had done that of her sister, and woke to find the pillow drenched in tears. These dreams softened her heart too much, and cast a deep shadow over her young days; for then, and later, the life of dreams,—probably because there was in it less to distract the mind from its own earnestness,—has often seemed to her more real, and been remembered with more interest, than that of waking hours.

Poor child! Far remote in time, in thought, from that period, I look back on these glooms and terrors, wherein I was enveloped, and perceive that I had no natural childhood!

Books

Thus passed my first years. My mother was in delicate health, and much absorbed in the care of her younger children. In the house was neither dog nor bird, nor any graceful animated form of existence. I saw no persons who took my fancy, and real life offered no attraction. Thus my already over-excited mind found no relief from without, and was driven for refuge from itself to the world of books. I was taught Latin and English grammar at the same time, and began to read Latin at six years old, after which, for some years, I read it daily. In this branch of study, first by my father, and afterwards by a tutor, I was trained to quite a high degree of precision. I was expected to understand the mechanism of the language thoroughly, and in translating to give the thoughts in as few well-arranged words as possible, and without breaks or hesitation, — for with these my father had absolutely no patience.

Indeed, he demanded accuracy and clearness in everything: you must not speak, unless you can make your meaning perfectly intelligible to the person addressed; must not express a thought, unless you can give a reason for it, if required; must not make a statement, unless sure of all particulars — such were his rules. "But," "if," "unless," "I am mistaken," and "it may be so," were words and phrases excluded from the province where he held sway. Trained to great dexterity in artificial methods, accurate, ready, with entire command of his resources, he had no belief in minds that listen, wait, and receive. He had no conception of the subtle and indirect motions of imagination and feeling. His influence on me was great, and opposed to the natural unfolding of my character, which was fervent, of strong grasp, and disposed to infatuation, and self-forgetfulness. He made the common prose world so present to me, that my natural bias was controlled. I did not go mad, as many would do, at being continually roused from my dreams. I had too much strength to be crushed, — and since I must put on the fetters, could not submit to let them impede my motions. My own world sank deep within, away from the surface of my life; in what I did and said I learned to have reference to other minds. But my true life was only the dearer that it was secluded and veiled over by a thick curtain of available intellect, and that coarse, but wearable stuff woven by the ages, — Common Sense.

In accordance with this discipline in heroic common sense, was the influence of those great Romans, whose thoughts and lives were my daily food during those plastic years. The genius of Rome displayed itself in Character, and scarcely needed an occasional wave of the torch of thought to show its lineaments, so marble strong they gleamed in every light. Who, that has lived with those men, but admires the plain force of fact, of thought passed into action? They take up things with their naked hands. There is just the man, and the block he casts before you, — no divinity, no demon, no unfulfilled aim, but just the man and Rome, and what he did for Rome. Everything turns your attention to what a man can become, not by yielding himself freely to impressions, not by letting nature play freely through him, but by a single thought, an earnest purpose, an indomitable will, by hardihood, self-command, and force of expression. Architecture was the art in which Rome excelled, and this corresponds with the feeling these men of Rome excite. They did not grow, — they built themselves up, or were built up by the fate of Rome, as a temple for Jupiter Stator.[2] The ruined Roman sits among the ruins; he flies to no green garden; he does not look to heaven; if his intent is defeated, if he is less than he meant to be, he lives no more. The names which end in "us," seem to speak with lyric cadence. That measured cadence, — that tramp and march, — which are not stilted, because they indicate real force, yet which seem so when compared with any other language, — make Latin a study in itself of mighty influence. The language alone, without the literature, would give one the *thought* of Rome. Man present in nature, commanding nature too sternly to be inspired by it, standing like the rock amid the sea, or moving like the fire over the land, either impassive, or irresistible; knowing not the soft mediums or fine flights of life, but by the force which he expresses, piercing to the centre.

We are never better understood than when we speak of a "Roman virtue," a "Roman outline." There is somewhat indefinite, somewhat yet unfulfilled in the thought of Greece, of Spain, of modern Italy; but ROME! it stands by itself, a clear Word. The power of will, the dignity of a fixed purpose is what it utters. Every Roman was an emperor. It is well that the infallible church should have been founded on this rock, that the presumptuous Peter[3] should hold the keys, as the conquering love did before his thunderbolts, to be seen of all the world. The Apollo tends flocks

---

[2]Jupiter, the chief Roman god, was the god of light, the sky, and the state. The Romans built a temple to Jupiter on the site where they were stopped in their flight from their enemies, the Sabines.

[3]According to the Bible, Peter (from *petrus,* "rock," in Latin) was chosen as the first pope by Jesus Christ and given the "keys to the kingdom of heaven" (Matthew 16.19).

with Admetus,[4] Christ teaches by the lonely lake, or plucks wheat as he wanders through the fields some Sabbath morning. They never come to this stronghold; they could not have breathed freely where all became stone as soon as spoken, where divine youth found no horizon for its all-promising glance, but every thought put on, before it dared issue to the day in action, its *toga virilis*.[5]

Suckled by this wolf,[6] man gains a different complexion from that which is fed by the Greek honey. He takes a noble bronze in camps and battle-fields; the wrinkles of council well beseem his brow, and the eye cuts its way like the sword. The Eagle should never have been used as a symbol by any other nation: it belonged to Rome.

The history of Rome abides in mind, of course, more than the literature. It was degeneracy for a Roman to use the pen; his life was in the day. The "vaunting" of Rome, like that of the North American Indians, is her proper literature. A man rises; he tells who he is, and what he has done; he speaks of his country and her brave men; he knows that a conquering god is there, whose agent is his own right hand; and he should end like the Indian, "I have no more to say."

It never shocks us that the Roman is self-conscious. One wants no universal truths from him, no philosophy, no creation, but only his life, his Roman life felt in every pulse, realized in every gesture. The universal heaven takes in the Roman only to make us feel his individuality the more. The Will, the Resolve of Man!—it has been expressed, — fully expressed!

I steadily loved this ideal in my childhood, and this is the cause, probably, why I have always felt that man must know how to stand firm on the ground, before he can fly. In vain for me are men more, if they are less, than Romans. Dante[7] was far greater than any Roman, yet I feel he was right to take the Mantuan as his guide through hell, and to heaven.

Horace[8] was a great deal to me then, and is so still. Though his words do not abide in memory, his presence does: serene, courtly, of darting hazel eye, a self-sufficient grace, and an appreciation of the world of stern

---

[4]According to Greek mythology, Apollo, the Greek god of the sun, was condemned to tend the herds of the king Admetus for a year after killing the giant Cyclopes.

[5]The white toga worn by adult Roman men (Latin).

[6]Legend holds that Romulus and Remus, the founders of Rome, were suckled by a wolf.

[7]Dante Alighieri (1265–1321), Italian poet, wrote the *Divine Comedy*, in which the poet is led by the classical poet Virgil (who was born in Mantua, Italy) through hell and then purgatory and finally to heaven. The three respective parts of the *Divine Comedy* are *Inferno, Purgatorio,* and *Paradiso.*

[8]Horace (65–68 B.C.), Roman poet and satirist.

realities, sometimes pathetic, never tragic. He is the natural man of the world; he is what he ought to be, and his darts never fail of their aim. There is a perfume and raciness, too, which makes life a banquet, where the wit sparkles no less that the viands were bought with blood.

Ovid[9] gave me not Rome, nor himself, but a view into the enchanted gardens of the Greek mythology. This path I followed, have been following ever since; and now, life half over, it seems to me, as in my childhood, that every thought of which man is susceptible, is intimated there. In those young years, indeed, I did not see what I now see, but loved to creep from amid the Roman pikes to lie beneath this great vine, and see the smiling and serene shapes go by, woven from the finest fibres of all the elements. I knew not why, at that time, — but I loved to get away from the hum of the forum, and the mailed clang of Roman speech, to these shifting shows of nature, these Gods and Nymphs born of the sunbeam, the wave, the shadows on the hill.

As with Rome I antedated the world of deeds, so I lived in those Greek forms the true faith of a refined and intense childhood. So great was the force of reality with which these forms impressed me, that I prayed earnestly for a sign, — that it would lighten in some particular region of the heavens, or that I might find a bunch of grapes in the path, when I went forth in the morning. But no sign was given, and I was left a waif stranded upon the shores of modern life!

Of the Greek language, I knew only enough to feel that the sounds told the same story as the mythology; —that the law of life in that land was beauty, as in Rome it was a stern composure. I wish I had learned as much of Greece as of Rome, — so freely does the mind play in her sunny waters, where there is no chill, and the restraint is from within out; for these Greeks, in an atmosphere of ample grace, could not be impetuous, or stern, but loved moderation as equable life always must, for it is the law of beauty.

With these books I passed my days. The great amount of study exacted of me soon ceased to be a burden, and reading became a habit and a passion. The force of feeling, which, under other circumstances, might have ripened thought, was turned to learn the thoughts of others. This was not a tame state, for the energies brought out by rapid acquisition gave glow enough. I thought with rapture of the all-accomplished man, him of the many talents, wide resources, clear sight, and omnipotent will. A

---

[9]Ovid (43 B.C.–A.D. 17), Roman poet, wrote *The Metamorphoses,* a collection of stories drawn in part from Greek mythology.

Caesar seemed great enough. I did not then know that such men impoverish the treasury to build the palace. I kept their statues as belonging to the hall of my ancestors, and loved to conquer obstacles, and fed my youth and strength for their sake.

Still, though the bias was so great that in earliest years I learned, in these ways, how the world takes hold of a powerful nature, I had yet other experiences. None of these were deeper than what I found in the happiest haunt of my childish years, — our little garden. Our house, though comfortable, was very ugly, and in a neighborhood which I detested, — every dwelling and its appurtenances having a mesquin[10] and huddled look. I liked nothing about us except the tall graceful elms before the house, and the dear little garden behind. Our back door opened on a high flight of steps, by which I went down to a green plot, much injured in my ambitious eyes by the presence of the pump and tool-house. This opened into a little garden, full of choice flowers and fruit-trees, which was my mother's delight, and was carefully kept. Here I felt at home. A gate opened thence into the fields, — a wooden gate made of boards, in a high, unpainted board wall, and embowered in the clematis creeper. This gate I used to open to see the sunset heaven; beyond this black frame I did not step, for I liked to look at the deep gold behind it. How exquisitely happy I was in its beauty, and how I loved the silvery wreaths of my protecting vine! I never would pluck one of its flowers at that time, I was so jealous of its beauty, but often since I carry off wreaths of it from the wild-wood, and it stands in nature to my mind as the emblem of domestic love.

Of late I have thankfully felt what I owe to that garden, where the best hours of my lonely childhood were spent. Within the house everything was socially utilitarian; my books told of a proud world, but in another temper were the teachings of the little garden. There my thoughts could lie callow in the nest, and only be fed and kept warm, not called to fly or sing before the time. I loved to gaze on the roses, the violets, the lilies, the pinks; my mother's hand had planted them, and they bloomed for me. I culled the most beautiful. I looked at them on every side. I kissed them, I pressed them to my bosom with passionate emotions, such as I have never dared express to any human being. An ambition swelled my heart to be as beautiful, as perfect as they. I have not kept my vow. Yet, forgive, ye wild asters, which gleam so sadly amid the fading grass; forgive me,

[10]Shabby (French).

ye golden autumn flowers, which so strive to reflect the glories of the departing distant sun; and ye silvery flowers, whose moonlight eyes I knew so well, forgive! Living and blooming in your unchecked law, ye know nothing of the blights, the distortions, which beset the human being; and which at such hours it would seem that no glories of free agency could ever repay! . . .

9

Dial Essays and Meditations

As the first editor of the Dial, *Margaret Fuller grasped the opportunity to shape the new Transcendentalist journal and to experiment in her own writing with a variety of subjects and modes of expression. Her contributions ranged from literary criticism to mystical meditations. Among her most ambitious review essays was "Goethe" (July 1841), which challenged her readers to recognize the artistic genius of an author considered highly immoral by most Americans. Many of Fuller's other disparate pieces shared a concern for women's powers and creativity. "Leila" (April 1841), one of Fuller's most distinctive articles, reflected the importance of her spiritual vision to her developing feminism. "Bettine Brentano and Her Friend Günderode" (January 1842), in form a more traditional review of the letters of two German women, complemented the feminism of Fuller's mystical meditation. This essay celebrated the egalitarian friendship and intellectual accomplishments of Bettine Brentano, a member of a wealthy commercial family, and Karoline Günderode, a canoness and poet. It might also be read as a further articulation of Fuller's ideal of friendship.*

19

Goethe

. . . The clear perception which was in Goethe's better nature of the beauty of that steadfastness, of that singleness and simple melody of soul, which he too much sacrificed to become "the many-sided One," is shown most distinctly in his two surpassingly beautiful works, The

Elective Affinities and Iphigenia.[1]

Not Werther, not the Nouvelle Heloise, have been assailed with such a storm of indignation as the first-named of these works, on the score of gross immorality.[2]

The reason probably is the subject; any discussion of the validity of the marriage vow making society tremble to its foundation; and, secondly, the cold manner in which it is done. All that is in the book would be bearable to most minds if the writer had had less the air of a spectator, and had larded his work here and there with ejaculations of horror and surprise.

These declarations of sentiment on the part of the author seem to be required by the majority of readers, in order to an interpretation of his purpose, as sixthly, seventhly, and eighthly were, in an old-fashioned sermon, to rouse the audience to a perception of the method made use of by the preacher.

But it has always seemed to me that those who need not such helps to their discriminating faculties, but read a work so thoroughly as to apprehend its whole scope and tendency, rather than hear what the author says it means, will regard the Elective Affinities as a work especially what is called moral in its outward effect, and religious even to piety in its spirit. The mental aberrations of the consorts from their plighted faith, though in the one case never indulged, and though in the other no veil of sophistry is cast over the weakness of passion, but all that is felt expressed with the openness of one who desires to legitimate what he feels, are punished by terrible griefs and a fatal catastrophe. Ottilia, that being of exquisite purity, with intellect and character so harmonized in feminine beauty, as they never before were found in any portrait of woman painted by the hand of man, perishes, on finding she has been breathed on by unhallowed passion, and led to err even by her ignorant wishes against what is held sacred. The only personage whom we do not

---

[1]Johann Wolfgang von Goethe (1749–1832) was Germany's most influential modern writer. Goethe's *Elective Affinities* (1809), the subject of this section of Fuller's review essay, takes passionate attraction and adultery as its central themes. In the novel, Edward, a happily married but selfish aristocrat, finds himself irresistibly attracted to his wife's visiting niece Ottilia. Following a tragic accident, the confused girl renounces both their mysterious "affinity" and her life. Most American critics and readers denounced the novel as dangerously immoral. Goethe's *Iphigenia* (1787), which Fuller treats later in her review, is a drama in the classical style.

[2]Goethe's first novel, *The Sorrows of Young Werther* (1774), shocked many readers with its romantic portrait of a lonely, sensitive young man who is crushed by the weight of his own passions and of a hopelessly conventional world. Fuller also refers here to the French author Jean-Jacques Rousseau's *Nouvelle Héloïse* (1761), another classic of European romantic literature.

pity is Edward, for he is the only one who stifles the voice of conscience.

There is indeed a sadness, as of an irresistible fatality, brooding over the whole. It seems as if only a ray of angelic truth could have enabled these men to walk wisely in this twilight, at first so soft and alluring, then deepening into blind horror.

But if no such ray came to prevent their earthly errors, it seems to point heavenward in the saintly sweetness of Ottilia. Her nature, too fair for vice, too finely wrought even for error, comes lonely, intense, and pale, like the evening star on the cold, wintry night. It tells of other worlds, where the meaning of such strange passages as this must be read to those faithful and pure like her, victims perishing in the green garlands of a spotless youth to atone for the unworthiness of others.

An unspeakable pathos is felt from the minutest trait of this character, and deepens with every new study of it. Not even in Shakespeare have I so felt the organizing power of genius. Through dead words I find the least gestures of this person, stamping themselves on my memory, betraying to the heart the secret of her life, which she herself, like all these divine beings, knew not. I feel myself familiarized with all beings of her order. I see not only what she was, but what she might have been, and live with her in yet untrodden realms.

Here is the glorious privilege of a form known only in the world of genius. There is on it no stain of usage or calculation to dull our sense of its immeasurable life. What in our daily walk, mid common faces and common places, fleets across us at moments from glances of the eye, or tones of the voice, is felt from the whole being of one of these children of genius.

This precious gem is set in a ring complete in its enamel. I cannot hope to express my sense of the beauty of this book as a work of art. I would not attempt it if I had elsewhere met any testimony to the same. The perfect picture, always before the mind, of the chateau, the moss hut, the park, the garden, the lake, with its boat and the landing beneath the platan trees; the gradual manner in which both localities and persons grow upon us, more living than life, inasmuch as we are, unconsciously, kept at our best temperature by the atmosphere of genius, and thereby more delicate in our perceptions than amid our customary fogs; the gentle unfolding of the central thought, as a flower in the morning sun; then the conclusion, rising like a cloud, first soft and white, but darkening as it comes, till with a sudden wind it bursts above our heads; the ease with which we every where find points of view all different, yet all bearing on the same circle, for, though we feel every hour new worlds, still before our eye lie the same objects, new, yet the same, unchangeable, yet always changing their aspects as we proceed, till at last we find we ourselves have traversed the circle, and know all we overlooked at first,—these things are worthy of our highest admiration.

For myself, I never felt so completely that very thing which genius should always make us feel—that I was in its circle, and could not get out till its spell was done, and its last spirit permitted to depart. I was not carried away, instructed, delighted more than by other works, but I was *there,* living there, whether as the platan tree, or the architect, or any other observing part of the scene. The personages live too intensely to let us live in them; they draw around themselves circles within the circle: we can only see them close, not be themselves.

Others, it would seem, on closing the book, exclaim, "What an immoral book!" I well remember my own thought, "It is a work of art!" At last I understood that world within a world, the ripest fruit of human nature, which is called art. With each perusal of the book my surprise and delight at this wonderful fulfilment of design grew. I understood why Goethe was well content to be called Artist, and his works, works of Art, rather than revelations. . . .

20

Leila

"In a deep vision's intellectual scene."[1]

I have often but vainly attempted to record what I know of Leila.[2] It is because she is a mystery, which can only be indicated by being reproduced. Had a Poet or Artist met her, each glance of hers would have suggested some form of beauty, for she is one of those rare beings who seem a key to all nature. Mostly those we know seem struggling for an individual existence. As the procession passes an observer like me, one seems a herald, another a basket-bearer, another swings a censer, and

---

[1] From "Liberty" (1829), by the English poet William Wordsworth (1770–1850).
[2] In a poem of 1844 entitled "To Sarah," Fuller wrote that Leila was her "chosen name": "I chose it by the sound, not knowing why, / But, since, I know that Leila stands for night, / I own that sable mantle of the sky / Through which pierce, gem-like, points of distant light." See also Fuller's poem "Leila in the Arabian Zone," of 1844 (Document 23, p. 153).

oft-times even priest and priestess suggest the ritual rather than the Divinity. Thinking of these men your mind dwells on the personalities at which they aim. But if you looked on Leila she was rather as the *fetiche*[3] which to the mere eye almost featureless, to the thought of the pious wild man suggests all the elemental powers of nature, with their regulating powers of conscience and retribution. The eye resting on Leila's eye, felt that it never reached the heart. Not as with other men did you meet a look which you could define as one of displeasure, scrutiny, or tenderness. You could not turn away, carrying with you some distinct impression, but your glance became a gaze from a perception of a boundlessness, of depth below depth, which seemed to say "in this being (couldst thou but rightly apprehend it) is the clasp to the chain of nature." Most men, as they gazed on Leila were pained; they left her at last baffled and well-nigh angry. For most men are bound in sense, time, and thought. They shrink from the overflow of the infinite; they cannot a moment abide in the coldness of abstractions; the weight of an idea is too much for their lives. They cry, "O give me a form which I may clasp to the living breast, fuel for the altars of the heart, a weapon for the hand." And who can blame them; it is almost impossible for time to bear this sense of eternity. Only the Poet, who is so happily organized as continually to relieve himself by reproduction, can bear it without falling into a kind of madness. And men called Leila mad, because they felt she made them so. But I, Leila, could look on thee;—to my restless spirit thou didst bring a kind of peace, for thou wert a bridge between me and the infinite; thou didst arrest the step, and the eye as the veil hanging before the Isis.[4] Thy nature seemed large enough for boundless suggestion. I did not love thee, Leila, but the desire for love was soothed in thy presence. I would fain have been nourished by some of thy love, but all of it I felt was only for the all.

We grew up together with name and home and parentage. Yet Leila ever seemed to me a spirit under a mask, which she might throw off at any instant. That she did not, never dimmed my perception of the unreality of her existence among us. She *knows* all, and *is* nothing. She stays here, I suppose, as a reminder to man of the temporary nature of his limitations. For she ever transcends sex, age, state, and all the barriers behind which man entrenches himself from the assaults of Spirit. You look on her, and she is the clear blue sky, cold and distant as the Pole-star; suddenly this sky opens and flows forth a mysterious wind that bears with

---

[3] Fetish (French), an object believed to possess magical power.
[4] Isis was a powerful Egyptian fertility goddess and the sister/wife of Osiris. A white veil customarily screened her image from the view of the profane.

it your last thought beyond the verge of all expectation, all association. Again, she is the mild sunset, and puts you to rest on a love-couch of rosy sadness, when on the horizon swells up a mighty sea and rushes over you till you plunge on its waves, affrighted, delighted, quite freed from earth.

When I cannot look upon her living form, I avail myself of the art magic. At the hour of high moon, in the cold silent night, I seek the centre of the park. My daring is my vow, my resolve my spell. I am a conjurer, for Leila is the vasty deep. In the centre of the park, perfectly framed in by solemn oaks and pines, lies a little lake, oval, deep, and still it looks up steadily as an eye of earth should to the ever promising heavens which are so bounteous, and love us so, yet never give themselves to us. As that lake looks at Heaven, so look I on Leila. At night I look into the lake for Leila.

If I gaze steadily and in the singleness of prayer, she rises and walks on its depths. Then know I each night a part of her life; I know where she passes the midnight hours.

In the days she lives among men; she observes their deeds, and gives them what they want of her, justice or love. She is unerring in speech or silence, for she is disinterested, a pure victim, bound to the altar's foot; God teaches her what to say.

In the night she wanders forth from her human investment, and travels amid those tribes, freer movers in the game of spirit and matter, to whom man is a supplement. I know not then whether she is what men call dreaming, but her life is true, full, and more single than by day.

I have seen her among the Sylphs' faint florescent forms that hang in the edges of life's rainbows. She is very fair, thus, Leila; and I catch, though edgewise, and sharp-gleaming as a sword, that bears down my sight, the peculiar light which she will be when she finds the haven of herself. But sudden is it, and whether king or queen, blue or yellow, I never can remember; for Leila is too deep a being to be known in smile or tear. Ever she passes sudden again from these hasty glories and tendernesses into the back-ground of being, and should she ever be detected it will be in the central secret of law. Breathless is my ecstasy as I pursue her in this region. I grasp to detain what I love, and swoon and wake and sigh again. On all such beauty transitoriness has set its seal. This sylph nature pierces through the smile of childhood. There is a moment of frail virginity on which it has set its seal, a silver star which may at any moment withdraw and leave a furrow on the brow it decked. Men watch these slender tapers which seem as if they would burn out next moment. They say that such purity is the seal of death. It is so; the condition of this ecstasy is, that it seems to die every moment, and even Leila has not force to die often; the electricity accumulates many days before the wild one comes, which leads to these sylph nights of tearful sweetness.

After one of these, I find her always to have retreated into the secret veins of earth. Then glows through her whole being the fire that so baffles men, as she walks on the surface of earth; the blood-red, heart's-blood-red of the carbuncle.[5] She is, like it, her own light, and beats with the universal heart, with no care except to circulate as the vital fluid; it would seem waste then for her to rise to the surface. There in these secret veins of earth she thinks herself into fine gold, or aspires for her purest self, till she interlaces the soil with veins of silver. She disdains not to retire upon herself in the iron ore. She knows that fires are preparing on upper earth to temper this sternness of her silent self. I venerate her through all this in awed silence. I wait upon her steps through the mines. I light my little torch and follow her through the caves where despair clings by the roof, as she trusts herself to the cold rushing torrents, which never saw the sun nor heard of the ocean. I know if she pauses, it will be to diamond her nature, transcending generations. Leila! thou hast never yet, I believe, penetrated to the central ices, nor felt the whole weight of earth. But thou searchest and searchest. Nothing is too cold, too heavy, nor too dark for the faith of the being whose love so late smiled and wept itself into the rainbow, and was the covenant of an only hope. Am I with thee on thy hours of deepest search? I think not, for still thou art an abyss to me, and the star which glitters at the bottom, often withdraws into newer darknesses. O draw me, Star, I fear not to follow; it is my eye and not my heart which is weak. Show thyself for longer spaces. Let me gaze myself into religion, then draw me down, — down.

As I have wished this, most suddenly Leila bursts up again in the fire. She greets the sweet moon with a smile so haughty, that the heavenly sky grows timid, and would draw back; but then remembering that the Earth also is planetary, and bound in one music with all its spheres, it leans down again and listens softly what this new, strange voice may mean. And it seems to mean wo, wo! for, as the deep thought bursts forth, it shakes the thoughts in which time was resting; the cities fall in ruins; the hills are rent asunder; and the fertile valleys ravaged with fire and water. Wo, wo! but the moon and stars smile denial, and the echo changes the sad, deep tone into divinest music. Wait thou, O Man, and walk over

[5]Fuller associated the carbuncle, a red gemstone, with the goddess and her own spiritual quest.

the hardened lava to fresh wonders. Let the chain be riven asunder; the gods will give a pearl to clasp it again.

Since these nights, Leila, Saint of Knowledge, I have been fearless, and utterly free. There are to me no requiems more, death is a name, and the darkest seeming hours sing Te Deum.[6]

See with the word the form of earth transfused to stellar clearness, and the Angel Leila showers down on man balm and blessing. One downward glance from that God-filled eye, and violets clothe the most ungrateful soil, fruits smile healthful along the bituminous lake, and the thorn glows with a crown of amaranth. Descend, thou of the silver sandals, to thy weary son; turn hither that swan-guided car. Not mine but thine, Leila. The rivers of bliss flow forth at thy touch, and the shadow of sin falls separate from the form of light. Thou art now pure ministry, one arrow from the quiver of God; pierce to the centre of things, and slay Dagon for evermore.[7] Then shall be no more sudden smiles, nor tears, nor searchings in secret caves, nor slow growths of centuries. But floating, hovering, brooding, strong-winged bliss shall fill eternity, roots shall not be clogged with earth, but God blossom into himself for evermore.

Straight at the wish the arrows divine of my Leila ceased to pierce. Love retired back into the bosom of chaos, and the Holy Ghost descended on the globes of matter. Leila, with wild hair scattered to the wind, bare and often bleeding feet, opiates and divining rods in each over-full hand, walked amid the habitations of mortals as a Genius, visited their consciences as a Demon.[8]

At her touch all became fluid, and the prison walls grew into Edens. Each ray of particolored light grew populous with beings struggling into divinity. The redemption of matter was interwoven into the coronal of thought, and each serpent form soared into a Phenix.[9]

Into my single life I stooped and plucked from the burning my divine children.[10] And ever, as I bent more and more with an unwearied benig-

---

[6]A Christian liturgical song of praise, the first line of which is "Te Deum laudamus," "Thee, God, we praise" (Latin).

[7]Dagon was a Philistine god destroyed by the Israelites' "ark of God," which the Philistines had captured (1 Samuel 5.1–4). The ark, containing the stone tablets inscribed with the law that Moses had received from God, symbolized for the Israelites the power of God.

[8]For Fuller, as for the German writer Goethe, the Demon symbolized the instinctive powers that defy human understanding.

[9]In Greek mythology, a phoenix was a bird that lived five hundred years, burned itself to ashes on a pyre, and rose from the ashes to live again.

[10]According to legend, while acting as a nurse to a royal infant, Isis secretly burned away the child's mortal parts each night to create a divine child.

nity, an elected pain, like that of her, my wild-haired Genius; more beauteous forms, unknown before to me, nay, of which the highest God had not conscience as shapes, were born from that suddenly darting flame, which had threatened to cleave the very dome of my being. And Leila, she, the moving principle; O, who can speak of the immortal births of her unshrinking love. Each surge left Venus Urania[11] at her feet; from each abjured blame, rose floods of solemn incense, that strove in vain to waft her to the sky. And I heard her voice, which ever sang, "I shrink not from the baptism, from slavery let freedom, from parricide piety, from death let birth be known."

Could I but write this into the words of earth, the secret of moral and mental alchymy[12] would be discovered, and all Bibles have passed into one Apocalypse; but not till it has all been lived can it be written.

Meanwhile cease not to whisper of it, ye pines, plant here the hope from age to age; blue dome, wait as tenderly as now; cease not, winds, to bear the promise from zone to zone; and thou, my life, drop the prophetic treasure from the bud of each day, — Prophecy.

Of late Leila kneels in the dust, yea, with her brow in the dust. I know the thought that is working in her being. To be a child, yea, a human child, perhaps man, perhaps woman, to bear the full weight of accident and time, to descend as low as ever the divine did, she is preparing. I also kneel. I would not avail myself of all this sight. I cast aside my necromancy, and yield all other prowess for the talisman of humility. But Leila, wondrous circle, who hast taken into thyself all my thought, shall I not meet thee on the radius of human nature? I will be thy fellow pilgrim, and we will learn together the bliss of gratitude.

Should this ever be, I shall seek the lonely lake no more, for in the eye of Leila I shall find not only the call to search, but the object sought. Thou hast taught me to recognize all powers; now let us be impersonated, and traverse the region of forms together. *Together,* CAN that be, thinks Leila, can one be with any but God? Ah! it is so, but only those who have known the one can know the two. Let us pass out into nature, and she will give us back to God yet wiser, and worthier, than when clinging to his footstool as now. "Have I ever feared," said Leila. Never! but the hour is come for still deeper trust. Arise! let us go forth!

---

[11]Urania was the Greek Muse of astronomy. "Venus Urania" refers to the "Celestial Venus," the Roman goddess of productivity, love, and beauty.

[12]Alchemy, or the power to transform something common into something precious.

21

Bettine Brentano and Her Friend Günderode

Bettine Brentano's letters to Goethe, published under the title of Goethe's correspondence with a Child,[1] are already well known among us and met with a more cordial reception from readers in general than could have been expected. Even those who are accustomed to measure the free movements of art by the conventions that hedge the path of daily life, who, in great original creations, seek only intimations of the moral character borne by the author in his private circle, . . . suffered themselves to be surprised in their intrenchments, by the exuberance and wild, youthful play of Bettine's genius, and gave themselves up to receive her thoughts and feelings in the spirit which led her to express them. They felt that here was one whose only impulse was to live, — to unfold and realize her nature, and they forgot to measure what she did by her position in society. . . .

Yet, while we enjoyed this picture of a mind tuned to its highest pitch by the desire of daily ministering to an idolized object; while we were enriched by the results of the Child's devotion to him, hooted at by the Philistines[2] as the "Old Heathen," but to her poetic apprehension "Jupiter, Apollo, all in one," we must feel that the relation in which she stands to Goethe is not a beautiful one. Idolatries are natural to youthful hearts noble enough for a passion beyond the desire for sympathy or the instinct of dependence, and almost all aspiring natures can recall a period when some noble figure, whether in life or literature, stood for them at the gate of heaven, and represented all the possible glories of nature and art. This worship is in most instances, a secret worship; the still, small voice constantly rising in the soul to bid them harmonize the discords of the world, and distill beauty from imperfection, for another of kindred nature has done so. This figure whose achievements they admire is their St. Peter, holding for them the keys of Paradise, their model, their excitement to fulness and purity of life, their external conscience. When this devotion is silent, or only spoken out through our private acts, it is most likely to make the stair to heaven, and lead men on till suddenly they find the golden gate will open at their own touch, and they need neither media-

---

[1] *Goethe's Correspondence with a Child* was published in English translation in 1837.
[2] Those who are uninformed or ignorant of intellectual matters.

Dial, January 1842, 313–57.

tor nor idol more. The same course is observable in the religion of nations, where the worship of Persons rises at last into free thought in the minds of Philosophers.

But when this worship is expressed, there must be singular purity and strength of character on the part both of Idol and Idolater, to prevent its degenerating into a mutual excitement of vanity or mere infatuation.

"Thou art the only one worthy to inspire me;" cries one.

"Thou art the only one capable of understanding my inspiration," smiles back the other.

And clouds of incense rise to hide from both the free breath of heaven! . . .

But the letters to Goethe are not my present subject; and those before me with the same merits give us no cause however trifling for regret. They are letters which passed between Bettine, and the Canoness Günderode, the friend to whom she was devoted several years previous to her acquaintance with Goethe.

The readers of the Correspondence with a Child will remember the history of this intimacy, and of the tragedy with which it closed,[3] as one of the most exquisite passages in the volumes. The filling out of the picture is not unworthy the outline there given.

Günderode was a Canoness in one of the orders described by Mrs. Jameson,[4] living in the house of her order, but mixing freely in the world at her pleasure. But as she was eight or ten years older than her friend, and of a more delicate and reserved nature, her letters describe a narrower range of outward life. She seems to have been intimate with several men of genius and high cultivation, especially in philosophy, as well as with Bettine; these intimacies afforded stimulus to her life, which passed, at the period of writing, either in her little room with her books and her pen, or in occasional visits to her family and to beautiful country-places.

Bettine, belonging to a large and wealthy family of extensive commercial connexions, and seeing at the house of grandmother Me. La Roche,[5] most of the distinguished literati of the time, as well as those noble and princely persons who were proud to do honor to letters, if they did not professedly cultivate them, brings before us a much wider circle. The letters would be of great interest, if only for the distinct pictures they present of the two modes of life; and the two beautiful figures

<hr>

[3] Fuller refers to Günderode's suicide.
[4] Anna Brownell Jameson (1794–1860) was a popular Irish essayist. Her *Sacred and Legendary Art* described various clerical orders.
[5] Sophie von La Roche (1731–1807) wrote the first known German novel by a woman.

which animate and portray these modes of life are in perfect harmony with them. . . .

The relation before us presents all that is lovely between woman and woman, adorned by great genius and beauty on both sides. The advantage in years, the higher culture, and greater harmony of Günderode's nature is counterbalanced, by the ready spring impulse, richness and melody of the other.

And not only are these letters interesting as presenting this view of the interior of German life, and of an ideal relation realized, but the high state of culture in Germany which presented to the thoughts of those women themes of poesy and philosophy as readily, as to the English or American girl come the choice of a dress, the last concert or assembly, has made them expressions of the noblest aspirations, filled them with thoughts and oftentimes deep thoughts on the great subjects. Many of the poetical fragments from the pen of Günderode are such as would not have been written had she not been the contemporary of Schelling and Fichte, yet are they native and original, the atmosphere of thought reproduced in the brilliant and delicate hues of a peculiar plant. This transfusion of such energies as are manifested in Goethe, Kant, and Schelling[6] into these private lives is a creation not less worthy our admiration, than the forms which the muse has given them to bestow on the world through their immediate working by their chosen means. These are not less the children of the genius than his statue or the exposition of his method. Truly, as regards the artist, the immortal offspring of the Muse,

"Loves where (art) has set its seal,"

are objects of clearer confidence than the lives on which he has breathed; they are safe as the poet tells us death alone can make the beauty of the actual; they will ever bloom as sweet and fair as now, ever thus radiate pure light, nor degrade the prophecy of high moments, by compromise, fits of inanity, or folly, as the living poems do. But to the universe, which will give time and room to correct the bad lines in those living poems, it is given to wait as the artist with his human feelings cannot, though secure that a true thought never dies, but once gone forth must work and live forever.

We know that cant and imitation must always follow a bold expression of thought in any wise, and reconcile ourself as well as we can to those

[6]Friedrich Wilhelm Joseph von Schelling (1775–1854), Johann Gottlieb Fichte (1762–1814), and Immanuel Kant (1724–1804) were all prominent German philosophers whose work inspired the American Transcendentalists.

insects called by the very birth of the rose to prey upon its sweetness. But pleasure is unmingled, where thought has done its proper work and fertilized while it modified each being in its own kind. Let him who has seated himself beneath the great German oak, and gazed upon the growth of poesy, of philosophy, of criticism, of historic painting, of the drama, till the life of the last fifty years seems well worth man's living, pick up also these little acorns which are dropping gracefully on the earth, and carry them away to be planted in his own home, for in each fairy form may be read the story of the national tree, the promise of future growths as noble.

The talisman of this friendship may be found in Günderode's postscript to one of her letters, "If thou findest Muse, write soon again," I have hesitated whether this might not be, "if thou findest Musse (leisure) write soon again;" then had the letters wound up like one of our epistles here in America. But, in fine, I think there can be no mistake. They waited for the Muse. Here the pure products of public and private literature are on a par. That inspiration which the poet finds in the image of the ideal man, the man of the ages, of whom nations are but features, and Messiahs the voice, the friend finds in the thought of his friend, a nature in whose positive existence and illimitable tendencies he finds the mirror of his desire, and the spring of his conscious growth. For those who write in the spirit of sincerity, write neither to the public nor the individual, but to the soul made manifest in the flesh, and publication or correspondence only furnish them with the occasion for bringing their thoughts to a focus.

The day was made rich to Bettine and her friend by hoarding its treasures for one another. If we have no object of the sort, we cannot live at all in the day, but thoughts stretch out into eternity and find no home. We feel of these two that they were enough to one another to be led to indicate their best thoughts, their fairest visions, and therefore theirs was a true friendship. They needed not "descend to meet."[7]

Sad are the catastrophes of friendships, for they are mostly unequal, and it is rare that more than one party keeps true to the original covenant. Happy the survivor if in losing his friend, he loses not the idea of friendship, nor can be made to believe, because those who were once to him the angels of his life, sustaining the aspiration of his nobler nature, and calming his soul by the gleams of pure beauty that for a time were seen in their deeds, in their desires, unexpectedly grieve the spirit, and baffle the trust which had singled them out as types of excellence amid a sullied race, by infirmity of purpose, shallowness of heart and mind, selfish

---

[7]Fuller refers to a phrase to which she objected in Ralph Waldo Emerson's essay "Friendship" (1841).

absorption or worldly timidity, that there is no such thing as true intimacy, as harmonious development of mind by mind, two souls prophesying to one another, two minds feeding one another, two human hearts sustaining and pardoning one another! Be not faithless, thou whom I see wandering alone amid the tombs of thy buried loves. The relation thou hast thus far sought in vain is possible even on earth to calm, profound, tender, and unselfish natures; it is assured in heaven, where only chastened spirits can enter, — pilgrims dedicate to Perfection. . . .

10

Summer on the Lakes

Following a four-month journey with friends through Illinois, Wisconsin, and Michigan in the summer of 1843, Margaret Fuller published her first original book. Summer on the Lakes, in 1843 *(1844) was both more and less than a traditional travel narrative: skimming over the physical description of the places she visited, Fuller focused on their impact on her own intellectual and spiritual development. As the following selections reveal, that inner journey moved her toward a new perspective as a cultural "outsider," as she questioned ever more forcefully her society's rigid and confining gender boundaries. Inserting the quasi-autobiographical story of Mariana into the heart of the book, Fuller displayed her empathy with the frontier women she met, and her desire to analyze "the defect in the position of woman." Her gender analysis also led her to consider the position of those American Indians whom she found dispossessed of their land, their power, and their hope. At journey's end, she could only wonder "how far this blood shall be required" at American hands. Despite the natural beauty and plenty all around her, she had seen few traces of the promised freedom and equality of the American frontier.*

22

Summer on the Lakes, in 1843

Chapter I

Niagara, June 10, 1843

Since you are to share with me such foot-notes as may be made on the pages of my life during this summer's wanderings, I should not be quite silent as to this magnificent prologue to the, as yet, unknown drama. Yet

S. M. Fuller, *Summer on the Lakes, in 1843* (Boston, 1844).

I, like others, have little to say where the spectacle is, for once, great enough to fill the whole life, and supersede thought, giving us only its own presence. "It is good to be here," is the best as the simplest expression that occurs to the mind.

We have been here eight days, and I am quite willing to go away. So great a sight soon satisfies, making us content with itself, and with what is less than itself. Our desires, once realized, haunt us again less readily. Having "lived one day" we would depart, and become worthy to live another.

We have not been fortunate in weather, for there cannot be too much, or too warm sunlight for this scene, and the skies have been lowering, with cold, unkind winds. My nerves, too much braced up by such an atmosphere, do not well bear the continual stress of sight and sound. For here there is no escape from the weight of a perpetual creation; all other forms and motions come and go, the tide rises and recedes, the wind, at its mightiest, moves in gales and gusts, but here is really an incessant, an indefatigable motion. Awake or asleep, there is no escape, still this rushing round you and through you. It is in this way I have most felt the grandeur—somewhat eternal, if not infinite.

At times a secondary music rises; the cataract seems to seize its own rhythm and sing it over again, so that the ear and soul are roused by a double vibration. This is some effect of the wind, causing echoes to the thundering anthem. It is very sublime, giving the effect of a spiritual repetition through all the spheres.

When I first came I felt nothing but a quiet satisfaction. I found that drawings, the panorama, &c. had given me a clear notion of the position and proportions of all objects here; I knew where to look for everything, and everything looked as I thought it would.

Long ago, I was looking from a hill-side with a friend at one of the finest sunsets that ever enriched this world. A little cow-boy, trudging along, wondered what we could be gazing at. After spying about some time, he found it could only be the sunset, and looking, too, a moment, he said approvingly "that sun looks well enough;" a speech worthy of Shakspeare's Cloten,[1] or the infant Mercury, up to everything from the cradle, as you please to take it.

Even such a familiarity, worthy of Jonathan,[2] our national hero, in a prince's palace, or "stumping" as he boasts to have done, "up the Vatican

---

[1]A character in William Shakespeare's *Cymbeline.*

[2]"Brother Jonathan," a stock serio-comic character of the early American theater, was a simple Yankee yeoman farmer. Never able to understand the attractions of sophisticated European culture, he remained morally pure and uncorrupted in the face of all temptations.

stairs, into the Pope's presence, in my old boots," I felt here; it looks really *well enough,* I felt, and was inclined, as you suggested, to give my approbation as to the one object in the world that would not disappoint.

But all great expression, which, on a superficial survey, seems so easy as well as so simple, furnishes, after a while, to the faithful observer its own standard by which to appreciate it. Daily these proportions widened and towered more and more upon my sight, and I got, at last, a proper foreground for these sublime distances. Before coming away, I think I really saw the full wonder of the scene. After awhile it so drew me into itself as to inspire an undefined dread, such as I never knew before, such as may be felt when death is about to usher us into a new existence. The perpetual trampling of the waters seized my senses. I felt that no other sound, however near, could be heard, and would start and look behind me for a foe. I realized the identity of that mood of nature in which these waters were poured down with such absorbing force, with that in which the Indian was shaped on the same soil. For continually upon my mind came, unsought and unwelcome, images, such as never haunted it before, of naked savages stealing behind me with uplifted tomahawks; again and again this illusion recurred, and even after I had thought it over, and tried to shake it off, I could not help starting and looking behind me.

As picture, the Falls can only be seen from the British side. There they are seen in their veils, and at sufficient distance to appreciate the magical effects of these, and the light and shade. From the boat, as you cross, the effects and contrasts are more melodramatic. On the road back from the whirlpool, we saw them as a reduced picture with delight. But what I liked best was to sit on Table Rock, close to the great fall. There all power of observing details, all separate consciousness, was quite lost.

Once, just as I had seated myself there, a man came to take his first look. He walked close up to the fall, and, after looking at it a moment, with an air as if thinking how he could best appropriate it to his own use, he spat into it.

This trait seemed wholly worthy of an age whose love of *utility* is such that the Prince Puckler Muskau[3] suggests the probability of men coming to put the bodies of their dead parents in the fields to fertilize them, and of a country such as Dickens[4] has described; but these will not, I hope, be seen on the historic page to be truly the age or truly the America. A little leaven is leavening the whole mass for other bread. . . .

[3]Hermann Ludwig Heinrich Furst von Pückler-Muskau (1785–1871) was a German travel writer.
[4]The English author Charles Dickens (1812–1870) had found little to admire in his recent tour of the United States.

Chapter II. The Lakes

... Coming up the river St. Clair, we saw Indians for the first time. They were camped out on the bank. It was twilight, and their blanketed forms, in listless groups or stealing along the bank, with a lounge and a stride so different in its wildness from the rudeness of the white settler, gave me the first feeling that I really approached the West.

The people on the boat were almost all New Englanders, seeking their fortunes. They had brought with them their habits of calculation, their cautious manners, their love of polemics. It grieved me to hear these immigrants who were to be the fathers of a new race, all, from the old man down to the little girl, talking not of what they should do, but of what they should get in the new scene. It was to them a prospect, not of the unfolding nobler energies, but of more ease, and larger accumulation. It wearied me, too, to hear Trinity and Unity discussed in the poor, narrow doctrinal way on these free waters; but that will soon cease, there is not time for this clash of opinions in the West, where the clash of material interests is so noisy. They will need the spirit of religion more than ever to guide them, but will find less time than before for its doctrine. This change was to me, who am tired of the war of words on these subjects, and believe it only sows the wind to reap the whirlwind, refreshing, but I argue nothing from it; there is nothing real in the freedom of thought at the West, it is from the position of men's lives, not the state of their minds. So soon as they have time, unless they grow better meanwhile, they will cavil and criticise, and judge other men by their own standard, and outrage the law of love every way, just as they do with us. . . .

Chapter III

In the afternoon of this day we reached the Rock river, in whose neighborhood we proposed to make some stay, and crossed at Dixon's ferry.

This beautiful stream flows full and wide over a bed of rocks, traversing a distance of near two hundred miles, to reach the Mississippi. Great part of the country along its banks is the finest region of Illinois, and the scene of some of the latest romance of Indian warfare. To these beautiful regions Black Hawk[5] returned with his band "to pass the summer," when he drew upon himself the warfare in which he was finally vanquished. No wonder he could not resist the longing, unwise though its indulgence might be, to return in summer to this home of beauty. . . .

[5]The Sac chief Black Hawk (1767–1838) was defeated by U.S. troops in the "Black Hawk War" of 1832.

There was a peculiar charm in coming here, where the choice of location, and the unobtrusive good taste of all the arrangements, showed such intelligent appreciation of the spirit of the scene, after seeing so many dwellings of the new settlers, which showed plainly that they had no thought beyond satisfying the grossest material wants. Sometimes they looked attractive, the little brown houses, the natural architecture of the country, in the edge of the timber. But almost always when you came near, the slovenliness of the dwelling and the rude way in which objects around it were treated, when so little care would have presented a charming whole, were very repulsive. Seeing the traces of the Indians, who chose the most beautiful sites for their dwellings, and whose habits do not break in on that aspect of nature under which they were born, we feel as if they were the rightful lords of a beauty they forbore to deform. But most of these settlers do not see it at all; it breathes, it speaks in vain to those who are rushing into its sphere. Their progress is Gothic, not Roman, and their mode of cultivation will, in the course of twenty, perhaps ten, years, obliterate the natural expression of the country. . . .

Here a man need not take a small slice from the landscape, and fence it in from the obtrusions of an uncongenial neighbor, and there cut down his fancies to miniature improvements which a chicken could run over in ten minutes. He may have water and wood and land enough, to dread no incursions on his prospect from some chance Vandal that may enter his neighborhood. He need not painfully economise and manage how he may use it all; he can afford to leave some of it wild, and to carry out his own plans without obliterating those of nature.

Here, whole families might live together, if they would. The sons might return from their pilgrimages to settle near the parent hearth; the daughters might find room near their mother. Those painful separations, which already desecrate and desolate the Atlantic coast, are not enforced here by the stern need of seeking bread; and where they are voluntary, it is no matter. To me, too, used to the feelings which haunt a society of struggling men, it was delightful to look upon a scene where nature still wore her motherly smile and seemed to promise room not only for those favored or cursed with the qualities best adapting for the strifes of competition, but for the delicate, the thoughtful, even the indolent or eccentric. She did not say, Fight or starve; nor even, Work or cease to exist; but, merely showing that the apple was a finer fruit than the wild crab, gave both room to grow in the garden.

A pleasant society is formed of the families who live along the banks of this stream upon farms. They are from various parts of the world, and have much to communicate to one another. Many have cultivated minds and refined manners, all a varied experience, while they have in common the interests of a new country and a new life. They must traverse some space to get at one another, but the journey is through scenes that make it a separate pleasure. They must bear inconveniences to stay in one another's houses; but these, to the well-disposed, are only a source of amusement and adventure.

The great drawback upon the lives of these settlers, at present, is the unfitness of the women for their new lot. It has generally been the choice of the men, and the women follow, as women will, doing their best for affection's sake, but too often in heartsickness and weariness. Beside it frequently not being a choice or conviction of their own minds that it is best to be here, their part is the hardest, and they are least fitted for it. The men can find assistance in field labor, and recreation with the gun and fishing-rod. Their bodily strength is greater, and enables them to bear and enjoy both these forms of life.

The women can rarely find any aid in domestic labor. All its various and careful tasks must often be performed, sick or well, by the mother and daughters, to whom a city education has imparted neither the strength nor skill now demanded.

The wives of the poorer settlers, having more hard work to do than before, very frequently become slatterns; but the ladies, accustomed to a refined neatness, feel that they cannot degrade themselves by its absence, and struggle under every disadvantage to keep up the necessary routine of small arrangements.

With all these disadvantages for work, their resources for pleasure are fewer. When they can leave the housework, they have not learnt to ride, to drive, to row, alone. Their culture has too generally been that given to women to make them "the ornaments of society." They can dance, but not draw; talk French, but know nothing of the language of flowers; neither in childhood were allowed to cultivate them, lest they should tan their complexions. Accustomed to the pavement of Broadway, they dare not tread the wildwood paths for fear of rattlesnakes!

Seeing much of this joylessness, and inaptitude, both of body and mind, for a lot which would be full of blessings for those prepared for it, we could not but look with deep interest on the little girls, and hope they would grow up with the strength of body, dexterity, simple tastes, and resources that would fit them to enjoy and refine the western farmer's life.

But they have a great deal to war with in the habits of thought acquired by their mothers from their own early life. Everywhere the fatal spirit of imitation, of reference to European standards, penetrates, and threatens to blight whatever of original growth might adorn the soil.

If the little girls grow up strong, resolute, able to exert their faculties, their mothers mourn over their want of fashionable delicacy. Are they gay, enterprising, ready to fly about in the various ways that teach them so much, these ladies lament that "they cannot go to school, where they might learn to be quiet." They lament the want of "education" for their daughters, as if the thousand needs which call out their young energies, and the language of nature around, yielded no education.

Their grand ambition for their children, is to send them to school in some eastern city, the measure most likely to make them useless and unhappy at home. I earnestly hope that, ere long, the existence of good schools near themselves, planned by persons of sufficient thought to meet the wants of the place and time, instead of copying New York or Boston, will correct this mania. Instruction the children want to enable them to profit by the great natural advantages of their position; but methods copied from the education of some English Lady Augusta, are as ill suited to the daughter of an Illinois farmer, as satin shoes to climb the Indian mounds. An elegance she would diffuse around her, if her mind were opened to appreciate elegance; it might be of a kind new, original, enchanting, as different from that of the city belle as that of the prairie torchflower from the shopworn article that touches the cheek of that lady within her bonnet.

To a girl really skilled to make home beautiful and comfortable, with bodily strength to enjoy plenty of exercise, the woods, the streams, a few studies, music, and the sincere and familiar intercourse, far more easily to be met here than elsewhere, would afford happiness enough. Her eyes would not grow dim, nor her cheeks sunken, in the absence of parties, morning visits, and milliner's shops. . . .

Chapter IV. Chicago Again

. . . At the hotel table were daily to be seen new faces, and new stories to be learned. And any one who has a large acquaintance may be pretty sure of meeting some of them here in the course of a few days.

Among those whom I met was Mrs. Z., the aunt of an old schoolmate, to whom I impatiently hastened, as soon as the meal was over, to demand news of Mariana.[6] The answer startled me. Mariana, so full of life, was dead. That form, the most rich in energy and coloring of any I had ever seen, had faded from the earth. The circle of youthful associations had given way in the part, that seemed the strongest. What I now learned of

---

[6]In a letter to her friend William H. Channing in June 1844, Fuller claimed Mariana as a quasi-autobiographical character. She wrote that she would always see herself in Mariana, although "nobody dreams of its being like me." See Margaret Fuller to William H. Channing, [June ? 1844], *Letters*, 3:198–99.

the story of this life, and what was by myself remembered, may be bound together in this slight sketch.

At the boarding-school to which I was too early sent, a fond, a proud, and timid child, I saw among the ranks of the gay and graceful, bright or earnest girls, only one who interested my fancy or touched my young heart; and this was Mariana. She was, on the father's side, of Spanish Creole blood, but had been sent to the Atlantic coast, to receive a school education under the care of her aunt, Mrs. Z.

This lady had kept her mostly at home with herself, and Mariana had gone from her house to a dayschool; but the aunt, being absent for a time in Europe, she had now been unfortunately committed for some time to the mercies of a boarding-school.

A strange bird she proved there, — a lonely swallow that could not make for itself a summer. At first, her schoolmates were captivated with her ways; her love of wild dances and sudden song, her freaks of passion and of wit. She was always new, always surprising, and, for a time, charming.

But, after awhile, they tired of her. She could never be depended on to join in their plans, yet she expected them to follow out hers with their whole strength. She was very loving, even infatuated in her own affections, and exacted from those who had professed any love for her, the devotion she was willing to bestow.

Yet there was a vein of haughty caprice in her character; a love of solitude, which made her at times wish to retire entirely, and at these times she would expect to be thoroughly understood, and let alone, yet to be welcomed back when she returned. She did not thwart others in their humors, but she never doubted of great indulgence from them.

Some singular habits she had which, when new, charmed, but, after acquaintance, displeased her companions. She had by nature the same habit and power of excitement that is described in the spinning dervishes of the East. Like them, she would spin until all around her were giddy, while her own brain, instead of being disturbed, was excited to great action. Pausing, she would declaim verse of others or her own; act many parts, with strange catch-words and burdens that seemed to act with mystical power on her own fancy, sometimes stimulating her to convulse the hearer with laughter, sometimes to melt him to tears. When her power began to languish, she would spin again till fired to recommence her singular drama, into which she wove figures from the scenes of her earlier childhood, her companions, and the dignitaries she sometimes saw, with fantasies unknown to life, unknown to heaven or earth.

This excitement, as may be supposed, was not good for her. It oftenest came on in the evening, and often spoiled her sleep. She would wake in the night, and cheat her restlessness by inventions that teazed, while they sometimes diverted her companions.

She was also a sleep-walker; and this one trait of her case did somewhat alarm her guardians, who, otherwise, showed the same profound stupidity as to this peculiar being, usual in the overseers of the young. They consulted a physician, who said she would outgrow it, and prescribed a milk diet.

Meantime, the fever of this ardent and too early stimulated nature was constantly increased by the restraints and narrow routine of the boarding school. She was always devising means to break in upon it. She had a taste which would have seemed ludicrous to her mates, if they had not felt some awe of her, from a touch of genius and power that never left her, for costume and fancy dresses, always some sash twisted about her, some drapery, something odd in the arrangement of her hair and dress, so that the methodical preceptress dared not let her go out without a careful scrutiny and remodelling, whose soberizing effects generally disappeared the moment she was in the free air.

At last, a vent for her was found in private theatricals. Play followed play, and in these and the rehearsals she found entertainment congenial with her. The principal parts, as a matter of course, fell to her lot; most of the good suggestions and arrangements came from her, and for a time she ruled masterly and shone triumphant.

During these performances the girls had heightened their natural bloom with artificial red; this was delightful to them—it was something so out of the way. But Mariana, after the plays were over, kept her carmine saucer on the dressing-table, and put on her blushes regularly as the morning.

When stared and jeered at, she at first said she did it because she thought it made her look prettier; but, after a while, she became quite petulant about it,—would make no reply to any joke, but merely kept on doing it.

This irritated the girls, as all eccentricity does the world in general, more than vice or malignity. They talked it over among themselves, till they got wrought up to a desire of punishing, once for all, this sometimes amusing, but so often provoking nonconformist.

Having obtained the leave of the mistress, they laid, with great glee, a plan one evening, which was to be carried into execution next day at dinner.

Among Mariana's irregularities was a great aversion to the meal-time ceremonial. So long, so tiresome she found it, to be seated at a certain moment, to wait while each one was served at so large a table, and one where there was scarcely any conversation; from day to day it became more heavy to her to sit there, or go there at all. Often as possible she excused herself on the ever-convenient plea of headache, and was hardly ever ready when the dinnerbell rang.

To-day it found her on the balcony, lost in gazing on the beautiful prospect. I have heard her say afterwards, she had rarely in her life been so happy, — and she was one with whom happiness was a still rapture. It was one of the most blessed summer days; the shadows of great white clouds empurpled the distant hills for a few moments only to leave them more golden; the tall grass of the wide fields waved in the softest breeze. Pure blue were the heavens, and the same hue of pure contentment was in the heart of Mariana.

Suddenly on her bright mood jarred the dinner bell. At first rose her usual thought, I will not, cannot go; and then the must, which daily life can always enforce, even upon the butterflies and birds, came, and she walked reluctantly to her room. She merely changed her dress, and never thought of adding the artificial rose to her cheek.

When she took her seat in the dining-hall, and was asked if she would be helped, raising her eyes, she saw the person who asked her was deeply rouged, with a bright glaring spot, perfectly round, in either cheek. She looked at the next, same apparition! She then slowly passed her eyes down the whole line, and saw the same, with a suppressed smile distorting every countenance. Catching the design at once, she deliberately looked along her own side of the table, at every schoolmate in turn; every one had joined in the trick. The teachers strove to be grave, but she saw they enjoyed the joke. The servants could not suppress a titter.

When Warren Hastings stood at the bar of Westminster Hall[7]—when the Methodist preacher walked through a line of men, each of whom greeted him with a brickbat or a rotten egg, they had some preparation for the crisis, and it might not be very difficult to meet it with an impassive brow. Our little girl was quite unprepared to find herself in the midst of a world which despised her, and triumphed in her disgrace.

She had ruled, like a queen, in the midst of her companions; she had shed her animation through their lives, and loaded them with prodigal favors, nor once suspected that a powerful favorite might not be loved.

---

[7]Warren Hastings (1732–1818), the first British governor general of India, was tried for high crimes and misdemeanors before the House of Lords in 1788–1795. He was ultimately acquitted.

Now, she felt that she had been but a dangerous plaything in the hands of those whose hearts she never had doubted.

Yet, the occasion found her equal to it, for Mariana had the kind of spirit, which, in a better cause, had made the Roman matron truly say of her death-wound, "It is not painful, Poetus." She did not blench — she did not change countenance. She swallowed her dinner with apparent composure. She made remarks to those near her, as if she had no eyes.

The wrath of the foe of course rose higher, and the moment they were freed from the restraints of the dining-room, they all ran off, gaily calling, and sarcastically laughing, with backward glances, at Mariana, left alone.

She went alone to her room, locked the door, and threw herself on the floor in strong convulsions. These had sometimes threatened her life, as a child, but of later years, she had outgrown them. School-hours came, and she was not there. A little girl, sent to her door, could get no answer. The teachers became alarmed, and broke it open. Bitter was their penitence and that of her companions at the state in which they found her. For some hours, terrible anxiety was felt; but, at last, nature, exhausted, relieved herself by a deep slumber.

From this Mariana rose an altered being. She made no reply to the expressions of sorrow from her companions, none to the grave and kind, but undiscerning comments of her teacher. She did not name the source of her anguish, and its poisoned dart sank deeply in. It was this thought which stung her so. What, not one, not a single one, in the hour of trial, to take my part, not one who refused to take part against me. Past words of love, and caresses, little heeded at the time, rose to her memory, and gave fuel to her distempered thoughts. Beyond the sense of universal perfidy, of burning resentment, she could not get. And Mariana, born for love, now hated all the world.

The change, however, which these feelings made in her conduct and appearance bore no such construction to the careless observer. Her gay freaks were quite gone, her wildness, her invention. Her dress was uniform, her manner much subdued. Her chief interest seemed now to lie in her studies, and in music. Her companions she never sought, but they, partly from uneasy remorseful feelings, partly that they really liked her much better now that she did not oppress and puzzle them, sought her continually. And here the black shadow comes upon her life, the only stain upon the history of Mariana.

They talked to her, as girls, having few topics, naturally do, of one another. And the demon rose within her, and spontaneously, without design, generally without words of positive falsehood, she became a genius of discord among them. She fanned those flames of envy and jealousy which a wise, true word from a third will often quench forever; by a glance, or a seemingly light reply, she planted the seeds of dissension, till there was scarce a peaceful affection, or sincere intimacy in the circle where she lived, and could not but rule, for she was one whose nature was to that of the others as fire to clay.

It was at this time that I came to the school, and first saw Mariana. Me she charmed at once, for I was a sentimental child, who, in my early ill health, had been indulged in reading novels, till I had no eyes for the common greens and browns of life. The heroine of one of these, "The Bandit's Bride,"[8] I immediately saw in Mariana. Surely the Bandit's Bride had just such hair, and such strange, lively ways, and such a sudden flush of the eye. The Bandit's Bride, too, was born to be "misunderstood" by all but her lover. But Mariana, I was determined, should be more fortunate, for, until her lover appeared, I myself would be the wise and delicate being who could understand her.

It was not, however, easy to approach her for this purpose. Did I offer to run and fetch her handkerchief, she was obliged to go to her room, and would rather do it herself. She did not like to have people turn over for her the leaves of the music book as she played. Did I approach my stool to her feet, she moved away, as if to give me room. The bunch of wild flowers which I timidly laid beside her plate was left there.

After some weeks my desire to attract her notice really preyed upon me, and one day meeting her alone in the entry, I fell upon my knees, and kissing her hand, cried, "O Mariana, do let me love you, and try to love me a little." But my idol snatched away her hand, and, laughing more wildly than the Bandit's Bride was ever described to have done, ran into her room. After that day her manner to me was not only cold, but repulsive; I felt myself scorned, and became very unhappy.

Perhaps four months had passed thus, when, one afternoon, it became obvious that something more than common was brewing. Dismay and mystery were written in many faces of the older girls; much whispering was going on in corners.

In the evening, after prayers, the principal bade us stay; and, in a grave, sad voice, summoned forth Mariana to answer charges to be made against her.

[8]Louisa Sidney Stanhope, *The Bandit's Bride, or The Maid of Saxony, a Romance* (1807).

Mariana came forward, and leaned against the chimney-piece. Eight of the older girls came forward, and preferred against her charges, alas, too well-founded, of calumny and falsehood.

My heart sank within me, as one after the other brought up their proofs, and I saw they were too strong to be resisted. I could not bear the thought of this second disgrace of my shining favorite. The first had been whispered to me, though the girls did not like to talk about it. I must confess, such is the charm of strength to softer natures, that neither of these crises could deprive Mariana of hers in my eyes.

At first, she defended herself with self-possession and eloquence. But when she found she could no more resist the truth, she suddenly threw herself down, dashing her head, with all her force, against the iron hearth, on which a fire was burning, and was taken up senseless.

The affright of those present was great. Now that they had perhaps killed her, they reflected it would have been as well, if they had taken warning from the former occasion, and approached very carefully a nature so capable of any extreme. After awhile she revived, with a faint groan, amid the sobs of her companions. I was on my knees by the bed, and held her cold hand. One of those most aggrieved took it from me to beg her pardon, and say it was impossible not to love her. She made no reply.

Neither that night, nor for several days, could a word be obtained from her, nor would she touch food; but, when it was presented to her, or any one drew near for any cause, she merely turned away her head, and gave no sign. The teacher saw that some terrible nervous affection had fallen upon her, that she grew more and more feverish. She knew not what to do.

Meanwhile a new revolution had taken place in the mind of the passionate, but nobly-tempered child. All these months nothing but the sense of injury had rankled in her heart. She had gone on in one mood, doing what the demon prompted, without scruple and without fear.

But, at the moment of detection, the tide ebbed, and the bottom of her soul lay revealed to her eye. How black, how stained and sad. Strange, strange that she had not seen before the baseness and cruelty of falsehood, the loveliness of truth. Now, amid the wreck, uprose the moral nature which never before had attained the ascendant. "But," she thought, "too late, sin is revealed to me in all its deformity, and, sin-defiled, I will not, cannot live. The mainspring of life is broken."

And thus passed slowly by her hours in that black despair of which only youth is capable. In older years men suffer more dull pain, as each sorrow that comes drops its leaden weight into the past, and, similar features of character bringing similar results, draws up a heavy burden buried in those depths. But only youth has energy, with fixed unwinking gaze, to contemplate grief, to hold it in the arms and to the heart, like a child which makes it wretched, yet is indubitably its own.

The lady who took charge of this sad child had never well understood her before, but had always looked on her with great tenderness. And now love seemed, when all around were in greatest distress, fearing to call in medical aid, fearing to do without it, to teach her where the only balm was to be found that could have healed this wounded spirit.

One night she came in, bringing a calming draught. Mariana was sitting, as usual, her hair loose, her dress the same robe they had put on her at first, her eyes fixed vacantly upon the whited wall. To the proffers and entreaties of her nurse she made no reply.

The lady burst into tears, but Mariana did not seem even to observe it.

The lady then said, "O my child, do not despair, do not think that one great fault can mar a whole life. Let me trust you, let me tell you the griefs of my sad life. I will tell to you, Mariana, what I never expected to impart to any one."

And so she told her tale: it was one of pain, of shame, borne, not for herself, but for one near and dear as herself. Mariana knew the lady, knew the pride and reserve of her nature; she had often admired to see how the cheek, lovely, but no longer young, mantled with the deepest blush of youth, and the blue eyes were cast down at any little emotion. She had understood the proud sensibility of the character. She fixed her eyes on those now raised to hers, bright with fast falling tears. She heard the story to the end, and then, without saying a word, stretched out her hand for the cup.

She returned to life, but it was as one who has passed through the valley of death. The heart of stone was quite broken in her. The fiery life fallen from flame to coal. When her strength was a little restored, she had all her companions summoned, and said to them; "I deserved to die, but a generous trust has called me back to life. I will be worthy of it, nor ever betray the truth, or resent injury more. Can you forgive the past?"

And they not only forgave, but, with love and earnest tears, clasped in their arms the returning sister. They vied with one another in offices of humble love to the humbled one; and, let it be recorded as an instance of the pure honor of which young hearts are capable, that these facts, known to forty persons, never, so far as I know, transpired beyond those walls.

It was not long after this that Mariana was summoned home. She went thither a wonderfully instructed being, though in ways those who had sent her forth to learn little dreamed of.

Never was forgotten the vow of the returning prodigal. Mariana could not resent, could not play false. The terrible crisis, which she so early passed through, probably prevented the world from hearing much of her. A wild fire was tamed in that hour of penitence at the boarding school, such as has oftentimes wrapped court and camp in its destructive glow.

But great were the perils she had yet to undergo, for she was one of those barks which easily get beyond soundings, and ride not lightly on the plunging billow.

Her return to her native climate seconded the effects of inward revolutions. The cool airs of the north had exasperated nerves too susceptible for their tension. Those of the south restored her to a more soft and indolent state. Energy gave place to feeling, turbulence to intensity of character.

At this time love was the natural guest, and he came to her under a form that might have deluded one less ready for delusion.

Sylvain was a person well proportioned to her lot in years, family, and fortune. His personal beauty was not great, but of a noble character. Repose marked his slow gesture, and the steady gaze of his large brown eye, but it was a repose that would give way to a blaze of energy when the occasion called. In his stature, expression, and heavy coloring, he might not unfitly be represented by the great magnolias that inhabit the forests of that climate. His voice, like everything about him, was rich and soft, rather than sweet or delicate.

Mariana no sooner knew him than she loved, and her love, lovely as she was, soon excited his. But, oh! it is a curse to woman to love first, or most. In so doing she reverses the natural relations, and her heart can never, never be satisfied with what ensues.

Mariana loved first, and loved most, for she had most force and variety to love with. Sylvain seemed, at first, to take her to himself, as the deep southern night might some fair star. But it proved not so.

Mariana was a very intellectual being, and she needed companionship. This she could only have with Sylvain, in the paths of passion and action. Thoughts he had none, and little delicacy of sentiment. The gifts she loved to prepare of such for him, he took with a sweet, but indolent smile; he held them lightly, and soon they fell from his grasp. He loved to have her near him, to feel the glow and fragrance of her nature, but cared not to explore the little secret paths whence that fragrance was collected.

Mariana knew not this for a long time. Loving so much, she imagined all the rest, and, where she felt a blank, always hoped that further communion would fill it up. When she found this could never be; that there was absolutely a whole province of her being to which nothing in his answered, she was too deeply in love to leave him. Often after passing hours together, beneath the southern moon, when, amid the sweet intoxication of mutual love, she still felt the desolation of solitude, and a repression of her finer powers, she had asked herself, can I give him up? But the heart always passionately answered, no! I may be miserable with him, but I cannot live without him.

And the last miserable feeling of these conflicts was, that if the lover, soon to be the bosom friend, could have dreamed of these conflicts, he would have laughed, or else been angry, even enough to give her up.

Ah weakness of the strong. Of these strong only where strength is weakness. Like others she had the decisions of life to make, before she had light by which to make them. Let none condemn her. Those who have not erred as fatally, should thank the guardian angel who gave them more time to prepare for judgment, but blame no children who thought at arm's length to find the moon. Mariana, with a heart capable of highest Eros, gave it to one who knew love only as a flower or plaything, and bound her heartstrings to one who parted his as lightly as the ripe fruit leaves the bough. The sequel could not fail. Many console themselves for the one great mistake with their children, with the world. This was not possible to Mariana. A few months of domestic life she still was almost happy. But Sylvain then grew tired. He wanted business and the world; of these she had no knowledge, for them no faculties. He wanted in her the head of his house; she to make her heart his home. No compromise was possible between natures of such unequal poise, and which had met only on one or two points. Through all its stages she

> "felt
> The agonizing sense
> Of seeing love from passion melt
> Into indifference;
> The fearful shame that, day by day,
> Burns onward, still to burn,
> To have thrown her precious heart away,
> And met this black return,"

till death at last closed the scene. Not that she died of one downright blow on the heart. That is not the way such cases proceed. I cannot detail all the symptoms, for I was not there to watch them, and aunt Z. was neither so faithful an observer or narrator as I have shown myself in the school-day passages; but, generally, they were as follows.

Sylvain wanted to go into the world, or let it into his house. Mariana consented; but, with an unsatisfied heart, and no lightness of character, she played her part ill there. The sort of talent and facility she had displayed in early days, were not the least like what is called out in the social world by the desire to please and to shine. Her excitement had been muse-like, that of the improvisatrice,[9] whose kindling fancy seeks to create an atmosphere round it, and makes the chain through which to set free its electric sparks. That had been a time of wild and exuberant life. After her character became more tender and concentrated, strong affection or a pure enthusiasm might still have called out beautiful talents in her. But in the first she was utterly disappointed. The second was not roused within her thought. She did not expand into various life, and remained unequal; sometimes too passive, sometimes too ardent, and not sufficiently occupied with what occupied those around her to come on the same level with them and embellish their hours.

Thus she lost ground daily with her husband, who, comparing her with the careless shining dames of society, wondered why he had found her so charming in solitude.

At intervals, when they were left alone, Mariana wanted to open her heart, to tell the thoughts of her mind. She was so conscious of secret riches within herself, that sometimes it seemed, could she but reveal a glimpse of them to the eye of Sylvain, he would be attracted near her again, and take a path where they could walk hand in hand. Sylvain, in these intervals, wanted an indolent repose. His home was his castle. He wanted no scenes too exciting there. Light jousts and plays were well enough, but no grave encounters. He liked to lounge, to sing, to read, to sleep. In fine, Sylvain became the kind, but preoccupied husband, Mariana, the solitary and wretched wife. He was off continually, with his male companions, on excursions or affairs of pleasure. At home Mariana found that neither her books nor music would console her.

She was of too strong a nature to yield without a struggle to so dull a fiend as despair. She looked into other hearts, seeking whether she could there find such home as an orphan asylum may afford. This she did rather because the chance came to her, and it seemed unfit not to seize

---

[9]Literally, a female improviser (French). Derived from the novel *Corinne* (1807) by the French writer Mme. de Staël (1766–1817), the term referred to a wild, exuberant female genius.

the proffered plank, than in hope, for she was not one to double her stakes, but rather with Cassandra[10] power to discern early the sure course of the game. And Cassandra whispered that she was one of those.

"Whom men love not, but yet regret,"

And so it proved. Just as in her childish days, though in a different form, it happened betwixt her and these companions. She could not be content to receive them quietly, but was stimulated to throw herself too much into the tie, into the hour, till she filled it too full for them. Like Fortunio, who sought to do homage to his friends by building a fire of cinnamon, not knowing that its perfume would be too strong for their endurance, so did Mariana. What she wanted to tell, they did not wish to hear; a little had pleased, so much overpowered, and they preferred the free air of the street, even, to the cinnamon perfume of her palace.

However, this did not signify; had they staid, it would not have availed her! It was a nobler road, a higher aim she needed now; this did not become clear to her.

She lost her appetite, she fell sick, had fever. Sylvain was alarmed, nursed her tenderly; she grew better. Then his care ceased, he saw not the mind's disease, but left her to rise into health and recover the tone of her spirits, as she might. More solitary than ever, she tried to raise herself, but she knew not yet enough. The weight laid upon her young life was a little too heavy for it. One long day she passed alone, and the thoughts and presages came too thick for her strength. She knew not what to do with them, relapsed into fever, and died.

Notwithstanding this weakness, I must ever think of her as a fine sample of womanhood, born to shed light and life on some palace home. Had she known more of God and the universe, she would not have given way where so many have conquered. But peace be with her; she now, perhaps, has entered into a larger freedom, which is knowledge. With her died a great interest in life to me. Since her I have never seen a Bandit's Bride. She, indeed, turned out to be only a merchant's.—Sylvain is married again to a fair and laughing girl, who will not die, probably, till their marriage grows a "golden marriage."

Aunt Z. had with her some papers of Mariana's, which faintly shadow forth the thoughts that engaged her in the last days. One of these seems to have been written when some faint gleam had been thrown across the path, only to make its darkness more visible. It seems to have been sug-

---

[10]Cassandra was the daughter of Priam, the king of Troy during the Trojan War. Endowed with the gift of prophecy, she was fated never to be believed.

gested by remembrance of the beautiful ballad, *Helen of Kirconnel Lee,*[11] which once she loved to recite, and in tones that would not have sent a chill to the heart from which it came.

> "Death
> Opens her sweet white arms, and whispers Peace;
> Come, say thy sorrows in this bosom! This
> Will never close against thee, and my heart,
> Though cold, cannot be colder much than man's."

> "I wish I were where Helen lies,"
> A lover in the times of old,
> Thus vents his grief in lonely sighs,
> And hot tears from a bosom cold.

> But, mourner for thy martyred love,
> Could'st thou but know what hearts must feel,
> Where no sweet recollections move,
> Whose tears a desert fount reveal.

> When "in thy arms lyred Helen fell,"
> She died, sad man, she died for thee,
> Nor could the films of death dispel
> Her loving eye's sweet radiancy.

> Thou wert beloved, and she had loved,
> Till death alone the whole could tell,
> Death every shade of doubt removed,
> And steeped the star in its cold well.

> On some fond breast the parting soul
> Relies, — earth has no more to give;
> Who wholly loves has known the whole
> The wholly loved doth truly live

> But some, sad outcasts from this prize,
> Wither down to a lonely grave,
> All hearts their hidden love despise,
> And leave them to the whelming wave.

> They heart to heart have never pressed,
> Nor hands in holy pledge have given,
> By father's love were ne'er caressed,
> Nor in a mother's eye saw heaven

---

[11]A ballad of a lover's lament for the murdered Helen, whom he yearns to join.

A flowerless and fruitless tree,
A dried up stream, a mateless bird,
They live, yet never living be,
They die, their music all unheard.

I wish I were where Helen lies,
For there I could not be alone;
But now, when this dull body dies,
The spirit still will make its moan.

Love passed me by, nor touched my brow;
Life would not yield one perfect boon;
And all too late it calls me now,
O all too late, and all too soon.

. . . .

In temples sometimes she may rest,
In lonely groves, away from men,
There bend the head, by heats distrest,
Nor be by blows awoke again.

Nature is kind, and God is kind,
And, if she had not had a heart,
Only that great discerning mind,
She might have acted well her part.

But oh this thirst, that none can still,
Save those unfounden waters free;
The angel of my life should fill
And soothe me to Eternity!

It marks the defect in the position of woman that one like Mariana should have found reason to write thus. To a man of equal power, equal sincerity, no more!—many resources would have presented themselves. He would not have needed to seek, he would have been called by life, and not permitted to be quite wrecked through the affections only. But such women as Mariana are often lost, unless they meet some man of sufficiently great soul to prize them.

Van Artevelde's Elena,[12] though in her individual nature unlike my Mariana, is like her in a mind whose large impulses are disproportioned to the persons and occasions she meets, and which carry her beyond

---

[12]Philip van Artevelde, a merchant of the city of Ghent, led a fourteenth-century Flemish revolt against France. Killed in battle against the French, he became a folk hero and a symbol of artisanal independence and civic pride. During her trip, Fuller reread the dra-

those reserves which mark the appointed lot of woman. But, when she met Van Artevelde, he was too great not to revere her rare nature, without regard to the stains and errors of its past history; great enough to receive her entirely and make a new life for her; man enough to be a lover! But as such men come not so often as once an age, their presence should not be absolutely needed to sustain life.

At Chicago I read again Philip Van Artevelde, and certain passages in it will always be in my mind associated with the deep sound of the lake, as heard in the night. I used to read a short time at night, and then open the blind to look out. The moon would be full upon the lake, and the calm breath, pure light, and the deep voice harmonized well with the thought of the Flemish hero. When will this country have such a man? It is what she needs; no thin Idealist, no coarse Realist, but a man whose eye reads the heavens while his feet step firmly on the ground, and his hands are strong and dexterous for the use of human implements. A man religious, virtuous and—sagacious; a man of universal sympathies, but self-possessed; a man who knows the region of emotion, though he is not its slave; a man to whom this world is no mere spectacle, or fleeting shadow, but a great solemn game to be played with good heed, for its stakes are of eternal value, yet who, if his own play be true, heeds not what he loses by the falsehood of others. A man who hives from the past, yet knows that its honey can but moderately avail him; whose comprehensive eye scans the present, neither infatuated by its golden lures, nor chilled by its many ventures; who possesses prescience, as the wise man must, but not so far as to be driven mad to-day by the gift which discerns to-morrow. When there is such a man for America, the thought which urges her on will be expressed. . . .

Chapter V. Wisconsin

. . . One day we ladies gave, under the guidance of our host, to visiting all the beauties of the adjacent lakes—Nomabbin, Silver, and Pine Lakes. On the shore of Nomabbin had formerly been one of the finest Indian villages. Our host said that, one day, as he was lying there beneath the bank, he saw a tall Indian standing at gaze on the knoll. He lay a long time, curious to see how long the figure would maintain its statue-like absorption. But, at last, his patience yielded, and, in moving, he made a slight noise.

---

matic romance by Sir Henry Taylor (1800–1886), *Philip Van Artevelde* (1835), in which a heroic "Italian Lady," Elena della Torre, dies trying to protect the body of her slain hero.

The Indian saw him, gave a wild, snorting sound of indignation and pain, and strode away.

What feelings must consume their heart at such moments! I scarcely see how they can forbear to shoot the white man where he stands. . . .

This gentleman, though in other respects of most kindly and liberal heart, showed the aversion that the white man soon learns to feel for the Indian on whom he encroaches, the aversion of the injurer for him he has degraded. After telling the anecdote of his seeing the Indian gazing at the seat of his former home,

> "A thing for human feelings the most trying,"

and which, one would think, would have awakened soft compassion—almost remorse—in the present owner of that fair hill, which contained for the exile the bones of his dead, the ashes of his hopes,—he observed, "They cannot be prevented from straggling back here to their old haunts. I wish they could. They ought not to be permitted to drive away *our* game." OUR game—just heavens!

The same gentleman showed, on a slight occasion, the true spirit of the sportsman, or, perhaps I might say of Man, when engaged in any kind of chase. Showing us some antlers, he said, "This one belonged to a majestic creature. But this other was the beauty. I had been lying a long time at watch, when at last I heard them come crackling along. I lifted my head cautiously, as they burst through the trees. The first was a magnificent fellow; but then I saw coming one, the prettiest, the most graceful I ever beheld—there was something so soft and beseeching in its look. I chose him at once; took aim, and shot him dead. You see the antlers are not very large; it was young, but the prettiest creature!"

In the course of this morning's drive, we visited the gentlemen on their fishing party. They hailed us gaily, and rowed ashore to show us what fine booty they had. No disappointment there, no dull work. On the beautiful point of land from which we first saw them, lived a contented woman, the only one I heard of out there. She was English, and said she had seen so much suffering in her own country that the hardships of this seemed as nothing to her. But the others—even our sweet and gentle hostess—found their labors disproportioned to their strength, if not to their patience; and, while their husbands and brothers enjoyed the country in hunting or fishing, they found themselves confined to a comfortless and laborious indoor life. But it need not be so long. . . .

On the bank of Silver Lake we saw an Indian encampment. A shower threatened us, but we resolved to try if we could not visit it before it came on. We crossed a wide field on foot, and found them amid the trees on a shelving bank; just as we reached them the rain began to fall in torrents, with frequent thunder claps, and we had to take refuge in their lodges. These were very small, being for temporary use, and we crowded the occupants much, among whom were several sick, on the damp ground, or with only a ragged mat between them and it. But they showed all the gentle courtesy which marks them towards the stranger, who stands in any need; though it was obvious that the visit, which inconvenienced them, could only have been caused by the most impertinent curiosity, they made us as comfortable as their extreme poverty permitted. They seemed to think we would not like to touch them: a sick girl in the lodge where I was, persisted in moving so as to give me the dry place; a woman with the sweet melancholy eye of the race, kept off the children and wet dogs from even the hem of my garment.

Without, their fires smouldered, and black kettles, hung over them on sticks, smoked and seethed in the rain. An old theatrical looking Indian stood with arms folded, looking up to the heavens, from which the rain dashed and the thunder reverberated; his air was French-Roman, that is, more romanesque than Roman. The Indian ponies, much excited, kept careering through the wood, around the encampment, and now and then halting suddenly, would thrust in their intelligent, though amazed, phizzes, as if to ask their masters when this awful pother would cease, and then, after a moment, rush and trample off again.

At last we got off, well wetted, but with a picturesque scene for memory. At a house where we stopped to get dry, they told us that this wandering band (of Pottawattamies,) who had returned on a visit, either from homesickness, or need of relief, were extremely destitute. The women had been there to see if they could barter their head bands with which they club their hair behind into a form not unlike a Grecian knot, for food. They seemed, indeed, to have neither food, utensils, clothes, nor bedding; nothing but the ground, the sky, and their own strength. Little wonder if they drove off the game! . . .

Chapter VI. Mackinaw

Late at night we reached this island, so famous for its beauty, and to which I proposed a visit of some length. It was the last week in August, when a large representation from the Chippewa and Ottowa tribes are here to receive their annual payments from the American government. As their habits make travelling easy and inexpensive to them, neither being obliged to wait for steamboats, or write to see whether hotels are full, they come hither by thousands, and those thousands in families, secure of accommodation on the beach, and food from the lake, to make a long holiday out of the occasion. There were near two thousand encamped on the island already, and more arriving every day. . . .

Notwithstanding the homage paid to women, and the consequence allowed her in some cases, it is impossible to look upon the Indian women, without feeling that they do occupy a lower place than women among the nations of European civilization. The habits of drudgery expressed in their form and gesture, the soft and wild but melancholy expression of their eye, reminded me of the tribe mentioned by Mackenzie,[13] where the women destroy their female children, whenever they have a good opportunity; and of the eloquent reproaches addressed by the Paraguay woman to her mother, that she had not, in the same way, saved her from the anguish and weariness of her lot.

More weariness than anguish, no doubt, falls to the lot of most of these women. They inherit submission, and the minds of the generality accommodate themselves more or less to any posture. Perhaps they suffer less than their white sisters, who have more aspiration and refinement, with little power of self-sustenance. But their place is certainly lower, and their share of the human inheritance less.

Their decorum and delicacy are striking, and show that when these are native to the mind, no habits of life make any difference. Their whole gesture is timid, yet self-possessed. They used to crowd round me, to inspect little things I had to show them, but never press near; on the contrary, would reprove and keep off the children. Anything they took from my hand, was held with care, then shut or folded, and returned with an air of lady-like precision. They would not stare, however curious they might be, but cast sidelong glances. . . .

One day, as I was seated on one of the canoes, a woman came and sat beside me, with her baby in its cradle set up at her feet. She asked me by a gesture, to let her take my sun-shade, and then to show her how to open it. Then she put it into her baby's hand, and held it over its head, looking at me the while with a sweet, mischievous laugh, as much as to say, "you carry a thing that is only fit for a baby;" her pantomime was very pretty. She, like the other women, had a glance, and shy, sweet expression in the eye; the men have a steady gaze. . . .

---

[13]Sir Alexander Mackenzie (1763–1820), a Scottish fur trader and explorer in northwestern Canada, published an account of his explorations, *Voyages from Montreal on the River St. Lawrence, through the Continent of North America to the Frozen and Pacific Oceans in the Years 1789 and 1793*, in 1801. This was one of several earlier studies of American Indians that Fuller consulted in the Harvard College library as she prepared her book.

... It is also evident that, as Mrs. Schoolcraft[14] says, the women have great power at home. It can never be otherwise, men being dependent upon them for the comfort of their lives. Just so among ourselves, wives who are neither esteemed nor loved by their husbands, have great power over their conduct by the friction of every day, and over the formation of their opinions by the daily opportunities so close a relation affords, of perverting testimony and instilling doubts. But these sentiments should not come in brief flashes, but burn as a steady flame, then there would be more women worthy to inspire them. This power is good for nothing, unless the woman be wise to use it aright. Has the Indian, has the white woman, as noble a feeling of life and its uses, as religious a self-respect, as worthy a field of thought and action, as man? If not, the white woman, the Indian woman, occupies an inferior position to that of man. It is not so much a question of power, as of privilege.

The men of these subjugated tribes, now accustomed to drunkenness and every way degraded, bear but a faint impress of the lost grandeur of the race. They are no longer strong, tall, or finely proportioned. Yet as you see them stealing along a height, or striding boldly forward, they remind you of what was majestic in the red man.

On the shores of lake Superior, it is said, if you visit them at home, you may still see a remnant of the noble blood. The Pillagers— (Pilleurs)— a band celebrated by the old travellers, are still existant there.

"Still some, 'the eagles of their tribe,' may rush."

I have spoken of the hatred felt by the white man for the Indian: with white women it seems to amount to disgust, to loathing. How I could endure the dirt, the peculiar smell of the Indians, and their dwellings, was a great marvel in the eyes of my lady acquaintance; indeed, I wonder why they did not quite give me up, as they certainly looked on me with great distaste for it. "Get you gone, you Indian dog," was the felt, if not the breathed, expression towards the hapless owners of the soil. All their claims, all their sorrows quite forgot, in abhorrence of their dirt, their tawny skins, and the vices the whites have taught them.

A person who had seen them during [   ] great part of a life, expressed his prejudices to me with such violence, that I was no longer surprised that the Indian children threw sticks at him as he passed. A lady said, "do

[14]Jane Schoolcraft, an Ojibwa, was the wife of Henry Rowe Schoolcraft (1793–1864), the American explorer, ethnologist, and federal agent to the Indian tribes of the Lake Superior region. Fuller read Henry Rowe Schoolcraft's *Algic Researches, Comprising Inquiries Respecting the Mental Characteristics of the North American Indians* (1839) and especially valued Jane Schoolcraft's observations.

what you will for them, they will be ungrateful. The savage cannot be washed out of them. Bring up an Indian child and see if you can attach it to you." The next moment, she expressed, in the presence of one of those children whom she was bringing up, loathing at the odor left by one of her people, and one of the most respected, as he passed through the room. When the child is grown she will consider it basely ungrateful not to love her, as it certainly will not; and this will be cited as an instance of the impossibility of attaching the Indian.

Whether the Indian could, by any efforts of love and intelligence from the white man, have been civilized and made a valuable ingredient in the new state, I will not say; but this we are sure of; the French Catholics, at least, did not harm them, nor disturb their minds merely to corrupt them. The French they loved. But the stern Presbyterian, with his dogmas and his task-work, the city circle and the college, with their niggard concessions and unfeeling stare, have never tried the experiment. It has not been tried. Our people and our government have sinned alike against the first-born of the soil, and if they are the fated agents of a new era, they have done nothing—have invoked no god to keep them sinless while they do the hest of fate.

Worst of all, when they invoke the holy power only to mask their iniquity; when the felon trader, who, all the week, has been besotting and degrading the Indian with rum mixed with red pepper, and damaged tobacco, kneels with him on Sunday before a common altar, to tell the rosary which recalls the thought of him crucified for love of suffering men, and to listen to sermons in praise of "purity"!! . . .

"You say," said the Indian of the South to the missionary, "that Christianity is pleasing to God. How can that be?—Those men at Savannah are Christians."

Yes! slave-drivers and Indian traders are called Christians, and the Indian is to be deemed less like the Son of Mary than they! Wonderful is the deceit of man's heart! . . .

The Indian is steady to that simple creed, which forms the basis of all this mythology; that there is a God, and a life beyond this; a right and wrong which each man can see, betwixt which each man should choose; that good brings with it its reward and vice its punishment. Their moral code, if not refined as that of civilized nations, is clear and noble in the stress laid upon truth and fidelity. And all unprejudiced observers bear testimony that the Indians, until broken from their old anchorage by intercourse with the whites, who offer them, instead, a religion of which they furnish neither interpretation nor example, were singularly virtuous, if virtue be allowed to consist in a man's acting up to his own ideas of right. . . .

I have not wished to write sentimentally about the Indians, however moved by the thought of their wrongs and speedy extinction. I know that the Europeans who took possession of this country, felt themselves justified by their superior civilization and religious ideas. Had they been truly civilized or Christianized, the conflicts which sprang from the collision of the two races, might have been avoided; but this cannot be expected in movements made by masses of men. The mass has never yet been humanized, though the age may develop a human thought.

Since those conflicts and differences did arise, the hatred which sprang, from terror and suffering, on the European side, has naturally warped the whites still farther from justice.

The Indian, brandishing the scalps of his friends and wife, drinking their blood and eating their hearts, is by him viewed as a fiend, though, at a distant day, he will no doubt be considered as having acted the Roman or Carthaginian part of heroic and patriotic self-defence, according to the standard of right and motives prescribed by his religious faith and education. Looked at by his own standard, he is virtuous when he most injures his enemy, and the white, if he be really the superior in enlargement of thought, ought to cast aside his inherited prejudices enough to see this, — to look on him in pity and brotherly goodwill, and do all he can to mitigate the doom of those who survive his past injuries.

In McKenney's book,[15] is proposed a project for organizing the Indians under a patriarchal government, but it does not look feasible, even on paper. Could their own intelligent men be left to act unimpeded in their behalf, they would do far better for them than the white thinker, with all his general knowledge. But we dare not hope the designs of such will not always be frustrated by the same barbarous selfishness they were in Georgia.[16] There was a chance of seeing what might have been done, now lost forever.

[15]Thomas Loraine McKenney, *Sketches of a Tour to the Lakes, of the Character and Customs of the Chippeway Indians, and of Incidents Connected with the Treaty of Fond du Lac* (1827). Colonel McKenney (1785–1859) headed the new U.S. Bureau of Indian Affairs from 1824 to 1830.

[16]In the 1830s the state of Georgia, after harassing the Indians within the state's boundaries, forced the removal of the Cherokees to west of the Mississippi River. Many Americans considered the Cherokees the most assimilated, peaceful, and "civilized" Indian tribe.

Left: "Mackinaw Island." Etching by Sarah Clarke. This was one of the original illustrations for Margaret Fuller's *Summer on the Lakes, in 1843* (1844).

Yet let every man look to himself how far this blood shall be required at his hands. Let the missionary, instead of preaching to the Indian, preach to the trader who ruins him, of the dreadful account which will be demanded of the followers of Cain, in a sphere where the accents of purity and love come on the ear more decisively than in ours. Let every legislator take the subject to heart, and if he cannot undo the effects of past sin, try for that clear view and right sense that may save us from sinning still more deeply. And let every man and every woman, in their private dealings with the subjugated race, avoid all share in embittering, by insult or unfeeling prejudice, the captivity of Israel. . . .

11

The Poetry of 1844

Beset by anxieties about her family, friends, and especially her own ability to create a public role for herself as an author, Fuller determined to "turn all to Muse" in the summer and fall of 1844. In more than thirty poems that she composed during that period, she explored the personal and social sources of her pain and expressed her longing for wholeness and harmony. As the following selections demonstrate, she invoked a variety of powerful, creative goddesses in this intensely private poetry. With their inspiration, she recovered her balance, strength, and vision; in November 1844, she com-pleted her second book of the year, Woman in the Nineteenth Century.

23

Leila in the Arabian Zone

Leila in the Arabian zone
Dusky, languishing and lone
Yet full of light are her deep eyes
And her gales are lovers sighs.

Io in Egyptian clime[1]
Grows an Isis calm sublime[2]

[1] In Greek mythology, Io was a woman loved by Zeus, the king of the gods. When he transformed her into a cow to deceive his wife, Hera, Io swam to Egypt where, according to some legends, she was worshiped as the goddess Isis.

[2] Isis, an Egyptian fertility goddess, was often depicted with cow's horns. Her sistrum (which Fuller adopted as her talisman) was a rattle that she shook to frighten away the monster Typhon (the father of the Sphinx).

Margaret Fuller, Journal, 1844, Massachusetts Historical Society.

Blue black is her robe of night
But blazoned o'er with points of light
The horns that Io's brow deform
With Isis take a crescent form
And as a holy moon inform.

The magic Sistrum arms her hand
And at her deep eye's command
Brutes are raised to thinking men
Soul growing to her soul filled ken.

Dian of the lonely life
Hecate fed on gloom and strife
Phebe on her throne of air
Only Leila's children are.[3]

[3]Diana, or Artemis, the virgin goddess of the moon, was the daughter of Hecate (a Greek goddess of the underworld and witchcraft) and the granddaughter of Phoebe (one of the female Titans who ruled the earth until overthrown by the Olympian gods).

24

Winged Sphynx[1]

Through brute nature, upward rising,
Seed upstriving to the light,
Revelations still surprising
Inwardness is grown insight.
Still I slight not the first stages,
Dark, but God-directed ages;
In my nature leonine
Toiled and learned a soul divine,
Put forth an aspect chaste, serene
Nature's virgin mother queen
Assumes at last the destined wings
Earth and heaven together brings
While her own form the riddle tells
That baffled all the wizard spells

[1]In Greek mythology, the Sphynx was a winged monster with a lion's body and a woman's head. She would ask all comers a riddle and kill any who failed to answer it. In the drama *Oedipus Rex* by the Greek Sophocles (496–406 B.C.), Oedipus frees Thebes from the terror of the Sphynx by solving her riddle: "What has four feet, three feet, two feet, but one voice?"

Margaret Fuller, Journal, 1844, Massachusetts Historical Society.

Drawn from intellectual wells
Cold waters where Truth never dwells
It was fable told you so
Seek her in common daylight's glow.

25

Double Triangle, Serpent and Rays[1]

Patient serpent, circle round
Till in death thy life is found
Double form of godly prime
Holding the whole thought of time,
When the perfect two embrace,
Male and female, black and white
Soul is justified in space,
Dark made fruitful by the light,
And centred in the diamond Sun,
Time, eternity, are one.

[1]Fuller used the symbol of interlocking triangles surrounded by a serpent and the rays of a star as the frontispiece of *Woman in the Nineteenth Century.* (See p.157.)

12

Woman in the Nineteenth Century

Long considered a landmark in the history of American feminism, Woman in the Nineteenth Century *(1845) represents both the culmination of Fuller's Transcendental vision of self-culture and her first step beyond it. The selections reprinted here illustrate the breadth of Fuller's feminism in her most important book. Refusing to portray women merely as the victims of patriarchal norms, she drew upon history, literature, and mythology to create a pantheon of powerful heroines and goddesses. She also introduced another quasi-autobiographical character, the proud and independent Miranda. Together these female figures supported Fuller's claims that gender characteristics were naturally fluid, that "woman's nature" contained both the intellectual Minerva and the spiritual Muse, and that the rigid social construction of gender roles limited the full development of women and men alike. She urged women to take up Minerva's armor and javelin for a while to free themselves and all humanity. Luxuriating in different voices and modes of expression, Fuller wove her theory of Minerva and the Muse into the very fabric of her book. Upon completing it, she reflected, "I felt a delightful glow as if I had put a good deal of my true life in it, as if, suppose I went away now, the measure of my foot-print would be left on the earth."*

26

Woman in the Nineteenth Century

Preface

The following essay is a reproduction, modified and expanded, of an article published in "The Dial, Boston, July, 1843," under the title of "The Great Lawsuit. Man versus Men: Woman versus Women."

S. Margaret Fuller, *Woman in the Nineteenth Century* (NY, 1845).

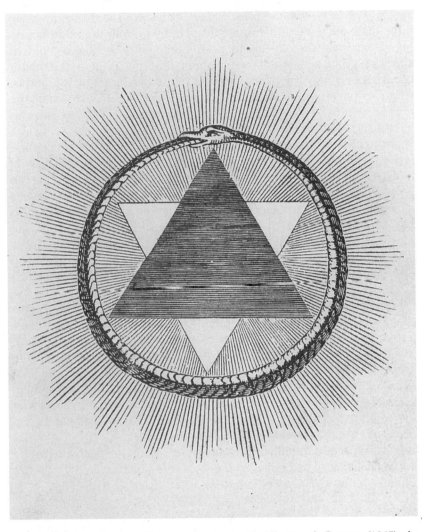

Frontispiece of Margaret Fuller's *Woman in the Nineteenth Century* (1845). As Fuller explained in her poem "Double Triangle, Serpent and Rays" of 1844 (Document 25), the interlocking triangles surrounded by a serpent and the rays of a star symbolized for her the overcoming of all oppositions.

This article excited a good deal of sympathy, and still more interest. It is in compliance with wishes expressed from many quarters, that it is prepared for publication in its present form.

Objections having been made to the former title, as not sufficiently easy to be understood, the present has been substituted as expressive of the main purpose of the essay; though, by myself, the other is preferred, partly for the reason others do not like it, *i. e.,* that it requires some thought to see what it means, and might thus prepare the reader to meet me on my own ground. Beside, it offers a larger scope, and is, in that way, more just to my desire. I meant, by that title, to intimate the fact that, while it is the destiny of Man, in the course of the Ages, to ascertain and fulfil the law of his being, so that his life shall be seen, as a whole, to be that of an angel or messenger, the action of prejudices and passions, which attend, in the day, the growth of the individual, is continually obstructing the holy work that is to make the earth a part of heaven. By Man I mean both man and woman: these are the two halves of one thought. I lay no especial stress on the welfare of either. I believe that the development of the one cannot be effected without that of the other. My highest wish is that this truth should be distinctly and rationally apprehended, and the conditions of life and freedom recognized as the same for the daughters and the sons of time; twin exponents of a divine thought.

I solicit a sincere and patient attention from those who open the following pages at all. I solicit of women that they will lay it to heart to ascertain what is for them the liberty of law. It is for this, and not for any, the largest, extension of partial privileges that I seek. I ask them, if interested by these suggestions, to search their own experience and intuitions for better, and fill up with fit materials the trenches that hedge them in. From men I ask a noble and earnest attention to any thing that can be offered on this great and still obscure subject, such as I have met from many with whom I stand in private relations.

And may truth, unpolluted by prejudice, vanity, or selfishness, be granted daily more and more, as the due inheritance, and only valuable conquest for us all!

Woman in the Nineteenth Century

> "Frailty, thy name is WOMAN."[1]
> "The Earth waits for her Queen."

The connection between these quotations may not be obvious, but it is strict. Yet would any contradict us, if we made them applicable to the other side, and began also

---

[1] William Shakespeare, *Hamlet* 1.2.146.

Frailty, thy name is MAN.
The Earth waits for its King.

Yet man, if not yet fully installed in his powers, has given much earnest of his claims. Frail he is indeed, how frail! how impure! Yet often has the vein of gold displayed itself amid the baser ores, and Man has appeared before us in princely promise worthy of his future.

If, oftentimes, we see the prodigal son feeding on the husks in the fair field no more his own, anon, we raise the eyelids, heavy from bitter tears, to behold in him the radiant apparition of genius and love, demanding not less than the all of goodness, power and beauty.[2] We see that in him the largest claim finds a due foundation. That claim is for no partial sway, no exclusive possession. He cannot be satisfied with any one gift of life, any one department of knowledge or telescopic peep at the heavens. He feels himself called to understand and aid nature, that she may, through his intelligence, be raised and interpreted; to be a student of, and servant to, the universe-spirit; and king of his planet, that as an angelic minister, he may bring it into conscious harmony with the law of that spirit. . . .

[Orpheus and Eurydice]

Orpheus was a law-giver by theocratic commission. He understood nature, and made her forms move to his music. He told her secrets in the form of hymns, nature as seen in the mind of God. His soul went forth toward all beings, yet could remain sternly faithful to a chosen type of excellence. Seeking what he loved, he feared not death nor hell, neither could any shape of dread daunt his faith in the power of the celestial harmony that filled his soul.[3] . . .

A better comment could not be made on what is required to perfect man, and place him in that superior position for which he was designed, than by the interpretation of Bacon[4] upon the legends of the Syren coast. When the wise Ulysses passed, says he, he caused his mariners to stop their ears with wax, knowing there was in them no power to resist the lure of that voluptuous song.[5] But he, the much experienced man, who

---

[2]Luke 15.11–32 contains the story of the prodigal son.
[3]In Greek mythology, Orpheus was a poet and musician who ventured into the underworld to rescue his wife, Eurydice, from Death. Although he charmed the gods of the underworld with his lyre, he lost Eurydice once more when he looked back to see if she followed as they returned to the land of the living.
[4]The English philosopher Sir Francis Bacon (1561–1626).
[5]In the *Odyssey* by the Greek poet Homer (fl. 850? B.C.), Ulysses (Odysseus) thus successfully passed the sirens, whose singing lured sailors to their deaths.

wished to be experienced in all, and use all to the service of wisdom, desired to hear the song that he might understand its meaning. Yet, distrusting his own power to be firm in his better purpose, he caused himself to be bound to the mast, that he might be kept secure against his own weakness. But Orpheus passed unfettered, so absorbed in singing hymns to the gods that he could not even hear those sounds of degrading enchantment.

Meanwhile not a few believe, and men themselves have expressed the opinion, that the time is come when Eurydice is to call for an Orpheus, rather than Orpheus for Eurydice: that the idea of Man, however imperfectly brought out, has been far more so than that of Woman, that she, the other half of the same thought, the other chamber of the heart of life, needs now to take her turn in the full pulsation, and that improvement in the daughters will best aid in the reformation of the sons of this age.

It should be remarked that, as the principle of liberty is better understood, and more nobly interpreted, a broader protest is made in behalf of Woman. As men become aware that few men have had a fair chance, they are inclined to say that no women have had a fair chance. . . .

[Woman's Rights]

Of all its banners, none has been more steadily upheld, and under none have more valor and willingness for real sacrifices been shown, than that of the champions of the enslaved African. And this band it is, which, partly from a natural following out of principles, partly because many women have been prominent in that cause, makes, just now, the warmest appeal in behalf of woman.[6]

Though there has been a growing liberality on this subject, yet society at large is not so prepared for the demands of this party, but that they are and will be for some time, coldly regarded as the Jacobins[7] of their day.

"Is it not enough," cries the irritated trader, "that you have done all you could to break up the national union, and thus destroy the prosperity of our country, but now you must be trying to break up family union, to take my wife away from the cradle and the kitchen hearth to vote at polls, and preach from a pulpit? Of course, if she does such things, she cannot attend to those of her own sphere. She is happy enough as she is. She has more leisure than I have, every means of improvement, every indulgence."

[6]Woman's rights was one of the most divisive issues that American abolitionists faced.
[7]Jacobins were the radical republicans of the French Revolution. Americans generally associated them with the Reign of Terror (1793–1794), in which thousands of French men and women were executed (many by guillotine) as enemies of the republic.

"Have you asked her whether she was satisfied with these *indulgences?*"

"No, but I know she is. She is too amiable to wish what would make me unhappy, and too judicious to wish to step beyond the sphere of her sex. I will never consent to have our peace disturbed by any such discussions."

" 'Consent—you?' it is not consent from you that is in question, it is assent from your wife."

"Am not I the head of my house?"

"You are not the head of your wife. God has given her a mind of her own."

"I am the head and she the heart."

"God grant you play true to one another then. I suppose I am to be grateful that you did not say she was only the hand. If the head represses no natural pulse of the heart, there can be no question as to your giving your consent. Both will be of one accord, and there needs but to present any question to get a full and true answer. There is no need of precaution, of indulgence, or consent. But our doubt is whether the heart does consent with the head, or only obeys its decrees with a passiveness that precludes the exercise of its natural powers, or a repugnance that turns sweet qualities to bitter, or a doubt that lays waste the fair occasions of life. It is to ascertain the truth, that we propose some liberating measures."

Thus vaguely are these questions proposed and discussed at present. But their being proposed at all implies much thought and suggests more. Many women are considering within themselves, what they need that they have not, and what they can have, if they find they need it. Many men are considering whether women are capable of being and having more than they are and have, *and,* whether, if so, it will be best to consent to improvement in their condition. . . .

It may well be an Anti-Slavery party that pleads for woman, if we consider merely that she does not hold property on equal terms with men; so that, if a husband dies without making a will, the wife, instead of taking at once his place as head of the family, inherits only a part of his fortune, often brought him by herself, as if she were a child, or ward only, not an equal partner.

We will not speak of the innumerable instances in which profligate and idle men live upon the earnings of industrious wives; or if the wives leave them, and take with them the children, to perform the double duty of mother and father, follow from place to place, and threaten to rob them of the children, if deprived of the rights of a husband, as they call them, planting themselves in their poor lodgings, frightening them into paying tribute by taking from them the children, running into debt at the expense of these otherwise so overtasked helots. Such instances count up by scores within my own memory. I have seen the husband who had stained himself by a long course of low vice, till his wife was wearied from her heroic forgiveness, by finding that his treachery made it useless, and that if she would provide bread for herself and her children, she must be separate from his ill fame. I have known this man come to instal himself in the chamber of a woman who loathed him and say she should never take food without his company. I have known these men steal their children whom they knew they had no means to maintain, take them into dissolute company, expose them to bodily danger, to frighten the poor woman, to whom, it seems, the fact that she alone had borne the pangs of their birth and nourished their infancy, does not give an equal right to them. I do believe that this mode of kidnapping, and it is frequent enough in all classes of society, will be by the next age viewed as it is by Heaven now, and that the man who avails himself of the shelter of men's laws to steal from a mother her own children, or arrogate any superior right in them, save that of superior virtue, will bear the stigma he deserves, in common with him who steals grown men from their mother land, their hopes, and their homes.

I said, we will not speak of this now, yet I have spoken, for the subject makes me feel too much. I could give instances that would startle the most vulgar and callous, but I will not, for the public opinion of their own sex is already against such men, and where cases of extreme tyranny are made known, there is private action in the wife's favor. But she ought not to need this, nor, I think, can she long. Men must soon see that, on their own ground, that woman is the weaker party, she ought to have legal protection, which would make such oppression impossible. But I would not deal with "atrocious instances" except in the way of illustration, neither demand from men a partial redress in some one matter, but go to the root of the whole. If principles could be established, particulars would adjust themselves aright. Ascertain the true destiny of woman, give her legitimate hopes, and a standard within herself; marriage and all other relations would by degrees be harmonized with these.

But to return to the historical progress of this matter. Knowing that there exists in the minds of men a tone of feeling towards women as towards slaves, such as is expressed in the common phrase, "Tell that to women and children," that the infinite soul can only work through them in already ascertained limits; that the gift of reason, man's highest prerogative, is allotted to them in much lower degree; that they must be kept from mischief and melancholy by being constantly engaged in active labor, which is to be furnished and directed by those better able to think,

&c. &c.; we need not multiply instances, for who can review the experience of last week without recalling words which imply, whether in jest or earnest, these views or views like these; knowing this, can we wonder that many reformers think that measures are not likely to be taken in behalf of women, unless their wishes could be publicly represented by women?

That can never be necessary, cry the other side. All men are privately influenced by women; each has his wife, sister, or female friends, and is too much biased by these relations to fail of representing their interests, and, if this is not enough, let them propose and enforce their wishes with the pen. The beauty of home would be destroyed, the delicacy of the sex be violated, the dignity of halls of legislation degraded by an attempt to introduce them there. Such duties are inconsistent with those of a mother; and then we have ludicrous pictures of ladies in hysterics at the polls, and senate chambers filled with cradles.

But if, in reply, we admit as truth that woman seems destined by nature rather for the inner circle, we must add that the arrangements of civilized life have not been, as yet, such as to secure it to her. Her circle, if the duller, is not the quieter. If kept from "excitement," she is not from drudgery. Not only the Indian squaw carries the burdens of the camp, but the favorites of Louis the Fourteenth[8] accompany him in his journeys, and the washerwoman stands at her tub and carries home her work at all seasons, and in all states of health. Those who think the physical circumstances of woman would make a part in the affairs of national government unsuitable, are by no means those who think it impossible for the negresses to endure field work, even during pregnancy, or the sempstresses to go through their killing labors.

As to the use of the pen, there was quite as much opposition to woman's possessing herself of that help to free agency, as there is now to her seizing on the rostrum or the desk; and she is likely to draw, from a permission to plead her cause that way, opposite inferences to what might be wished by those who now grant it.

As to the possibility of her filling with grace and dignity, any such position, we should think those who had seen the great actresses, and heard the Quaker preachers of modern times,[9] would not doubt, that woman can express publicly the fulness of thought and creation, without losing any of the peculiar beauty of her sex. What can pollute and tarnish is to act thus from any motive except that something needs to be said or

[8]Louis XIV (1638–1715) was king of France from 1643 to 1715. He was known for his extravagance and his mistresses, among other things.

[9]Fuller particularly admired the great French actress Mlle. Rachel (1820–1858) and the Quaker and abolitionist speaker Abby Kelley (1810–1887).

done. Women could take part in the processions, the songs, the dances of old religion; no one fancied their delicacy was impaired by appearing in public for such a cause.

As to her home, she is not likely to leave it more than she now does for balls, theatres, meetings for promoting missions, revival meetings, and others to which she flies, in hope of an animation for her existence, commensurate with what she sees enjoyed by men. Governors of ladies' fairs are no less engrossed by such a change, than the Governor of the state by his; presidents of Washingtonian societies no less away from home than presidents of conventions. If men look straitly to it, they will find that, unless their lives are domestic, those of the women will not be. A house is no home unless it contain food and fire for the mind as well as for the body. The female Greek, of our day, is as much in the street as the male to cry, What news? We doubt not it was the same in Athens of old. The women, shut out from the market place, made up for it at the religious festivals. For human beings are not so constituted that they can live without expansion. If they do not get it one way, they must another, or perish.

As to men's representing women fairly at present, while we hear from men who owe to their wives not only all that is comfortable or graceful, but all that is wise in the arrangement of their lives, the frequent remark, "You cannot reason with a woman," when from those of delicacy, nobleness, and poetic culture, the contemptuous phrase "women and children," and that in no light sally of the hour, but in works intended to give a permanent statement of the best experiences, when not one man, in the million, shall I say? no, not in the hundred million, can rise above the belief that woman was made *for man,* when such traits as these are daily forced upon the attention, can we feel that man will always do justice to the interests of woman? Can we think that he takes a sufficiently discerning and religious view of her office and destiny, *ever* to do her justice, except when prompted by sentiment, accidentally or transiently, that is, for the sentiment will vary according to the relations in which he is placed. The lover, the poet, the artist, are likely to view her nobly. The father and the philosopher have some chance of liberality; the man of the world, the legislator for expediency, none.

Under these circumstances, without attaching importance, in themselves, to the changes demanded by the champions of woman, we hail them as signs of the times. We would have every arbitrary barrier thrown down. We would have every path laid open to woman as freely as to man. Were this done and a slight temporary fermentation allowed to subside, we should see crystallizations more pure and of more various beauty. We believe the divine energy would pervade nature to a degree unknown in the history of former ages, and that no discordant collision, but a ravishing harmony of the spheres would ensue.

Yet, then and only then, will mankind be ripe for this, when inward and outward freedom for woman as much as for man shall be acknowledged as a right, not yielded as a concession. As the friend of the negro assumes that one man cannot by right, hold another in bondage, so should the friend of woman assume that man cannot, by right, lay even well-meant restrictions on woman. If the negro be a soul, if the woman be a soul, appareled in flesh, to one Master only are they accountable. There is but one law for souls, and if there is to be an interpreter of it, he must come not as man, or son of man, but as son of God.

Were thought and feeling once so far elevated that man should esteem himself the brother and friend, but nowise the lord and tutor of woman, were he really bound with her in equal worship, arrangements as to function and employment would be of no consequence. What woman needs is not as a woman to act or rule, but as a nature to grow, as an intellect to discern, as soul to live freely and unimpeded, to unfold such powers as were given her when we left our common home. If fewer talents were given her, yet if allowed the free and full employment of these, so that she may render back to the giver his own with usury[10] she will not complain; nay I dare to say she will bless and rejoice in her earthly birth-place, her earthly lot. Let us consider what obstructions impede this good era, and what signs give reason to hope that it draws near.

[Miranda]

I was talking on this subject with Miranda, a woman, who, if any in the world could, might speak without heat and bitterness of the position of her sex.[11] Her father was a man who cherished no sentimental reverence for woman, but a firm belief in the equality of the sexes. She was his eldest child, and came to him at an age when he needed a companion. From the time she could speak and go alone, he addressed her not as a plaything, but as a living mind. Among the few verses he ever wrote was a copy addressed to this child, when the first locks were cut from her head, and the reverence expressed on this occasion for that cherished

---

[10]See Luke 25.14–30 for the parable of the talents.

[11]Fuller created Miranda as another portrait of herself, according to her journal of 1844: "Last year at this time I wrote of Woman, and proudly painted myself as Miranda." By naming this autobiographical character after Prospero's daughter in Shakespeare's *The Tempest,* Fuller also paid homage to her father—in sharp contrast to her unpublished "Autobiographical Sketch" (see Document 18). Quotation marks have been silently added to the dialogue with Miranda that follows.

head, he never belied. It was to him the temple of immortal intellect. He respected his child, however, too much to be an indulgent parent. He called on her for clear judgment, for courage, for honor and fidelity; in short, for such virtues as he knew. In so far as he possessed the keys to the wonders of this universe, he allowed free use of them to her, and by the incentive of a high expectation, he forbade, as far as possible, that she should let the privilege lie idle.

Thus this child was early led to feel herself a child of the spirit. She took her place easily, not only in the world of organized being, but in the world of mind. A dignified sense of self-dependence was given as all her portion, and she found it a sure anchor. Herself securely anchored, her relations with others were established with equal security. She was fortunate in a total absence of those charms which might have drawn to her bewildering flatteries, and in a strong electric nature, which repelled those who did not belong to her, and attracted those who did. With men and women her relations were noble, affectionate without passion, intellectual without coldness. The world was free to her, and she lived freely in it. Outward adversity came, and inward conflict, but that faith and self-respect had early been awakened which must always lead at last, to an outward serenity and an inward peace.

Of Miranda I had always thought as an example, that the restraints upon the sex were insuperable only to those who think them so, or who noisily strive to break them. She had taken a course of her own, and no man stood in her way. Many of her acts had been unusual, but excited no uproar. Few helped, but none checked her, and the many men, who knew her mind and her life, showed to her confidence, as to a brother, gentleness as to a sister. And not only refined, but very coarse men approved and aided one in whom they saw resolution and clearness of design. Her mind was often the leading one, always effective.

When I talked with her upon these matters, and had said very much what I have written, she smilingly replied: "And yet we must admit that I have been fortunate, and this should not be. My good father's early trust gave the first bias, and the rest followed of course. It is true that I have had less outward aid, in after years, than most women, but that is of little consequence. Religion was early awakened in my soul, a sense that what the soul is capable to ask it must attain, and that, though I might be aided and instructed by others, I must depend on myself as the only constant friend. This self dependence, which was honored in me, is deprecated as a fault in most women. They are taught to learn their rule from without, not to unfold it from within.

"This is the fault of man, who is still vain, and wishes to be more important to woman than, by right, he should be."

"Men have not shown this disposition toward you," I said.

"No! because the position I early was enabled to take was one of self-reliance. And were all women as sure of their wants as I was, the result would be the same. But they are so overloaded with precepts by guardians, who think that nothing is so much to be dreaded for a woman as originality of thought or character, that their minds are impeded by doubts till they lose their chance of fair free proportions. The difficulty is to get them to the point from which they shall naturally develop self-respect, and learn self-help.

"Once I thought that men would help to forward this state of things more than I do now. I saw so many of them wretched in the connections they had formed in weakness and vanity. They seemed so glad to esteem women whenever they could.

" 'The soft arms of affection,' said one of the most discerning spirits, 'will not suffice for me, unless on them I see the steel bracelets of strength.'

"But early I perceived that men never, in any extreme of despair, wished to be women. On the contrary they were ever ready to taunt one another at any sign of weakness with,

'Art thou not like the women, who'—

The passage ends various ways, according to the occasion and rhetoric of the speaker. When they admired any woman they were inclined to speak of her as 'above her sex.' Silently I observed this, and feared it argued a rooted scepticism, which for ages had been fastening on the heart, and which only an age of miracles could eradicate. Ever I have been treated with great sincerity; and I look upon it as a signal instance of this, that an intimate friend of the other sex said, in a fervent moment, that I 'deserved in some star to be a man.' He was much surprised when I disclosed my view of my position and hopes, when I declared my faith that the feminine side, the side of love, of beauty, of holiness, was now to have its full chance, and that, if either were better, it was better now to be a woman, for even the slightest achievement of good was furthering an especial work of our time. He smiled incredulous. 'She makes the best she can of it,' thought he. 'Let Jews believe the pride of Jewry, but I am of the better sort, and know better.'

"Another used as highest praise, in speaking of a character in literature, the words 'a manly woman.'

"So in the noble passage of Ben Jonson:

'I meant the day-star should not brighter ride,
Nor shed like influence from its lucent seat;
I meant she should be courteous, facile, sweet,
Free from that solemn vice of greatness, pride;

> I meant each softest virtue there should meet,
> Fit in that softer bosom to abide,
> Only a learned and a *manly* soul,
> I purposed her, that should with even powers,
> The rock, the spindle, and the shears control
> Of destiny, and spin her own free hours.' "[12]

"Methinks," said I, "you are too fastidious in objecting to this. Jonson in using the word 'manly' only meant to heighten the picture of this, the true, the intelligent fate, with one of the deeper colors." "And yet," said she, "so invariable is the use of this word where a heroic quality is to be described, and I feel so sure that persistence and courage are the most womanly no less than the most manly qualities, that I would exchange these words for others of a larger sense at the risk of marring the fine tissue of the verse. Read, 'a heavenward and instructed soul,' and I should be satisfied. Let it not be said, wherever there is energy or creative genius, 'She has a masculine mind.' "

This by no means argues a willing want of generosity toward woman. Man is as generous toward her, as he knows how to be.

Wherever she has herself arisen in national or private history, and nobly shone forth in any form of excellence, men have received her, not only willingly, but with triumph. Their encomiums indeed, are always, in some sense, mortifying; they show too much surprise. Can this be you? he cries to the transfigured Cinderella; well I should never have thought it, but I am very glad. We will tell every one that you have "*surpassed your sex.*"

In every-day life the feelings of the many are stained with vanity. Each wishes to be lord in a little world, to be superior at least over one; and he does not feel strong enough to retain a life-long ascendancy over a strong nature. Only a Theseus could conquer before he wed the Amazonian Queen. Hercules wished rather to rest with Dejanira, and received the poisoned robe, as a fit guerdon.[13] The tale should be interpreted to all those who seek repose with the weak.

But not only is man vain and fond of power, but the same want of development, which thus affects him morally, prevents his intellectually discerning the destiny of woman. The boy wants no woman, but only a girl to play ball with him, and mark his pocket handkerchief. . . .

---

[12] From "On Lucy Countess of Bedford" by the English dramatist and poet laureate Ben Jonson (1572–1637).

[13] According to legend, Theseus, a king of Athens, defeated the Amazons and married their queen, Hippolyte. Hercules, the mythical Greek hero fabled for his tremendous strength, was killed by his jealous wife Deianira, who gave him a poisoned robe that ate away his flesh. A guerdon was a reward won by a knight in contest.

[Heroines and Goddesses]

No! man is not willingly ungenerous. He wants faith and love, because he is not yet himself an elevated being. He cries, with sneering skepticism, Give us a sign. But if the sign appears, his eyes glisten, and he offers not merely approval, but homage.

The severe nation which taught that the happiness of the race was forfeited through the fault of a woman, and showed its thought of what sort of regard man owed her, by making him accuse her on the first question to his God; who gave her to the patriarch as a handmaid, and by the Mosaical law, bound her to allegiance like a self; even they greeted, with solemn rapture, all great and holy women as heroines, prophetesses, judges in Israel; and if they made Eve listen to the serpent, gave Mary as a bride to the Holy Spirit.[14] In other nations it has been the same down to our day. To the woman who could conquer, a triumph was awarded. And not only those whose strength was recommended to the heart by association with goodness and beauty, but those who were bad, if they were steadfast and strong, had their claims allowed. In any age a Semiramis, an Elizabeth of England, a Catharine of Russia, makes her place good, whether in a large or small circle.[15] . . .

Whatever may have been the domestic manners of the ancients, the idea of woman was nobly manifested in their mythologies and poems, where she appears as Sita in the Ramayana, a form of tender purity, as the Egyptian Isis, of divine wisdom never yet surpassed.[16] In Egypt, too, the Sphynx, walking the earth with lion tread, looked out upon its marvels in the calm, inscrutable beauty of a virgin's face, and the Greek could only add wings to the great emblem.[17] In Greece, Ceres, and Proserpine, significantly termed "the great goddesses," were seen seated, side by side.[18] They needed not to rise for any worshipper or any change; they were prepared for all things, as those initiated to their mysteries knew. More obvious is the meaning of these three forms, the Diana, Minerva, and Vesta.[19] Unlike in the expression of their beauty, but alike in this,—

---

[14]See Genesis 3.1–6 for the story of Eve and the serpent. Mary becomes the bride of the Holy Spirit in Luke 1.35.

[15]Semiramis was a ninth-century B.C. Assyrian queen. Elizabeth of England was Queen Elizabeth I (1533–1603), daughter of Henry VIII, who ruled from 1558 to 1603. Catharine of Russia was Empress Catherine the Great (1729–1796), who reigned from 1762 to 1796.

[16]Sita was a Hindu fertility goddess, and Isis an Egyptian fertility goddess.

[17]The Sphynx was a legendary winged monster, with a lion's body and a woman's head.

[18]According to legend, the earth goddess Ceres journeyed into the underworld to rescue her daughter, Proserpine, who had been abducted by Death.

[19]Diana was the Roman goddess of the moon and the hunt. The Roman goddess of wisdom and war, Minerva (Athena in Greek mythology), was born from the head of her fa-

that each was self-sufficing. Other forms were only accessories and illustrations, none the complement to one like these. Another might, indeed, be the companion, and the Apollo and Diana set off one another's beauty.[20] Of the Vesta, it is to be observed, that not only deep-eyed, deep-discerning Greece, but ruder Rome, who represents the only form of good man, (the always busy warrior), that could be indifferent to woman, confided the permanence of its glory to a tutelary goddess, and her wisest legislator spoke of meditation as a nymph. . . .

We are told of the Greek nations in general, that woman occupied there an infinitely lower place than man. It is difficult to believe this when we see such range and dignity of thought on the subject in the mythologies, and find the poets producing such ideals as Cassandra, Iphiginia, Antigone, Macaria,[21] where Sibylline priestesses told the oracle of the highest god, and he could not be content to reign with a court of fewer than nine muses. Even victory wore a female form.

But whatever were the facts of daily life, I cannot complain of the age and nation, which represents its thought by such a symbol as I see before me at this moment. It is a zodiac of the busts of gods and goddesses, arranged in pairs. The circle breathes the music of a heavenly order. Male and female heads are distinct in expression, but equal in beauty, strength and calmness. Each male head is that of a brother and a king—each female of a sister and a queen. Could the thought, thus expressed, be lived out, there would be nothing more to be desired. There would be unison in variety, congeniality in difference.

Coming nearer our own time, we find religion and poetry no less true in their revelations. The rude man, just disengaged from the sod, the Adam, accuses woman to his God, and records her disgrace to their posterity. He is not ashamed to write that he could be drawn from heaven by one beneath him, one made, he says, from but a small part of himself. But in the same nation, educated by time, instructed by a succession of prophets, we find woman in as high a position as she has ever occupied. No figure that has ever arisen to greet our eyes has been received with more fervent reverence than that of the Madonna. Heine calls her the

---

ther, Jupiter, the king of the gods. Vesta was the Roman goddess of the hearth fire and the state, whose shrine in Rome was tended by the vestal virgins.

[20]As the god of the sun, Apollo complemented the moon's beauty.

[21]The Greek dramatist Euripides (ca. 484–406 B.C.) wrote about Cassandra (the prophetic, misunderstood daughter of the king of Troy), Iphigenia (whose father, the Greek king Agamemnon, sacrificed her to the gods), and Macaria (a daughter of Hercules). The Greek dramatist Sophocles (ca. 496–406 B.C.) created Antigone, who sacrificed her own life to bury her brother's body.

Dame du Comptoir[22] of the Catholic church, and this jeer well expresses a serious truth.

And not only this holy and significant image was worshipped by the pilgrim, and the favorite subject of the artist, but it exercised an immediate influence on the destiny of the sex. The empresses who embraced the cross, converted sons and husbands. Whole calendars of female saints, heroic dames of chivalry, binding the emblem of faith on the heart of the best-beloved, and wasting the bloom of youth in separation and loneliness, for the sake of duties they thought it religion to assume, with innumerable forms of poesy, trace their lineage to this one. Nor, however imperfect may be the action, in our day, of the faith thus expressed, and though we can scarcely think it nearer this ideal, than that of India or Greece was near their ideal, is it in vain that the truth has been recognized, that woman is not only a part of man, bone of his bone, and flesh of his flesh, born that men might not be lonely, but that women are in themselves possessors of and possessed by immortal souls. This truth undoubtedly received a greater outward stability from the belief of the church that the earthly parent of the Saviour of souls was a woman. . . .

[Love and Marriage]

The ideal of love and marriage rose high in the mind of all the Christian nations who were capable of grave and deep feeling. We may take as examples of its English aspect, the lines,

> "I could not love thee, dear, so much,
> Loved I not honor more."[23]

Or the address of the Commonwealth's man to his wife, as she looked out from the Tower window to see him for the last time, on his way to the scaffold. He stood up in the cart, waved his hat, and cried, "To Heaven, my love, to Heaven, and leave you in the storm?"

Such was the love of faith and honor, a love which stopped, like Colonel Hutchinson's, "on this side idolatry," because it was religious. The meeting of two such souls Donne describes as giving birth to an "abler soul."[24] . . .

---

[22]Counter woman or salesclerk (French). The German-Jewish author Heinrich Heine (1797–1856) spent most of his life in exile in Paris.

[23]From "To Lucasta, Going to the Warres" by the English poet Richard Lovelace (1618–1657).

[24]From "The Ecstasy" by the English poet John Donne (1572–1631). Thomas Hutchinson (1711–1780) was the last civilian royal governor of colonial Massachusetts and a prominent Loyalist.

Centuries have passed since, but civilized Europe is still in a transition state about marriage; not only in practice, but in thought. It is idle to speak with contempt of the nations where polygamy is an institution, or seraglios a custom, when practices far more debasing haunt, well nigh fill, every city and every town. And so far as union of one with one is believed to be the only pure form of marriage, a great majority of societies and individuals are still doubtful whether the earthly bond must be a meeting of souls, or only supposes a contract of convenience and utility. Were woman established in the rights of an immortal being, this could not be. She would not, in some countries, be given away by her father, with scarcely more respect for her feelings than is shown by the Indian chief, who sells his daughter for a horse, and beats her if she runs away from her new home. Nor, in societies where her choice is left free, would she be perverted, by the current of opinion that seizes her, into the belief that she must marry, if it be only to find a protector, and a home of her own.

Neither would man, if he thought the connection of permanent importance, form it so lightly. He would not deem it a trifle, that he was to enter into the closest relations with another soul, which, if not eternal in themselves, must eternally affect his growth.

Neither, did he believe woman capable of friendship, would he, by rash haste, lose the chance of finding a friend in the person who might, probably, live half a century by his side. Did love, to his mind, stretch forth into infinity, he would not miss his chance of its revelations, that he might, the sooner, rest from his weariness by a bright fireside, and secure a sweet and graceful attendant "devoted to him alone." Were he a step higher, he would not carelessly enter into a relation where he might not be able to do the duty of a friend, as well as a protector from external ill, to the other party, and have a being in his power pining for sympathy, intelligence and aid, that he could not give.

What deep communion, what real intercourse is implied by the sharing the joys and cares of parentage, when any degree of equality is admitted between the parties! It is true that, in a majority of instances, the man looks upon his wife as an adopted child, and places her to the other children in the relation of nurse or governess, rather than of parent. Her influence with them is sure, but she misses the education which should enlighten that influence, by being thus treated. It is the order of nature that children should complete the education, moral and mental, of parents, by making them think what is needed for the best culture of human beings, and conquer all faults and impulses that interfere with their giving this to these dear objects, who represent the world to them. Father and mother should assist one another to learn what is required for this sublime priesthood of nature. But, for this, a religious recognition of equality is required.

Where this thought of equality begins to diffuse itself, it is shown in four ways.

The household partnership. In our country, the woman looks for a "smart but kind" husband; the man for a "capable, sweet-tempered" wife.

The man furnishes the house; the woman regulates it. Their relation is one of mutual esteem, mutual dependence. Their talk is of business, their affection shows itself by practical kindness. They know that life goes more smoothly and cheerfully to each for the other's aid; they are grateful and content. The wife praises her husband as a "good provider;" the husband, in return, compliments her as a "capital housekeeper." This relation is good, as far as it goes.

Next comes a closer tie, which takes the two forms, either of mutual idolatry, or of intellectual companionship. The first, we suppose, is to no one a pleasing subject of contemplation. . . .

The other form, of intellectual companionship, has become more and more frequent. Men engaged in public life, literary men, and artists, have often found in their wives companions and confidants in thought no less than in feeling. And as the intellectual development of woman has spread wider and risen higher, they have, not unfrequently, shared the same employment. As in the case of Roland and his wife, who were friends in the household and in the nation's councils, read, regulated home affairs, or prepared public documents together, indifferently.[25]

It is very pleasant, in letters begun by Roland, and finished by his wife, to see the harmony of mind, and the difference of nature; one thought, but various ways of treating it. . . .

The fourth and highest grade of marriage union, is the religious, which may be expressed as pilgrimage towards a common shrine. This includes the others; home sympathies and household wisdom, for these pilgrims must know how to assist each other along the dusty way; intellectual communion, for how sad it would be on such a journey to have a companion to whom you could not communicate thoughts and aspirations as they sprang to life; who would have no feeling for the prospects that open, more and more glorious as we advance; who would never see the flowers that may be gathered by the most industrious traveller. It must

---

[25] Jean-Marie Roland de La Platière (1734–1793) and Manon Philipon Roland (1754–1793) were French intellectuals and revolutionaries who died during the Reign of Terror, she by execution and he by suicide. Mme. Roland's last words were "O Liberty, what crimes are committed in thy name!"

include all these. Such a fellow-pilgrim Count Zinzendorf[26] seems to have found in his Countess, of whom he thus writes:

"Twenty-five years' experience has shown me that just the helpmate whom I have, is the only one that could suit my vocation. Who else could have so carried through my family affairs? Who lived so spotlessly before the world? Who so wisely aided me in my rejection of a dry morality? . . . Who, without a murmur, have seen her husband encounter such dangers by land and sea? Who undertaken with him, and sustained such astonishing pilgrimages? Who, amid such difficulties, always held up her head and supported me? Who found such vast sums of money, and acquitted them on her own credit? And, finally, who, of all human beings, could so well understand and interpret to others my inner and outer being as this one, of such nobleness in her way of thinking, such great intellectual capacity, and free from the theological perplexities that enveloped me!"

Let any one peruse, with all their power, the lineaments of this portrait, and see if the husband had not reason, with this air of solemn rapture and conviction, to challenge comparison? We are reminded of the majestic cadence of the line whose feet step in the just proportions of Humanity,

"Daughter of God and Man, accomplished Eve!"[27]

An observer adds this testimony:

"We may, in many marriages, regard it as the best arrangement, if the man has so much advantage over his wife, that she can, without much thought of her own, be, by him, led and directed as by a father. But it was not so with the Count and his consort. She was not made to be a copy; she was an original; and, while she loved and honored him, she thought for herself, on all subjects, with so much intelligence, that he could and did look on her as sister and friend also."

Compare with this refined specimen of a religiously civilized life, the following imperfect sketch of a North American Indian, and we shall see that the same causes will always produce the same results. The Flying Pigeon (Ratchewaine)[28] was the wife of a barbarous chief, who had six others, but she was his only true wife, because the only one of a strong and pure character, and, having this, inspired a veneration, as like as the mind of the man permitted, to that inspired by the Countess Zinzendorf. She died when her son was only four years old, yet left on his mind a feel-

---

[26]Count Nikolaus Ludwig von Zinzendorf (1700–1760) organized the Moravian Brethren, a religious sect, in Germany and established Moravian congregations in Pennsylvania in 1741.

[27]From *Paradise Lost* (1667) by the English poet John Milton (1608–1674).

[28]Ratchewaine, or Flying Pigeon, was the wife of Mahaskah, an Iowa chief.

ing of reverent love worthy the thought of Christian chivalry. Grown to manhood, he shed tears on seeing her portrait.

THE FLYING PIGEON

"Ratchewaine was chaste, mild, gentle in her disposition, kind, generous, and devoted to her husband. A harsh word was never known to proceed from her mouth; nor was she ever known to be in a passion. Mahaskah used to say of her, after her death, that her hand was shut, when those, who did not want, came into her presence; but when the really poor came in, it was like a strainer full of holes, letting all she held in it pass through. In the exercise of generous feeling she was uniform. It was not indebted for its exercise to whim, or caprice, or partiality. No matter of what nation the applicant for her bounty was, or whether at war or peace with her nation; if he were hungry, she fed him; if naked, she clothed him; and if houseless, she gave him shelter. The continued exercise of this generous feeling kept her poor. And she has been known to give away her last blanket—all the honey that was in the lodge, the last bladder of bear's oil, and the last piece of dried meat.

"She was scrupulously exact in the observance of all the religious rites which her faith imposed upon her. Her conscience is represented to have been extremely tender. She often feared that her acts were displeasing to the Great Spirit, when she would blacken her face, and retire to some lone place, and fast and pray."[29]

To these traits should be added, but for want of room, anecdotes which show the quick decision and vivacity of her mind. Her face was in harmony with this combination. Her brow is as ideal and the eyes and lids as devout and modest as the Italian pictures of the Madonna, while the lower part of the face has the simplicity and childish strength of the Indian race. Her picture presents the finest specimen of Indian beauty we have ever seen.

Such a woman is the sister and friend of all beings, as the worthy man is their brother and helper. . . .

[Educated Women]

Another sign of the times is furnished by the triumphs of female authorship. These have been great and constantly increasing. Women have taken possession of so many provinces for which men had pronounced them unfit, that though these still declare there are some inaccessible to them, it is difficult to say just *where* they must stop.

---

[29]From Thomas L. McKenney and James Hall, *The History of the Indian Tribes of North America, with Biographical Sketches and Anecdotes of the Principal Chiefs*, vol. 1 (1838). Fuller had consulted this popular work as she prepared her *Summer on the Lakes, in 1843.*

The shining names of famous women have cast light upon the path of the sex, and many obstructions have been removed. When a Montague could learn better than her brother, and use her lore afterward to such purpose, as an observer, it seemed amiss to hinder women from preparing themselves to see, or from seeing all they could, when prepared. Since Somerville has achieved so much, will any young girl be prevented from seeking a knowledge of the physical sciences, if she wishes it?[30] . . .

Whether much or little has been done or will be done, whether women will add to the talent of narration, the power of systematizing, whether they will carve marble, as well as draw and paint, is not important. But that it should be acknowledged that they have intellect which needs developing, that they should not be considered complete, if beings of affection and habit alone, is important.

Yet even this acknowledgment, rather conquered by woman than proffered by man, has been sullied by the usual selfishness. So much is said of women being better educated, that they may become better companions and mothers *for men.* They should be fit for such companionship, and we have mentioned, with satisfaction, instances where it has been established. Earth knows no fairer, holier relation than that of a mother. It is one which, rightly understood, must both promote and require the highest attainments. But a being of infinite scope must not be treated with an exclusive view to any one relation. Give the soul free course, let the organization, both of body and mind, be freely developed, and the being will be fit for any and every relation to which it may be called. The intellect, no more than the sense of hearing, is to be cultivated merely that she may be a more valuable companion to man, but because the Power who gave a power, by its mere existence, signifies that it must be brought out towards perfection.

In this regard of self-dependence, and a greater simplicity and fulness of being, we must hail as a preliminary the increase of the class contemptuously designated as old maids. . . .

[Minerva and the Muse]

There are two aspects of woman's nature, represented by the ancients as Muse and Minerva. . . .

Male and female represent the two sides of the great radical dualism. But, in fact, they are perpetually passing into one another. Fluid hardens

---

[30]Lady Mary Wortley Montagu (1689–1762) was an English author; Mary Somerville (1780–1872) was a Scottish mathematician and scientist.

to solid, solid rushes to fluid. There is no wholly masculine man, no purely feminine woman.

History jeers at the attempts of physiologists to bind great original laws by the forms which flow from them. They make a rule; they say from observation, what can and cannot be. In vain! Nature provides exceptions to every rule. She sends women to battle, and sets Hercules[31] spinning; she enables women to bear immense burdens, cold, and frost; she enables the man, who feels maternal love, to nourish his infant like a mother. Of late she plays still gayer pranks. Not only she deprives organizations, but organs, of a necessary end. She enables people to read with the top of the head, and see with the pit of the stomach. Presently she will make a female Newton,[32] and a male Syren.

Man partakes of the feminine in the Apollo, woman of the masculine as Minerva.

What I mean by the Muse is the unimpeded clearness of the intuitive powers which a perfectly truthful adherence to every admonition of the higher instincts would bring to a finely organized human being. It may appear as prophecy or as poesy. It enabled Cassandra to foresee the results of actions passing round her; the Seeress[33] to behold the true character of the person through the mask of his customary life. (Sometimes she saw a feminine form behind the man, sometimes the reverse.) It enabled the daughter of Linnaeus[34] to see the soul of the flower exhaling from the flower. . . . Sight must be verified by life before it can deserve the honors of piety and genius. Yet sight comes first, and of this sight of the world of causes, this approximation to the region of primitive motions, women I hold to be especially capable. Even without equal freedom with the other sex, they have already shown themselves so, and should these faculties have free play, I believe they will open new, deeper and purer sources of joyous inspiration than have as yet refreshed the earth.

Let us be wise and not impede the soul. Let her work as she will. Let us have one creative energy, one incessant revelation. Let it take what form it will, and let us not bind it by the past to man or woman, black or white. Jove sprang from Rhea, Pallas from Jove.[35] So let it be.

---

[31] Hercules was a mythical Greek hero fabled for his great strength.

[32] Sir Isaac Newton (1642–1727), an English mathematician and natural philosopher, was known as the greatest genius of his time.

[33] The powers of the German mystic Friederike Hauffe (d. 1829) were described in *Die Seherin von Prevorst* (The Seeress of Prevorst) of 1829 by the German physician and poet Andreas Justinus Kerner (1786–1862). Fuller was impressed by the story, which figured largely in *Summer on the Lakes, in 1843*.

[34] The Swedish botanist Carolus Linnaeus (1707–1778) was a master of classification.

[35] Jove, or Jupiter (Zeus in Greek), was the king of the gods; Rhea was one of the earliest Greek mother goddesses; and Pallas was another name for Athena or Minerva.

If it has been the tendency of these remarks to call woman rather to the Minerva side,—if I, unlike the more generous writer, have spoken from society no less than the soul,—let it be pardoned! It is love that has caused this, love for many incarcerated souls, that might be freed, could the idea of religious self-dependence be established in them, could the weakening habit of dependence on others be broken up.

Proclus teaches that every life has, in its sphere, a totality or wholeness of the animating powers of the other spheres; having only, as its own characteristic, a predominance of some one power. Thus Jupiter comprises, within himself, the other twelve powers, which stand thus: The first triad is *demiurgic or fabricative,* i.e., Jupiter, Neptune, Vulcan; the second, *defensive,* Vesta, Minerva, Mars; the third, *vivific,* Ceres, Juno, Diana; and the fourth, Mercury, Venus, Apollo, *elevating and harmonic.*[36] In the sphere of Jupiter, energy is predominant—with Venus, beauty; but each comprehends and apprehends all the others.

When the same community of life and consciousness of mind begins among men, humanity will have, positively and finally, subjugated its brute elements and Titanic childhood;[37] criticism will have perished; arbitrary limits and ignorant censure be impossible; all will have entered upon the liberty of law, and the harmony of common growth.

Then Apollo will sing to his lyre what Vulcan forges on the anvil, and the Muse weave anew the tapestries of Minerva.

It is, therefore, only in the present crisis that the preference is given to Minerva. The power of continence must establish the legitimacy of freedom, the power of self-poise the perfection of motion.

Every relation, every gradation of nature is incalculably precious, but only to the soul which is poised upon itself, and to whom no loss, no change, can bring dull discord, for it is in harmony with the central soul.

If any individual live too much in relations, so that he becomes a stranger to the resources of his own nature, he falls, after a while, into a distraction, or imbecility, from which he can only be cured by a time of isolation, which gives the renovating fountains time to rise up. With a society it is the same. Many minds, deprived of the traditionary or instinctive means of passing a cheerful existence, must find help in self-impulse, or perish. It is therefore that, while any elevation, in the view of union, is to be hailed with joy, we shall not decline celibacy as the great fact of the

---

[36]Proclus (410–485) was a Greek Neoplatonic philosopher. Neptune was the god of the sea, Vulcan of fire, and Mars of war; Juno was the queen of the goddesses; Venus was a fertility goddess; and Mercury was the messenger of the gods.

[37]According to legend, the giant Titans ruled the earth until they were overthrown by the Olympian gods.

time. It is one from which no vow, no arrangement, can at present save a thinking mind. For now the rowers are pausing on their oars; they wait a change before they can pull together. All tends to illustrate the thought of a wise contemporary. Union is only possible to those who are units. To be fit for relations in time, souls, whether of man or woman, must be able to do without them in the spirit.

It is therefore that I would have woman lay aside all thought, such as she habitually cherishes, of being taught and led by men. I would have her, like the Indian girl, dedicate herself to the Sun, the Sun of Truth, and go no where if his beams did not make clear the path. I would have her free from compromise, from complaisance, from helplessness, because I would have her good enough and strong enough to love one and all beings, from the fulness, not the poverty of being.

Men, as at present instructed, will not help this work, because they also are under the slavery of habit. I have seen with delight their poetic impulses. A sister is the fairest ideal, and how nobly Wordsworth, and even Byron, have written of a sister.[38]

There is no sweeter sight than to see a father with his little daughter. Very vulgar men become refined to the eye when leading a little girl by the hand. At that moment the right relation between the sexes seems established, and you feel as if the man would aid in the noblest purpose, if you ask him in behalf of his little daughter. Once two fine figures stood before me, thus. The father of very intellectual aspect, his falcon eye softened by affection as he looked down on his fair child, she the image of himself, only more graceful and brilliant in expression. I was reminded of Southey's Kehama;[39] when lo, the dream was rudely broken. They were talking of education, and he said,

"I shall not have Maria brought too forward. If she knows too much, she will never find a husband; superior women hardly ever can."

"Surely," said his wife, with a blush, "you wish Maria to be as good and wise as she can, whether it will help her to marriage or not."

"No," he persisted, "I want her to have a sphere and a home, and some one to protect her when I am gone."

It was a trifling incident, but made a deep impression. I felt that the holiest relations fail to instruct the unprepared and perverted mind. If this man, indeed, could have looked at it on the other side, he was the last that would have been willing to have been taken himself for the home

---

[38] See "To My Sister" and "Tintern Abbey" by the English poet laureate William Wordsworth (1770–1850) and "Epistle to Augusta" by the English poet George Gordon, Lord Byron (1788–1824).

[39] *The Curse of Kehama* (1810) by the English poet Robert Southey (1774–1843).

and protection he could give, but would have been much more likely to repeat the tale of Alcibiades with his phials.[40]

But men do *not* look at both sides, and women must leave off asking them and being influenced by them, but retire within themselves, and explore the groundwork of life till they find their peculiar secret. Then, when they come forth again, renovated and baptized, they will know how to turn all dross to gold, and will be rich and free though they live in a hut, tranquil, if in a crowd. Then their sweet singing shall not be from passionate impulse, but the lyrical overflow of a divine rapture, and a new music shall be evolved from this many-chorded world.

Grant her, then, for a while, the armor and the javelin. Let her put from her the press of other minds and meditate in virgin loneliness. The same idea shall re-appear in due time as Muse, or Ceres, the all-kindly patient Earth-Spirit. . . .

[Prostitution and Chastity]

Mrs. Jameson[41] is a sentimentalist, and, therefore, suits us ill in some respects, but she is full of talent, has a just and refined perception of the beautiful, and a genuine courage when she finds it necessary. She does not appear to have thought out, thoroughly, the subject on which we are engaged, and her opinions, expressed as opinions, are sometimes inconsistent with one another. But from the refined perception of character, admirable suggestions are given in her "Women of Shak[e]speare," and "Loves of the Poets."

But that for which I most respect her is the decision with which she speaks on a subject which refined women are usually afraid to approach, for fear of the insult and scurril jest they may encounter; but on which she neither can nor will restrain the indignation of a full heart. I refer to the degradation of a large portion of women into the sold and polluted slaves of men, and the daring with which the legislator and man of the world lifts his head beneath the heavens, and says "this must be; it cannot be helped; it is a necessary accompaniment of *civilization*."

So speaks the *citizen*. Man born of woman, the father of daughters, declares that he will and must buy the comforts and commercial advantages of his London, Vienna, Paris, New-York, by conniving at the moral death, the damnation, so far as the action of society can insure it, of thousands of women for each splendid metropolis.

---

[40]Alcibiades (ca. 450–404 B.C.) was a dissolute Athenian aristocrat and general who was accused of profaning the mysteries of the goddesses.

[41]Anna Brownell Jameson (1794–1860) was a popular Irish author.

O men! I speak not to you. It is true that your wickedness (for you must not deny that, at least, nine thousand out of the ten fall through the vanity you have systematically flattered, or the promises you have treacherously broken;) yes, it is true that your wickedness is its own punishment. Your forms degraded and your eyes clouded by secret sin; natural harmony broken and fineness of perception destroyed in your mental and bodily organization; God and love shut out from your hearts by the foul visitants you have permitted there; incapable of pure marriage; incapable of pure parentage; incapable of worship; oh wretched men, your sin is its own punishment! You have lost the world in losing yourselves. Who ruins another has admitted the worm to the root of his own tree, and the fuller ye fill the cup of evil, the deeper must be your own bitter draught. But I speak not to you—you need to teach and warn one another. And more than one voice rises in earnestness. And all that *women* say to the heart that has once chosen the evil path, is considered prudery, or ignorance, or perhaps, a feebleness of nature which exempts from similar temptations.

But to you, women, American women, a few words may not be addressed in vain. One here and there may listen. . . .

A little while since, I was at one of the most fashionable places of public resort. I saw there many women, dressed without regard to the season or the demands of the place, in apery, or, as it looked, in mockery of European fashions. I saw their eyes restlessly courting attention. I saw the way in which it was paid, the style of devotion, almost an open sneer, which it pleased those ladies to receive from men whose expression marked their own low position in the moral and intellectual world. Those women went to their pillows with their heads full of folly, their hearts of jealousy, or gratified vanity: those men, with the low opinion they already entertained of woman confirmed. These were American *ladies;* i. e., they were of that class who have wealth and leisure to make full use of the day, and confer benefits on others. They were of that class whom the possession of external advantages makes of pernicious example to many, if these advantages be misused.

Soon after, I met a circle of women, stamped by society as among the most degraded of their sex. "How," it was asked of them, "did you come here?" for, by the society that I saw in the former place, they were shut up in a prison. The causes were not difficult to trace: love of dress, love of flattery, love of excitement. They had not dresses like the other ladies, so they stole them; they could not pay for flattery by distinctions, and the dower of a worldly marriage, so they paid by the profanation of their persons. In excitement, more and more madly sought from day to day, they drowned the voice of conscience.

Now I ask you, my sisters, if the women at the fashionable house be not answerable for those women being in the prison?

As to position in the world of souls, we may suppose the women of the prison stood fairest, both because they had misused less light, and because loneliness and sorrow had brought some of them to feel the need of better life, nearer truth and good. This was no merit in them, being an effect of circumstance, but it was hopeful. But you, my friends, (and some of you I have already met,) consecrate yourselves without waiting for reproof, in free love and unbroken energy, to win and to diffuse a better life. Offer beauty, talents, riches, on the altar; thus shall ye keep spotless your own hearts, and be visibly or invisibly the angels to others.

I would urge upon those women who have not yet considered this subject, to do so. Do not forget the unfortunates who dare not cross your guarded way. If it do not suit you to act with those who have organized measures of reform, then hold not yourself excused from acting in private. Seek out these degraded women, give them tender sympathy, counsel, employment. Take the place of mothers, such as might have saved them originally.

If you can do little for those already under the ban of the world, and the best considered efforts have often failed, from a want of strength in those unhappy ones to bear up against the sting of shame and the prejudices of the world, which makes them seek oblivion again in their old excitements, you will at least leave a sense of love and justice in their hearts that will prevent their becoming utterly imbittered and corrupt. And you may learn the means of prevention for those yet uninjured. There will be found in a diffusion of mental culture, simple tastes, best taught by your example, a genuine self-respect, and above all, what the influence of man tends to hide from woman, the love and fear of a divine, in preference to a human tribunal.

But suppose you save many who would have lost their bodily innocence (for as to mental, the loss of that is incalculably more general,) through mere vanity and folly; there still remain many, the prey and spoil of the brute passions of man. For the stories frequent in our newspapers outshame antiquity, and vie with the horrors of war.

As to this, it must be considered that, as the vanity and proneness to seduction of the imprisoned women represented a general degradation in their sex; so do these acts a still more general and worse in the male. Where so many are weak it is natural there should be many lost, where legislators admit that ten thousand prostitutes are a fair proportion to one city, and husbands tell their wives that it is folly to expect chastity from men, it is inevitable that there should be many monsters of vice. . . .

[Las Exaltadas]

On this subject, let every woman, who has once begun to think, examine herself, see whether she does not suppose virtue possible and necessary to man, and whether she would not desire for her son a virtue which aimed at a fitness for a divine life, and involved, if not asceticism, that degree of power over the lower self, which shall "not exterminate the passions, but keep them chained at the feet of reason." The passions, like fire, are a bad master; but confine them to the hearth and the altar, and they give life to the social economy, and make each sacrifice meet for heaven.

When many women have thought upon this subject, some will be fit for the Senate, and one such Senate in operation would affect the morals of the civilized world.

At present I look to the young. As preparatory to the Senate, I should like to see a society of novices, such as the world has never yet seen, bound by no oath, wearing no badge. In place of an oath they should have a religious faith in the capacity of man for virtue; instead of a badge, should wear in the heart a firm resolve not to stop short of the destiny promised him as a son of God. Their service should be action and conservatism, not of old habits, but of a better nature, enlightened by hopes that daily grow brighter.

If sin was to remain in the world, it should not be by their connivance at its stay, or one moment's concession to its claims.

They should succor the oppressed, and pay to the upright the reverence due in hero-worship by seeking to emulate them. They would not denounce the willingly bad, but they could not be with them, for the two classes could not breathe the same atmosphere.

They would heed no detention from the time-serving, the worldly and the timid.

They could love no pleasures that were not innocent and capable of good fruit.

I saw, in a foreign paper, the title now given to a party abroad, "Los Exaltados."[42] Such would be the title now given these children by the world: Los Exaltados, Las Exaltadas; but the world would not sneer always, for from them would issue a virtue by which it would, at last, be exalted too.

I have in my eye a youth and a maiden whom I look to as the nucleus of such a class. They are both in early youth, both as yet uncontaminated, both aspiring, without rashness, both thoughtful, both capable of deep

---

[42] In the 1820s, *Los Exaltados* (literally, "hot headed"), a Spanish radical political party, advocated taxing the rich rather than the poor.

affection, both of strong nature and sweet feelings, both capable of large mental development. They reside in different regions of earth, but their place in the soul is the same. To them I look, as, perhaps, the harbingers and leaders of a new era, for never yet have I known minds so truly virgin, without narrowness or ignorance.

When men call upon women to redeem them, they mean such maidens. But such are not easily formed under the present influences of society. As there are more such young men to help give a different tone, there will be more such maidens. . . .

[Slavery and Freedom]

I now touch on my own place and day, and, as I write, events are occurring that threaten the fair fabric approached by so long an avenue. Week before last the Gentile was requested to aid the Jew to return to Palestine, for the Millennium, the reign of the Son of Mary, was near. Just now, at high and solemn mass, thanks were returned to the Virgin for having delivered O'Connell from unjust imprisonment, in requital of his having consecrated to her the league formed in behalf of Liberty on Tara's Hill.[43] But, last week brought news which threatens that a cause identical with the enfranchisement of Jews, Irish, women, ay, and of Americans in general, too, is in danger, for the choice of the people threatens to rivet the chains of slavery and the leprosy of sin permanently on this nation, through the annexation of Texas![44]

Ah! if this should take place, who will dare again to feel the throb of heavenly hope, as to the destiny of this country? The noble thought that gave unity to all our knowledge, harmony to all our designs;—the thought that the progress of history had brought on the era, the tissue of prophecies pointed out the spot, where humanity was, at last, to have a fair chance to know itself, and all men be born free and equal for the eagle's flight, flutters as if about to leave the breast, which, deprived of it, will have no more a nation, no more a home on earth.

Women of my country!—Exaltadas! if such there be,—Women of English, old English nobleness, who understand the courage of Boadicea, the sacrifice of Godiva, the power of Queen Emma to tread the red hot iron unharmed. Women who share the nature of Mrs. Hutchinson, Lady Russell, and the mothers of our own revolution: have you nothing to do

---

[43]The Irish nationalist leader Daniel O'Connell (1775–1847) was arrested for demanding repeal of the union of Great Britain and Ireland.

[44]Many northerners opposed the U.S. annexation of Texas in 1844, which expanded the territory of slavery and provoked a war with Mexico.

with this?[45] You see the men, how they are willing to sell shamelessly, the happiness of countless generations of fellow-creatures, the honor of their country, and their immortal souls, for a money market and political power. Do you not feel within you that which can reprove them, which can check, which can convince them? You would not speak in vain; whether each in her own home, or banded in unison.

Tell these men that you will not accept the glittering baubles, spacious dwellings, and plentiful service, they mean to offer you through these means. Tell them that the heart of women demands nobleness and honor in man, and that, if they have not purity, have not mercy, they are no longer fathers, lovers, husbands, sons of yours.

This cause is your own, for as I have before said, there is a reason why the foes of African slavery seek more freedom for women; but put it not upon that ground, but on the ground of right.

If you have a power, it is a moral power. The films of interest are not so close around you as around the men. If you will but think, you cannot fail to wish to save the country from this disgrace. Let not slip the occasion, but do something to lift off the curse incurred by Eve. . . .

[Summary]

And now I have designated in outline, if not in fullness, the stream which is ever flowing from the heights of my thought.

In the earlier tract, I was told, I did not make my meaning sufficiently clear. In this I have consequently tried to illustrate it in various ways, and may have been guilty of much repetition. Yet, as I am anxious to leave no room for doubt, I shall venture to retrace, once more, the scope of my design in points, as was done in old-fashioned sermons.

Man is a being of two-fold relations, to nature beneath, and intelligence above him. The earth is his school, if not his birth-place: God his object: life and thought, his means of interpreting nature, and aspiring to God.

Only a fraction of this purpose is accomplished in the life of any one man. Its entire accomplishment is to be hoped only from the sum of the lives of men, or man considered as a whole.

---

[45]The British queen Boadicea (d. 60 A.D.) led a rebellion against the Roman conquest of Britain; the English Lady Godiva (ca. 1140–1180) rode naked through Coventry to force her husband to lower taxes; the British Queen Emma (d. 1052) withstood torture by hot iron; Anne Hutchinson (1591–1643) was banished from Massachusetts Bay Colony in 1637 for her religious views; and Lady Rachel Russell (1636–1723) criticized the corruption of English society.

As this whole has one soul and one body, any injury or obstruction to a part, or to the meanest member, affects the whole. Man can never be perfectly happy or virtuous, till all men are so.

To address man wisely, you must not forget that his life is partly animal, subject to the same laws with nature.

But you cannot address him wisely unless you consider him still more as soul, and appreciate the conditions and destiny of soul.

The growth of man is two-fold, masculine and feminine.

As far as these two methods can be distinguished they are so as

Energy and Harmony.

Power and Beauty.

Intellect and Love.

Or by some such rude classification, for we have not language primitive and pure enough to express such ideas with precision.

These two sides are supposed to be expressed in man and woman, that is, as the more and less, for the faculties have not been given pure to either, but only in preponderance. There are also exceptions in great number, such as men of far more beauty than power, and the reverse. But as a general rule, it seems to have been the intention to give a preponderance on the one side, that is called masculine, and on the other, one that is called feminine.

There cannot be a doubt that, if these two developments were in perfect harmony, they would correspond to and fulfil one another, like hemispheres, or the tenor and bass in music.

But there is no perfect harmony in human nature; and the two parts answer one another only now and then, or, if there be a persistent consonance, it can only be traced, at long intervals, instead of discoursing an obvious melody.

What is the cause of this?

Man, in the order of time, was developed first; as energy comes before harmony; power before beauty.

Woman was therefore under his care as an elder. He might have been her guardian and teacher.

But as human nature goes not straight forward, but by excessive action and then reaction in an undulated course, he misunderstood and abused his advantages, and became her temporal master instead of her spiritual sire.

On himself came the punishment. He educated woman more as a servant than a daughter, and found himself a king without a queen.

The children of this unequal union showed unequal natures, and, more and more, men seemed sons of the hand-maid, rather than princes.

At last there were so many Ishmaelites that the rest grew frightened and indignant. They laid the blame on Hagar, and drove her forth into the wilderness.[46]

But there were none the fewer Ishmaelites for that.

At last men became a little wiser, and saw that the infant Moses was, in every case, saved by the pure instincts of woman's breast. For, as too much adversity is better for the moral nature than too much prosperity, woman, in this respect, dwindled less than man, though in other respects, still a child in leading strings.

So man did her more and more justice, and grew more and more kind.

But yet, his habits and his will corrupted by the past, he did not clearly see that woman was half himself, that her interests were identical with his, and that, by the law of their common being, he could never reach his true proportions while she remained in any wise shorn of hers.

And so it has gone on to our day; both ideas developing, but more slowly than they would under a clearer recognition of truth and justice, which would have permitted the sexes their due influence on one another, and mutual improvement from more dignified relations.

Wherever there was pure love, the natural influences were, for the time, restored.

Wherever the poet or artist gave free course to his genius, he saw the truth, and expressed it in worthy forms, for these men especially share and need the feminine principle. The divine birds need to be brooded into life and song by mothers.

Wherever religion (I mean the thirst for truth and good, not the love of sect and dogma,) had its course, the original design was apprehended in its simplicity, and the dove presaged sweetly from Dodona's oak.[47]

I have aimed to show that no age was left entirely without a witness of the equality of the sexes in function, duty and hope.

Also that, when there was unwillingness or ignorance, which prevented this being acted upon, women had not the less power for their want of light and noble freedom. But it was power which hurt alike them and those against whom they made use of the arms of the servile: cunning, blandishment, and unreasonable emotion.

That now the time has come when a clearer vision and better action are possible. When man and woman may regard one another as brother and sister, the pillars of one porch, the priests of one worship.

I have believed and intimated that this hope would receive an ampler fruition, than ever before, in our own land.

---

[46]Genesis 21:9–21 tells of the expulsion of Hagar and Ishmael.

[47]Greek legend held that a dove flew from Thebes to Dodona, landed in an oak tree, and proclaimed in a human voice that an oracle of Zeus should be established there.

And it will do so if this land carry out the principles from which sprang our national life.

I believe that, at present, women are the best helpers of one another. Let them think; let them act; till they know what they need.

We only ask of men to remove arbitrary barriers. Some would like to do more. But I believe it needs for woman to show herself in her native dignity, to teach them how to aid her; their minds are so encumbered by tradition. . . .

[Prophecies]

You ask, what use will she make of liberty, when she has so long been sustained and restrained?

I answer; in the first place, this will not be suddenly given. I read yesterday a debate of this year on the subject of enlarging women's rights over property. It was a leaf from the class book that is preparing for the needed instruction. The men leaned visibly as they spoke. The champions of woman saw the fallacy of arguments, on the opposite side, and were startled by their own convictions. With their wives at home, and the readers of the paper, it was the same. And so the stream flows on; thought urging action, and action leading to the evolution of still better thought.

But, were this freedom to come suddenly, I have no fear of the consequences. Individuals might commit excesses, but there is not only in the sex a reverence for decorums and limits inherited and enhanced from generation to generation, which many years of other life could not efface, but a native love, in woman as woman, of proportion, of "the simple art of not too much," a Greek moderation, which would create immediately a restraining party, the natural legislators and instructors of the rest, and would gradually establish such rules as are needed to guard, without impeding life.

The Graces would lead the choral dance, and teach the rest to regulate their steps to the measure of beauty.

But if you ask me what offices they may fill; I reply — any. I do not care what case you put; let them be sea-captains, if you will. I do not doubt there are women well fitted for such an office, and, if so, I should be glad to see them in it, as to welcome the maid of Saragossa, or the maid of Missolonghi, or the Suliote heroine, or Emily Plater.[48]

[48]During the French siege of the Spanish city of Saragossa in 1808–1809, Augustina, the "maid of Saragossa," worked one of the city's guns when all of the male gunners had been killed. The English poet, Lord Byron (1788–1824), celebrated her courage in his long narrative poem, *Childe Harold's Pilgrimage* (1812–1818), canto i. 558–584. The Greek town of Missolonghi was besieged twice by the Turks during the Greek War of Independence

I think women need, especially at this juncture, a much greater range of occupation than they have, to rouse their latent powers. A party of travellers lately visited a lonely hut on a mountain. There they found an old woman that told them she and her husband had lived there forty years. "Why," they said, "did you choose so barren a spot? ["] She "did not know; *it was the man's notion.*"

And, during forty years, she had been content to act, without knowing why, upon "the man's notion." I would not have it so. . . .

I have no doubt, however, that a large proportion of women would give themselves to the same employments as now, because there are circumstances that must lead them. Mothers will delight to make the nest soft and warm. Nature would take care of that; no need to clip the wings of any bird that wants to soar and sing, or finds in itself the strength of pinion for a migratory flight unusual to its kind. The difference would be that *all* need not be constrained to employments, for which *some* are unfit.

I have urged upon the sex self-subsistence in its two forms of self-reliance and self-impulse, because I believe them to be the needed means of the present juncture.

I have urged on woman independence of man, not that I do not think the sexes mutually needed by one another, but because in woman this fact has led to an excessive devotion, which has cooled love, degraded marriage, and prevented either sex from being what it should be to itself or the other.

I wish woman to live, *first* for God's sake. Then she will not make an imperfect man her god, and thus sink to idolatry. Then she will not take what is not fit for her from a sense of weakness and poverty. Then, if she finds what she needs in man embodied, she will know how to love, and be worthy of being loved.

By being more a soul, she will not be less woman, for nature is perfected through spirit.

Now there is no woman, only an overgrown child.

That her hand may be given with dignity, she must be able to stand alone. I wish to see men and women capable of such relations as are depicted by Landor in his Pericles and Aspasia,[49] where grace is the natural garb of strength, and the affections are calm, because deep. The softness is that of a firm tissue, as when

---

in the 1820s; the Greek island of Suli rebelled against Turkish occupation in 1820. The Polish heroine Countess Emily Plater (1806–1831) joined the army to fight, unsuccessfully but valiantly, for Polish independence. Fuller noted that she would have liked a picture of Plater for the frontispiece of her book.

[49] *Pericles and Aspasia* (1836) by the English author Walter Savage Landor (1775–1864).

"The gods approve
The depths but not the tumult of the soul,
A fervent, not ungovernable love."[50]

A profound thinker has said, "no married woman can represent the female world, for she belongs to her husband. The idea of woman must be represented by a virgin."

But that is the very fault of marriage, and of the present relation between the sexes, that the woman does belong to the man, instead of forming a whole with him. Were it otherwise, there would be no such limitation to the thought.

Woman, self-centered, would never be absorbed by any relation; it would be only an experience to her as to man. It is a vulgar error that love, a love to woman is her whole existence; she also is born for Truth and Love in their universal energy. Would she but assume her inheritance, Mary would not be the only virgin mother. Not Manzoni alone would celebrate in his wife the virgin mind with the maternal wisdom and conjugal affections.[51] The soul is ever young, ever virgin.

And will not she soon appear? The woman who shall vindicate their birthright for all women; who shall teach them what to claim, and how to use what they obtain? Shall not her name be for her era Victoria, for her country and life Virginia? Yet predictions are rash; she herself must teach us to give her the fitting name.

An idea not unknown to ancient times has of late been revived, that, in the metamorphoses of life, the soul assumes the form, first of man, then of woman, and takes the chances, and reaps the benefits of either lot. Why then, say some, lay such emphasis on the rights or needs of woman? What she wins not, as woman, will come to her as man.

That makes no difference. It is not woman, but the law of right, the law of growth, that speaks in us, and demands the perfection of each being in its kind, apple as apple, woman as woman. Without adopting your theory I know that I, a daughter, live through the life of man; but what concerns me now is, that my life be a beautiful, powerful, in a word, a complete life in its kind. Had I but one more moment to live, I must wish the same.

Suppose, at the end of your cycle, your great world-year, all will be completed, whether I exert myself or not (and the supposition is *false,*) but suppose it true, am I to be indifferent about it? Not so! I must beat my own pulse true in the heart of the world; for *that* is virtue, excellence, health.

Thou, Lord, of Day! didst leave us to-night so calmly glorious, not dis-

---

[50]From "Laodamia" by William Wordsworth.
[51]The Italian author Alessandro Manzoni (1785–1873) praised his bride in his popular novel *I promessi sposi* (The Betrothed) of 1827.

mayed that cold winter is coming, not postponing thy beneficence to the fruitful summer! Thou didst smile on thy day's work when it was done, and adorn thy down-going as thy up-rising, for thou art loyal, and it is thy nature to give life, if thou canst, and shine at all events!

I stand in the sunny noon of life. Objects no longer glitter in the dews of morning, neither are yet softened by the shadows of evening. Every spot is seen, every chasm revealed. Climbing the dusty hill, some fair effigies that once stood for symbols of human destiny have been broken; those I still have with me, show defects in this broad light. Yet enough is left, even by experience, to point distinctly to the glories of that destiny; faint, but not to be mistaken streaks of the future day. I can say with the bard, "Though many have suffered shipwreck, still beat noble hearts."

Always the soul says to us all: Cherish your best hopes as a faith, and abide by them in action. Such shall be the effectual fervent means to their fulfilment,

> For the Power to whom we bow
> Has given its pledge that, if not now,
> They of pure and stedfast mind,
> By faith exalted, truth refined,
> Shall hear all music loud and clear,
> Whose first notes they ventured here.
> Then fear not thou to wind the horn,
> Though elf and gnome thy courage scorn;
> Ask for the Castle's King and Queen;
> Though rabble rout may rush between,
> Beat thee senseless to the ground,
> In the dark beset thee round;
> Persist to ask and it will come,
> Seek not for rest in humbler home;
> So shalt thou see what few have seen,
> The palace home of King and Queen.[52]

15th November 1844.

[52]This is another of Fuller's poems of 1844. (See Documents 23–25.)

13

New York Journalism

In December 1844, Margaret Fuller moved to New York City to become the first literary editor of Horace Greeley's progressive Whig newspaper, the New-York Daily Tribune. As one of the first female members of the working press and the first woman to serve on the editorial staff of a leading American newspaper, she found her audience and interests expanding. During her twenty months on the job, she published 250 articles with her byline (marked by a star rather than her name) and many more unsigned columns. She interpreted her position broadly, reviewing the latest European and American literature (Documents 27 and 28), but also addressing a wide range of social and cultural issues in the nation's largest city. Often her journalistic investigations began with a focus on the condition and concerns of women. Yet, as Documents 29–32 demonstrate, her keen consciousness of gender inequalities also led her to critique class and race relations in America. Whether her subject was poverty, prostitution, class tensions, or racism, she asked her readers to dig to the root of the problem and to empathize with others. She dared a city seething with nativist resentment of immigrants to "learn from all nations" and to build understanding across class, gender, and racial lines.

27

Emerson's Essays[1]

At the distance of three years this volume follows the first series of Essays, which have already made to themselves a circle of readers, attentive, thoughtful, more and more intelligent, and this circle is a large one if we

---

[1]Ralph Waldo Emerson (1803–1882), a prominent American essayist and lecturer, was a leading Transcendentalist and a close friend of Margaret Fuller. Here she reviews Emerson's *Essays: Second Series* (Boston, 1844).

New-York Daily Tribune, December 7, 1844.

consider the circumstances of this country, and of England, also, at this time.

In England it would seem there are a larger number of persons waiting for an invitation to calm thought and sincere intercourse than among ourselves. Copies of Mr. Emerson's first published little volume called "Nature," have there been sold by thousands in a short time, while one edition has needed seven years to get circulated here. Several of his Orations and Essays from "The Dial" have also been republished there, and met with a reverent and earnest response.

We suppose that while in England the want of such a voice is as great as here, a larger number are at leisure to recognize that want; a far larger number have set foot in the speculative region and have ears refined to appreciate these melodious accents.

Our people, heated by a partisan spirit, necessarily occupied in these first stages by bringing out the material resources of the land, not generally prepared by early training for the enjoyment of books that require attention and reflection, are still more injured by a large majority of writers and speakers, who lend all their efforts to flatter corrupt tastes and mental indolence, instead of feeling it their prerogative and their duty to admonish the community of the danger and arouse it to nobler energy. The aim of the writer or lecturer is not to say the best he knows in as few and well-chosen words as he can, making it his first aim to do justice to the subject. Rather he seeks to beat out a thought as thin as possible, and to consider what the audience will be most willing to receive.

The result of such a course is inevitable. Literature and Art must become daily more degraded; Philosophy cannot exist. A man who feels within his mind some spark of genius, or a capacity for the exercises of talent, should consider himself as endowed with a sacred commission. He is the natural priest, the shepherd of the people. He must raise his mind as high as he can toward the heaven of truth, and try to draw up with him those less gifted by nature with ethereal lightness. If he does not so, but rather employs his powers to flatter them in their poverty, and to hinder aspiration by useless words, and a mere seeming of activity, his sin is great, he is false to God, and false to man.

Much of this sin indeed is done ignorantly. The idea that literature calls men to the genuine hierarchy is almost forgotten. One, who finds himself able, uses his pen, as he might a trowel, solely to procure himself bread, without having reflected on the position in which he thereby places himself.

Apart from the troop of mercenaries, there is one, still larger, of those who use their powers merely for local and temporary ends, aiming at no excellence other than may conduce to these. Among these, rank persons of honor and the best intentions, but they neglect the lasting for the transient, as a man neglects to furnish his mind that he may provide the better for the house in which his body is to dwell for a few years.

When these sins and errors are prevalent, and threaten to become more so, how can we sufficiently prize and honor a mind which is quite pure from such? When, as in the present case, we find a man whose only aim is the discernment and interpretation of the spiritual laws by which we live and move and have our being, all whose objects are permanent, and whose every word stands for a fact.

If only as a representative of the claims of individual culture in a nation which tends to lay such stress on artificial organization and external results, Mr. Emerson would be invaluable here. History will inscribe his name as a father of the country, for he is one who pleads her cause against herself. . . .

The Essays have also been obnoxious[2] to many charges. To that of obscurity, or want of perfect articulation. Of 'Euphuism,' as an excess of fancy in proportion to imagination, and an inclination, at times, to subtlety at the expense of strength, has been styled.[3] The human heart complains of inadequacy, either in the nature or experience of the writer, to represent its full vocation and its deeper needs. Sometimes it speaks of this want as "under-development" or a want of expansion which may yet be remedied; sometimes doubts whether "in this mansion there be either hall or portal to receive the loftier of the Passions." Sometimes the soul is deified at the expense of nature, then again nature at that of man, and we are not quite sure that we can make a true harmony by balance of the statements.—This writer has never written one good work, if such a work be one where the whole commands more attention than the parts. If such an one be produced only where, after an accumulation of materials, fire enough be applied to fuse the whole into one new substance. This second series is superior in this respect to the former, yet in no one essay is the main stress so obvious as to produce on the mind the harmonious effect of a noble river or a tree in full leaf. Single passages and sentences engage our attention too much in proportion. These essays, it has been justly said, tire like a string of mosaics or a house built of medals. We miss what we expect in the work of the great

---

[2]"Obnoxious" is used here in its archaic sense of "exposed to."
[3]Euphuism is a very ornate prose style.

poet, or the great philosopher, the liberal air of all the zones: the glow, uniform yet various in tint, which is given to a body by free circulation of the heart's blood from the hour of birth. Here is, undoubtedly, the man of ideas, but we want the ideal man also; want the heart and genius of human life to interpret it, and here our satisfaction is not so perfect. We doubt this friend raised himself too early to the perpendicular and did not lie along the ground long enough to hear the secret whispers of our parent life. We could wish he might be thrown by conflicts on the lap of mother earth, to see if he would not rise again with added powers.

All this we may say, but it cannot excuse us from benefitting by the great gifts that have been given, and assigning them their due place.

Some painters paint on a red ground. And this color may be supposed to represent the ground work most immediately congenial to most men, as it is the color of blood and represents human vitality. The figures traced upon it are instinct with life in its fulness and depth.

But other painters paint on a gold ground. And a very different, but no less natural, because also a celestial beauty, is given to their works who choose for their foundation the color of the sunbeam, which nature has preferred for her most precious product, and that which will best bear the test of purification, gold.

If another simile may be allowed, another no less apt is at hand. Wine is the most brilliant and intense expression of the powers of earth.—It is her potable fire, her answer to the sun. It exhilarates, it inspires, but then it is liable to fever and intoxicate too the careless partaker.

Mead was the chosen drink of the Northern gods. And this essence of the honey of the mountain bee was not thought unworthy to revive the souls of the valiant who had left their bodies on the fields of strife below.

Nectar should combine the virtues of the ruby wine, the golden mead, without their defects or dangers.

Two high claims our writer can vindicate on the attention of his contemporaries. One from his sincerity. You have his thought just as it found place in the life of his own soul. Thus, however near or relatively distant its approximation to absolute truth, its action on you cannot fail to be healthful. It is a part of the free air.

He belongs to that band of whom there may be found a few in every age, and who now in human history may be counted by hundreds, who worship the one God only, the God of Truth. They worship, not saints, not creeds, nor churches, nor reliques, nor idols in any form. The mind is kept open to truth, and life only valued as a tendency toward it. This must be illustrated by acts and words of love, purity and intelligence. Such are the salt of the earth; let the minutest crystal of that salt be willingly by us held in solution.

The other is through that part of his life, which, if sometimes obstructed or chilled by the critical intellect, is yet the prevalent and the main source of his power. It is that by which he imprisons his hearer only to free him again as a "liberating God" (to use his own words).[4] But indeed let us use them altogether, for none other, ancient or modern, can more worthily express how, making present to us the courses and destinies of nature, he invests himself with her serenity and animates us with her joy.

"Poetry was all written before time was, and whenever we are so finely organized that we can penetrate into that region where the air is music, we hear those primal warblings, and attempt to write them down, but we lose ever and anon a word, or a verse, and substitute something of our own, and thus miswrite the poem. The men of more delicate ear write down these cadences more faithfully, and these transcripts, though imperfect, become the songs of the nations.

"As the eyes of the Lyncaeus were said to see through the earth, so the poet turns the world to glass, and shows us all things in their right series and procession.[5] For, through that better perception, he stands one step nearer to things, and sees the flowing or metamorphosis; perceives that thought is multiform; that within the form of every creature is a force impelling it to ascend into a higher form; and following with his eyes the life, uses the forms which express that life, and so the speech flows with the flowing of nature."

Thus have we in a brief and unworthy manner indicated some views of these books. The only true criticism of these, or any good books, may be gained by making them the companions of our lives. Does every accession of knowledge or a juster sense of beauty make us prize them more? Then they are good, indeed, and more immortal than mortal. Let that test be applied to these; essays which will lead to great and complete poems—somewhere.

---

[4]This quotation and the one that follows are from "The Poet" in Emerson's *Essays: Second Series.*
[5]Lyncaeus was a legendary hero of ancient Greece, famous for his sharpness of sight.

28

[*George Sand's* Consuelo][1]

... In one respect the book is entirely successful, in showing how inward purity and honor may preserve a woman from bewilderment and danger, and secure her a genuine independence. Whoever aims at this is still considered by unthinking or prejudiced minds as wishing to despoil the female character of its natural and peculiar loveliness. It is supposed that delicacy must imply weakness, and that only an Amazon can stand upright and have sufficient command of her faculties to confront the shock of adversity or resist the allurements of tenderness. Miss Bremer, Dumas, and the Northern novelist, Andersen, make women who have a tendency to the intellectual life of an artist fail and suffer the penalties of arrogant presumption, in the very first steps of a career to which an inward vocation called them in preference to the usual home duties.[2] Yet nothing is more obvious than that the circumstances of the time do, more and more frequently, call women to such lives, and that, if guardianship is absolutely necessary to women, many must perish for the want of it. There is, then, reason to hope that God may be a sufficient guardian to those who dare to rely on Him, and if the heroines of the novelists we have named ended as they did, it was for want of the purity of ambition and simplicity of character which do not permit such as Consuelo to be either unsexed and depraved, or unresisting victims and breaking reeds if left alone in the storm and crowd of life. To many women this picture will prove a true Consuelo, (consolation) and we think even very prejudiced men will not read it without being charmed with the expansion, sweetness and genuine force of a female character such as they have not met, but must, when painted, recognize as pos-

[1] George Sand was the pseudonym of the French author Amandine-Aurore-Lucile Dudevant (1804–1876). *Consuelo* and its sequel, *The Countess of Rudolstadt,* were written and published serially in Paris between 1842 and 1844. Generally considered Sand's most serious and ambitious work, the novel was loosely based on the life of the opera singer Pauline Garcia-Viardot (1821–1910), a friend and protégée of Sand and her lover, the pianist Frédéric Chopin (1810–1849). The novel's free-spirited heroine, Consuelo, dedicates her life and her music to the service of God and the love of humanity.

[2] Fredrika Bremer (1801–1865) introduced the domestic novel in Sweden. Alexandre Dumas (1802–1870) was a popular French novelist and dramatist. Known today for his fairy tales, the Danish author Hans Christian Andersen (1805–1875) also wrote many novels, plays, and travel books.

New-York Daily Tribune, June 24, 1846.

sible, and may be led to review their opinions, and, perhaps, to elevate and enlarge their hopes as to "woman's sphere" and "woman's mission." If such insist on what they have heard of the private life of this writer and refuse to believe that any good thing can come out of Nazareth, we reply that we do not know the true facts as to the history of George Sand, there has been no memoir or notice of her published on which any one can rely, and we have seen too much of life to accept the monsters of gossip in reference to any one.[3] But we know, through her works, that, whatever the stains on her life and reputation may have been, there is in her a soul so capable of goodness and honor as to depict them most successfully in her ideal forms.—It is her works and not her private life that we are considering. Of her works we have means of judging—of herself not; but among those who have passed unblamed through the walks of life, we have not often found a nobleness of purpose and feeling, a sincere religious hope to be compared with the spirit that breathes through the pages of *Consuelo. . . .*

[3]Most American critics and readers knew Sand only as a woman who smoked, wore masculine attire, and disregarded her marriage vows. Several of Fuller's literary reviews in the *Tribune* urged a morally outraged American public to judge Sand by her work rather than her private life.

29

Our City Charities

Visit to Bellevue Alms House, to the Farm School, the Asylum for the Insane, and Penitentiary on Blackwell's Island.

The aspect of Nature was sad; what is worse, it was dull and dubious, when we set forth on these visits. The sky was leaden and lowering, the air unkind and piercing, the little birds sat mute and astonished at the departure of the beautiful days which had lured them to premature song. It was a suitable day for such visits. The pauper establishments that belong to a great city take the place of the skeleton at the banquets of old.

New-York Daily Tribune, March 19, 1845.

They admonish us of stern realities, which must bear the same explanation as the frequent blight of Nature's bloom. They should be looked at by all, if only for their own sakes, that they may not sink listlessly into selfish ease, in a world so full of disease. They should be looked at by all who wish to enlighten themselves as to the means of aiding their fellow-creatures in any way, public or private. For nothing can really be done till the right principles are discovered, and it would seem they still need to be discovered or elucidated, so little is done, with a great deal of desire in the heart of the community to do what is right. Such visits are not yet calculated to encourage and exhilarate, as does the story of the Prodigal Son;[1] they wear a grave aspect and suit the grave mood of a *cold* Spring day.

At the Alms House there is every appearance of kindness in the guardians of the poor, and there was a greater degree of cleanliness and comfort than we had expected. But the want of suitable and sufficient employment is a great evil. The persons who find here either a permanent or temporary refuge have scarcely any occupation provided except to raise vegetables for the establishment, and prepare clothing for themselves. The men especially have the most vagrant, degraded air, and so much indolence must tend to confirm them in every bad habit. We were told that, as they are under no strict discipline, their labor at the various trades could not be made profitable; yet surely the means of such should be provided, even at some expense. Employments of various kinds must be absolutely needed, if only to counteract the bad effects of such a position. Every establishment in aid of the poor should be planned with a view to their education. There should be instruction, both practical and in the use of books, openings to a better intercourse than they can obtain from their miserable homes, correct notions, as to cleanliness, diet, and fresh air. A great deal of pains would be lost in their case, as with all other arrangements for the good of the many, but here and there the seed would fall into the right places, and some members of the downtrodden million, rising a little from the mud, would raise the whole body with them.

As we saw old women enjoying their dish of gossip and their dish of tea, and mothers able for a while to take care in peace of their poor little children, we longed and hoped for that genius, who shall teach how to

---

[1]The story of the prodigal son appears in Luke 15.11–32. A father welcomes home a son who had "wasted his substance with riotous living" in a distant land, with the command to "eat, and be merry" (Luke 15.13, 23).

make, of these establishments, places of rest and instruction, not of degradation.

The causes which make the acceptance of public charity so much more injurious to the receiver than that of private are obvious, but surely not such that the human mind which has just invented the magnetic telegraph and Anastatic printing,[2] may not obviate them. A deeper religion at the heart of Society would devise such means. Why should it be that the poor may still feel themselves men; paupers not? The poor man does not feel himself injured but benefitted by the charity of the doctor who gives him back the bill he is unable to pay, because the doctor is acting from intelligent sympathy—from love. Let Society do the same. She might raise the man, who is accepting her bounty, instead of degrading him.

Indeed, it requires great nobleness and faith in human nature, and God's will concerning it, for the officials not to take the tone toward these under their care, which their vices and bad habits prompt, but which must confirm them in the same. Men treated with respect are reminded of self-respect, and if there is a sound spot left in the character, the healthy influence spreads.

We were sorry to see mothers with their new-born infants exposed to the careless scrutiny of male visitors. In the hospital, those who had children scarce a day old were not secure from the gaze of the stranger. This cannot be pleasant to them, and, if they have not refinement to dislike it, those who have should teach it to them. But we suppose there is no woman who has so entirely lost sight of the feelings of girlhood as not to dislike the scrutiny of strangers at a time which is sacred, if any in life is. Women they may like to see, even strangers, if they can approach them with delicacy. . . .

Passing to the Penitentiary, we entered on one of the gloomiest scenes that deforms this great metropolis. Here are the twelve hundred, who receive the punishment due to the vices of so large a portion of the rest. And under what circumstances! Never was punishment treated more simply as a social convenience, without regard to pure right, or a hope of reformation.

Public attention is now so far awake to the state of the Penitentiary that it cannot be long, we trust, before proper means of classification are devised, a temporary asylum provided for those who leave this purgatory, even now, unwilling to return to the inferno from which it has for a time kept them, and means presented likely to lead some, at least, among the

---

[2]A technique of printing from etched plates.

many, who seem hardened, to better views and hopes. It must be that the more righteous feeling which has shown itself in regard to the prisons at Sing Sing and elsewhere, must take some effect as to the Penitentiary also. The present Superintendent enters into the necessity of such improvements, and, should he remain there, will do what he can to carry them into effect.

The want of proper matrons, or any matrons, to take the care so necessary for the bodily or mental improvement or even decent condition of the seven hundred women assembled here, is an offence that cries aloud. It is impossible to take the most cursory survey of this assembly of women; especially it is impossible to see them in the Hospital, where the circumstances are a little more favorable, without seeing how many there are in whom the feelings of innocent childhood are not dead, who need only good influences and steady aid to raise them from the pit of infamy and wo into which they have fallen. And, if there was not one that could be helped, at least Society owes them the insurance of a decent condition while here. We trust that interest on this subject will not slumber.

The recognized principles of all such institutions which have any higher object than the punishment of fault, (and we believe few among us are so ignorant as to avow that as the only object, though they may, from want of thought, act as if it were,) are—Classification as the first step, that the bad may not impede those who wish to do well; 2d. Instruction, practical, oral, and by furnishing books which may open entirely new hopes and thoughts to minds oftener darkened than corrupted; 3d. A good Sanitary system, which promotes self-respect, and, through health and purity of body, the same in mind. . . .

But nothing effectual can be achieved while both measures and men are made the sport of political changes. It is a most crying and shameful evil, which does not belong to our institutions, but is a careless distortion of them, that the men and measures are changed in these institutions with changes from Whig to Democrat, from Democrat to Whig. Churches, Schools, Colleges, the care of the Insane, and suffering Poor, should be preserved from the uneasy tossings of this delirium. The Country, the State, should look to it that only those fit for such officers should be chosen for such, apart from all considerations of political party. Let this be thought of; for without an absolute change in this respect no permanent good whatever can be effected; and farther, let not economy but utility be the rule of expenditure, for, here, parsimony is the worst prodigality.

30

Prevalent Idea That Politeness Is
Too Great a Luxury to Be Given to the Poor

A few days ago, a lady, crossing in one of the ferry boats that ply from this city, saw a young boy, poorly dressed, sitting with an infant in his arms on one of the benches. She observed that the child looked sickly and coughed. This, as the day was raw, made her anxious in its behalf, and she went to the boy and asked whether he was alone there with the baby, and if he did not think the cold breeze dangerous for it. He replied that he was sent out with the child to take care of it, and that his father said the fresh air from the water would do it good.

While he made this simple answer, a number of persons had collected around to listen, and one of them, a well-dressed woman, addressed the boy in a string of such questions and remarks as these:

"What is your name? Where do you live? Are you telling us the truth? It's a shame to have that baby out in such weather; you'll be the death of it. (To the bystanders:) I would go and see his mother and tell her about it, if I was sure he had told us the truth about where he lived. How do you expect to get back? Here, (in the rudest voice,) somebody says you have not told the truth as to where you live."

The child, whose only offence consisted in taking care of the little one in public, and answering when he was spoken to, began to shed tears at the accusations thus grossly preferred against him. The bystanders stared at both; but among them all there was not one with sufficiently clear notions of propriety and moral energy to say to this impudent questioner, "Woman! do you suppose, because you wear a handsome shawl, and that boy a patched jacket, that you have any right to speak to him at all, unless he wishes it, far less to prefer against him those rude accusations. Your vulgarity is unendurable; leave the place or alter your manner."

Many such instances have we seen of insolent rudeness or more insolent affability founded on no apparent grounds, except an apparent difference in pecuniary position, for no one can suppose in such cases the offending party has really enjoyed the benefit of refined education and society, but all present let them pass as matters of course. It was sad to see how the poor would endure—mortifying to see how the purse-proud

New-York Daily Tribune, May 31, 1845.

dared offend. An excellent man who was, in his early years, a missionary to the poor, used to speak afterwards with great shame of the manner in which he had conducted himself towards them.—"When I recollect," said he, "the freedom with which I entered their houses, inquired into all their affairs, commented on their conduct and disputed their statements I wonder I was never horsewhipped and feel that I ought to have been; it would have done me good, for I needed as severe a lesson on the universal obligations of politeness in its only genuine form of respect for man as man, and delicate sympathy with each in his peculiar position."

Charles Lamb, who was indeed worthy to be called a human being from those refined sympathies, said, "You call him a gentleman: does his washerwoman find him so?"[1] We may say, if she did so, she found him a *man,* neither treating her with vulgar abruptness, nor giving himself airs of condescending liveliness, but treating her with that genuine respect which a feeling of equality inspires.

To doubt the veracity of another is an insult which in most *civilized* communities must in the so-called higher classes be atoned for by blood, but, in those same communities, the same men will, with the utmost lightness, doubt the truth of one who wears a ragged coat, and thus do all they can to injure and degrade him by assailing his self-respect, and breaking the feeling of personal honor—a wound to which hurts a man as a wound to its bark does a tree.

Then how rudely are favors conferred, just as a bone is thrown to a dog. A gentleman indeed will not do *that* without accompanying signs of sympathy and regard. Just as this woman said, "If you have told the truth I will go and see your mother," are many acts performed on which the actors pride themselves as kind and charitable.

All men might learn from the French in these matters. That people, whatever be their faults, are really well-bred, and many acts might be quoted from their romantic annals, where gifts were given from rich to poor with a graceful courtesy, equally honorable and delightful to the giver and the receiver.

In Catholic countries there is more courtesy, for charity is there a duty, and must be done for God's sake; there is less room for a man to give himself the Pharisaical[2] tone about it. A rich man is not so surprised to find himself in contact with a poor one; nor is the custom of kneeling on the open pavement, the silk robe close to the beggar's rags, without

---

[1]Charles Lamb (1775–1834) was a popular English essayist.

[2]"Pharisaical" refers to the hypocritically self-righteous. The term is derived from the New Testament's portrayal of the Pharisees, Jewish religious leaders who frequently clashed with Jesus.

profit. The separation by pews, even on the day when all meet nearest, is as bad for the manners as the soul.

Blessed be he or she who has passed through this world, not only with an open purse and willingness to render the aid of mere outward benefits, but with an open eye and open heart, ready to cheer the downcast, and enlighten the dull by words of comfort and looks of love. The wayside charities are the most valuable both as to sustaining hope and diffusing knowledge, and none can render them who has not an expansive nature, a heart alive to affection, and some true notion, however imperfectly developed, of the nature of human brotherhood.

Such an one can never sauce the given meat with taunts, freeze the bread by a cold glance of doubt, or plunge the man who asked for his hand deeper back into the mud by any kind of rudeness.

In the little instance with which we begun, no help was asked, unless by the sight of the timid little boy's old jacket. But the license which this seemed to the well-clothed woman to give to rudeness was so characteristic of a deep fault now existing, that a volume of comments might follow and a host of anecdotes be drawn from almost any one's experience in exposition of it. These few words, perhaps, may awaken thought in those who have drawn tears from others eyes through an ignorance brutal, but not hopelessly so, if they are willing to rise above it.

31

Lyceum of New-Bedford, Massachusetts

Our readers may have noticed the act of exclusion by which the citizens of New-Bedford have shown the illiberal prejudice against people of color with an unblushing openness unusual even where it exists in its most unchristian form. The black population were denied, even in the case of the most respectable persons, the privilege of membership, and only allowed to hear lectures if they would confine themselves to a particular part of the house.—A minority protested in the strongest terms, but the majority persisted in the act of proscription. We rejoice to hear that, in consequence of these measures, R. W. Emerson and Charles Sumner,[1]

[1]Charles Sumner (1811–1874), a noted orator and U.S. senator from Massachusetts, strongly opposed the extension of slavery.

New-York Daily Tribune, December 9, 1845.

who were engaged as lecturers, have declined addressing an audience whose test of merit, or right to the privileges of a citizen consists not in intelligence or good character, but the color of the skin.

32

What Fits a Man to Be a Voter?
Is It to Be White Within, or White Without?

The country had been denuded of its forests, and men cried — "Come! we must plant anew, or there will be no shade for the homes of our children, or fuel for their hearths. Let us find the best kernels for a new growth."

And a basket of butternuts was offered.

But the planters rejected it with disgust. "What a black, rough coat it has," said they, "it is entirely unfit for the dishes on a nobleman's table, nor have we ever seen it in such places. It must have a greasy, offensive kernel; nor can fine trees grow up from such a nut."

"Friends," said one of the planters, "this decision may be rash. The chestnut has not a handsome outside; it is long encased in troublesome burrs, and, when disengaged, is almost as black as these nuts you despise. Yet from it grow trees of lofty stature, graceful form and long life. Its kernel is white and has furnished food to the most poetic and splendid nations of the older world."

"Don't tell me," says another, "brown is entirely different from black. I like brown very well; there is Oriental precedent for its respectability. Perhaps we will use some of your chestnuts, if we can get fine samples. But for the present I think we should use only English walnuts, such as our fore-fathers delighted to honor. Here are many basketsfull of them, quite enough for the present. We will plant them with a sprinkling between of the chestnut and acorn." "But," rejoined the other, "many butternuts are beneath the sod, and you cannot help a mixture of them being in your wood at any rate."

"Well! we will grub them up and cut them down wherever we find them. We can use the young shrubs for kindlings."

At that moment entered the council two persons of a darker complexion than most of those present, as if born beneath the glow of a more scorching sun. First came a Woman, beautiful in the mild, pure grandeur of her look; in whose large dark eye a prophetic intelligence was mingled with infinite sweetness. She looked at the assembly with an air of surprise, as if its aspect was strange to her. She threw quite back her veil, and stepping aside made room for her companion. His form was youthful, about the age of one we have seen in many a picture, produced by the thought of eighteen centuries, as of one "instructing the Doctors."[1] I need not describe the features; all minds have their own impressions of such an image,

"Severe in youthful beauty."[2]

In his hand, he bore a little white banner on which was embroidered PEACE AND GOOD WILL TO MEN.[3] And the words seemed to glitter and give out sparks, as he paused in the assembly.

"I came hither," said he, "an uninvited guest, because I read sculptured above the door—'All men born Free and Equal,' and in this dwelling hoped to find myself at home. What is the matter in dispute?"

Then they whispered one to another, and murmurs were heard—"He is a mere boy; young people are always foolish and extravagant;" or "He looks like a fanatic." But others said, "He looks like one whom we have been taught to honor. It will be best to tell the matter in dispute."

When he heard it, he smiled and said, "It will be needful first to ascertain which of the nuts is soundest *within.*" And with a hammer he broke one, two, and more of the English walnuts, and they were mouldy.

Then he tried the other nuts, but found most of them fresh and *white,* for they were fresh from the bosom of the earth, while the others had been kept in a damp cellar.

And he said, "You had better plant them together, lest none or few of the walnuts be sound. And why are you so reluctant? Has not Heaven permitted them both to grow on the same soil? and does not that show what is intended about it?"

And they said, "But they are black and ugly to look upon." He replied, "They do not seem so to me. What my Father has fashioned in such guise offends not mine eye."

And they said, "But from one of these trees flew a bird of prey who has done great wrong. We meant, therefore, to suffer no such tree among us."

And he replied, "Amid the band of my countrymen and friends there was one guilty of the blackest crime, that of selling for a price the life of

---

[1] In Luke 2.46, the young Jesus instructs the doctors in the temple.
[2] From *Paradise Lost* (1667), by the English poet John Milton (1608–1674).
[3] See Luke 2.14.

his dearest friend, yet all the others of his blood were not put under ban because of his guilt."

Then they said, "But in the Holy Book our teachers tell us, we are bid to keep in exile or distress whatsoever is black and unseemly in our eyes."

Then he put his hand to his brow and cried in a voice of the most penetrating pathos, "Have I been so long among ye and ye have not known me?"[4]—And the Woman turned from them, the majestic hope of her glance, and both forms suddenly vanished, but the banner was left trailing in the dust.

The men stood gazing at one another. After which one mounted on high and said:

"Perhaps, my friends, we carry too far this aversion to objects merely because they are black. I heard, the other day, a wise man say that black was the color of evil—marked as such by God, and that whenever a white man struck a black man he did an act of worship to God. I could not quite believe him. I hope, in what I am about to add, I shall not be misunderstood. I am no Abolitionist. I respect above all things, divine or human, the Constitution framed by our forefathers, and the peculiar institutions[5] hallowed by the usage of their sons. I have no sympathy with the black race in this country. I wish it to be understood that I feel toward negroes the purest personal antipathy. It is a family trait with us. My little son, scarce able to speak, will cry out 'Nigger! Nigger!' whenever he sees one, and try to throw things at them. He made a whole omnibus load laugh the other day by his cunning way of doing this. The child of my political antagonist, on the other hand, says 'he likes *tullared* children the best.' You see he is tainted in his cradle by the loose principles of his parents, even before he can say nigger or pronounce the more refined appellation. But that is no matter. I merely mention this by the way: not to prejudice you against Mr.———, but that you may appreciate the very different state of things in my family, and not misinterpret what I have to say. I was lately in one of our prisons where a somewhat injudicious indulgence had extended to one of the condemned felons, a lost and wretched outcast from society, the use of materials for painting, that having been his profession. He had completed at his leisure, a picture of the Lord's Supper. Most of the figures were well enough, but Judas he has represented as a black.—Now, gentlemen, I am of opinion that this is an unwarrantable liberty taken with the Holy Scriptures and shows *too much* prejudice in

[4]See John 14.9.
[5]Slavery was popularly known as the "peculiar institution."

the community. It is my wish to be moderate and fair, and preserve a medium, neither, on the one hand, yielding the wholesome antipathies planted in our breasts as a safeguard against degradation, and our constitutional obligations, which, as I have before observed, are, with me, more binding than any other; nor on the other hand forgetting that liberality and wisdom which are the prerogative of every citizen of this free Commonwealth. I agree then with our young visitor. I hardly know, indeed, why a stranger and one so young was permitted to mingle in this council, but it was certainly thoughtful in him to crack and examine the nuts. I agree that it may be well to plant some of the black nuts among the others, so that, if many of the walnuts fail, we may make use of this inferior tree."

At this moment arose a hubbub, and such a clamor of "dangerous innovation," "political capital," "low-minded demagogue," "infidel who denies the Bible," "lower link in the chain of creation," &c. that it is impossible to say what was the decision.

14

European Dispatches and Letters

In August 1846, more than a decade after she had first longed to go, Margaret Fuller departed for Europe. Traveling with friends through England, Scotland, France, and Italy, she also agreed to serve as a foreign correspondent for the New-York Daily Tribune *(another first for women in journalism). She sent home thirty-seven dispatches, published as* Things and Thoughts in Europe, *between August 1846 and January 1850. These dispatches offered a sharp critique of European society and politics and carried a warning to those "who have eyes and see not, ears and hear not, the convulsions and sobs of injured Humanity!" They also recorded her growing engagement with the Italian revolution of 1848–1849 (Documents 33–36). Unrivaled in dramatic intensity and vividness of detail, her accounts of the birth, siege, and fall of the Roman Republic remain valuable documents for students of European and American history. Read in conjunction with her last, private letters to her mother and her closest female friend, Caroline Sturgis Tappan (Documents 37–40), they also reveal the extraordinary richness and complexity of Margaret Fuller's final years.*

THINGS AND THOUGHTS IN EUROPE

33

No. XXIII. [A Revolutionary Spring]

ROME, 29 March 1848

It is long since I have written: my health entirely gave way beneath the Roman Winter. The rain was constant, commonly falling in torrents from the 16th December to the 19th March. Nothing could surpass the dirt,

New-York Daily Tribune, May 4, 1848.

the gloom, the desolation of Rome. Let no one fancy he has seen her who comes here only in the Winter. It is an immense mistake to do so. I cannot sufficiently rejoice that I did not first see Italy in the Winter.

The climate of Rome at this time of extreme damp I have found equally exasperating and weakening. I have had constant nervous headache without strength to bear it, nightly fever, want of appetite.[1] Some constitutions bear it better, but the complaint of weakness and extreme dejection of spirits is general among foreigners in the wet season. The English say they become acclimated in two or three years and cease to suffer, though never so strong as at home.

Now this long dark dream—to me the most idle and most suffering season of my life—seems past. The Italian heavens wear again their deep blue; the sun shines gloriously; the melancholy lustres are stealing again over the Campagna, and hundreds of larks sing unwearied above its ruins.

Nature seems in sympathy with the great events that are transpiring: with the emotions which are swelling the hearts of men. The morning sun is greeted by the trumpets of the Roman Legions marching out once more, but now not to oppress but to defend. The stars look down on their jubilees over the good news which nightly reaches them from their brothers of Lombardy.[2] This week has been one of nobler, sweeter feeling of a better hope and faith than Rome in her greatest days ever knew. How much has happened since I wrote!—First the victorious resistance of Sicily and the revolution of Naples.[3] This has led as yet only to half measures, but even these have been of great use to the progress of Italy. The Neapolitans will, probably, have to get rid at last of the stupid crowned head who is at present their puppet, but their bearing with him has led to the wiser sovereigns granting these Constitutions, which, if eventually inadequate to the wants of Italy, will be so useful, are so needed, to educate her to seek better, completer forms of administration. . . .

. . . The news of the dethronement of Louis Philippe reached us just after the close of the Carnival.[4] It was just a year from my leaving Paris. I did not think, as I looked with such disgust on the empire of sham he

---

[1] Fuller was in the first trimester of her pregnancy, which she kept hidden while in Rome.

[2] A popular uprising against the Austrian occupation of Lombardy led to violent street fighting in Milan. During the "Five Glorious Days" of Milan's resistance (March 18–22), the Milanese used homemade weapons and barricades to drive 20,000 Austrian troops from the city.

[3] In January 1848, revolution broke out in Palermo, Sicily. Threatened with uprisings in Naples and other towns in his kingdom of Sicily and Naples as well, Ferdinand II (1810–1859) granted his subjects a popular constitution.

[4] On February 22–24, 1848, Parisian workers, students, and artisans overthrew the monarchy of Louis-Philippe (1773–1850) and proclaimed France a republic.

had established in France, and saw the soul of the people imprisoned and held fast as in an iron vice, that it would burst its chains so soon. Whatever be the result, France has done gloriously; she has declared that she will not be satisfied with pretexts while there are facts in the world—that to stop her march is a vain attempt, though the onward path be dangerous and difficult. It is vain to cry Peace, peace, when there is no peace. The news from France, in these days, sounds ominous, though still vague; it would appear that the political is being merged in the social struggle: it is well; whatever blood is to be shed, whatever altars cast down. Those tremendous problems MUST be solved, whatever be the cost! That cost cannot fail to break many a bank, many a heart in Europe, before the good can bud again out of a mighty corruption. To you, people of America, it may perhaps be given to look on and learn in time for a preventive wisdom. You may learn the real meaning of the words FRATERNITY, EQUALITY:[5] you may, despite the apes of the Past, who strive to tutor you, learn the needs of a true Democracy. You may in time learn to reverence, learn to guard, the true aristocracy of a nation, the only real noble the LABORING CLASSES.

And Metternich, too, is crushed; the seed of the Woman has had his foot on the serpent.[6] I have seen the Austrian arms dragged through the streets of Rome and burned in the Piazza del Popolo.—The Italians embraced one another and cried, *Miracolo, Providenza!*[7] the modern Tribune Ciceronacchio fed the flame with faggots;[8] Adam Mickiewicz,[9] the great Poet of Poland, long exiled from his country or the hopes of a country, looked on, while Polish women, exiled too, or who, perhaps, like one nun who is here, had been daily scourged by the orders of a tyrant, brought little pieces that had been scattered in the street and threw into the flames—an offering received by the Italians with loud plaudits. It was a transport of the people, who found no way to vent their joy, but the symbol, the poesy, natural to the Italian mind; the ever-too-wise "upper classes" regret it, and the Germans choose to resent as an insult to Germany; but it was nothing of the kind; the insult was to the prisons of Spielberg, to

---

[5]The phrase "Liberty, Equality, Fraternity" was the inspirational cry of the French revolutionaries of 1789. It was widely echoed in subsequent European revolutions.

[6]Klemens Metternich (1773–1859), the Austrian minister of foreign affairs and the principal architect of Europe's conservative order, was driven from power by popular uprisings in Vienna. This fueled Italian hopes of unification and independence from the Austrian empire. For Fuller's biblical allusion, see Genesis 2.15.

[7]Good fortune (Italian).

[8]"Big Boy" (Italian) was the nickname of a popular leader in Rome. "Faggots" are bundles of sticks.

[9]Adam Mickiewicz (1798–1855), the Polish poet and revolutionary, was one of Fuller's European friends. He was in Rome in 1848 to organize a military unit to fight against Austrian troops in northern Italy.

those who commanded the massacres of Milan; a base tyranny little congenial to the native German heart, as the true Germans of Germany are at this moment showing by their struggles, by their resolves.

When the double-headed eagle was pulled down from above the lofty portal of the Palazzo di Venezia, the people placed there in its stead one of white and gold inscribed with the name ALTA ITALIA,[10] and quick upon the emblem followed the news that Milan was fighting against her tyrants—that Venice had driven them out and freed from their prisons the courageous Protestants in favor of truth, Tommasseo and Manin[11]—that Manin, descendant of the last Doge, had raised the Republican banner on the Place St. Mark—and that Modena, that Parma, were driving out the unfeeling and imbecile creatures who had mocked Heaven and Man by the pretence of Government there.

With indescribable rapture these news were received in Rome. Men were seen dancing, women weeping with joy along the street. The youth rushed to enrol themselves in regiments to go to the frontier. In the Colosseum their names were received. Father Gavazzi,[12] a truly patriotic monk, gave them the cross to carry on a new, a better, because defensive crusade. Sterbini,[13] long exiled, addressed them; he said, "Romans, do you wish to go; do you wish to go with all your hearts? If so, you *may,* and those who do not wish to go themselves may give money. To those who will go, the government gives bread and fifteen baiocchi a day." The people cried "We too wish to go, but we do not wish so much; the Government is very poor; we can live on a paul a day."[14] The princes answered by giving, one sixty thousand, others twenty, fifteen, ten thousand dollars. The people answered by giving at the benches which are opened in the piazzas literally everything; street-peddlers gave the gains of each day; women gave every ornament—from the splendid necklace and bracelet down to the poorest bit of coral; servant girls gave five pauls, two pauls, even half a paul, if they had no more; a man all in rags gave two

[10]Northern Italy (Italian). The double-headed eagle was the emblem of the Austrian empire. This image was superimposed on a red-white-red background that was declared the Austrian flag by Emperor Joseph II in 1786 and remained the national symbol and battle ensign of the dual monarchy of Austria-Hungary until 1918.

[11]Venice staged a successful revolt against Austria on March 22, 1848. The new Venetian Republic was headed by Daniele Manin (1804–1857), a popular leader. Manin and Niccolò Tommaseo (1802–1874), the Venetian Republic's minister of public education, had been in prison together earlier in 1848 for revolutionary activities.

[12]Alessandro Gavazzi (1809–1889) was a monk and supporter of Pope Pius IX (1792–1878).

[13]Pietro Sterbini (1795–1863), a follower of the Italian revolutionary Giuseppe Mazzini (1805–1872), was appointed a minister of state by the pope in November 1848.

[14]The *baiocchi* and the *paul* were small coins of little value.

pauls; "it is," said he, "all I have." "Then," said Torlonia,[15] "take from me this dollar;" the man of rags thanked him warmly and handed that also to the bench which refused to receive it. "No! that must stay with you," shouted all present. These are the people whom the traveler accuses of being unable to rise above selfish considerations. Nation, rich and glorious by nature as ever, capable, like all nations, all men, of being degraded by slavery, capable as are few nations, few men, of kindling into pure flame at the touch of a ray from the Sun of Truth, of Life. . . .

[15]Probably Prince Alessandro Torlonia (1800–1886), the director of a Roman bank.

34

No. XXVI. [The Birth of the Roman Republic]

ROME, 2 December 1848

Not till I saw the snow on the mountains grow rosy in the Autumn sunset did I turn my steps again toward Rome. I was very ready to return. After three or four years of constant excitement this six months of seclusion had been welcome; but now I felt the need of meeting other eyes beside those so bright and so shallow, of the Italian peasant. Indeed, I left what was most precious that I could not take with me; still it was a compensation that I was again to see Rome.[1] Rome that almost killed me with her cold breath of last Winter, yet still with that cold breath whispered a tale of import so divine. Rome so beautiful, so great; her presence stupifies, and one has to withdraw to prize the treasures she has given. City of the Soul! yes, it is *that;* the very dust magnetizes you, and thousand spells have been chaining you in every careless, every murmuring moment. Yes! Rome, however seen, thou must be still adored; and every hour of absence or presence must deepen love with one who has known what it is to repose in thy arms. . . .

I found Rome empty of foreigners: most of the English have fled in affright—the Germans and French are wanted at home—the Czar has recalled many of his younger subjects; he does not like the schooling they get here. That large part of the population which lives by the visits of

[1]Fuller's son was born on September 5, 1848, in northeastern Italy, where Fuller had gone for privacy. She returned to Rome without him in mid-November.

foreigners was suffering very much — trade, industry, for every reason, stagnant. The people were every moment becoming more exasperated by the impudent measures of the Minister Rossi, and their mortification at seeing Rome represented and betrayed by a foreigner. And what foreigner? A pupil of Guizot and Louis Philippe.[2] The news had just reached them of the bombardment and storm of Vienna. Zucchi, the Minister-of-War, left Rome to put down over-free manifestations in the Provinces, and impede the entrance of the troops of the Patriot Chief, Garibaldi, into Bologna.[3] From the Provinces came soldiery, called by Rossi to keep order at the opening of the Chamber of Deputies. He reviewed them in the face of the Civic Guard; the Press began to be restrained; men were arbitrarily seized and sent out of the kingdom; the public indignation rose to its height; the cup overflowed.

The 15th was a beautiful day and I had gone out for a long walk. Returning at night, the old Padrona[4] met me with her usual smile a little clouded, "Do you know," said she, "that the Minister Rossi has been killed?" (No Roman said *murdered*.)

"Killed!"

"Yes with a thrust in the back. A wicked man, surely, but is that the way to punish CHRISTIANS?"

"I cannot," observed a Philosopher, "sympathize under any circumstances with so immoral a deed; but surely the manner of doing it was. *grandiose.*"

The people at large was not so refined in their comments as either the Padrona or the Philosopher; but soldiers and populace alike ran up and down singing "Blessed the hand that rids the earth of a tyrant."

"Certainly, the manner was grandiose."

The Chamber was awaiting the entrance of Rossi. Had he lived to enter, he would have found the Assembly, without a single exception, ranged upon the Opposition benches. His carriage approached, attended by a howling, hissing multitude. He smiled, affected unconcern, but must have felt relieved when his horses entered the courtyard gate of the *Can-*

---

[2]Pellegrino Rossi (1787–1848) was an Italian political exile who became a naturalized French citizen. François-Pierre-Guillaume Guizot (1787–1874), the French premier forced into retirement by the revolution of 1848, appointed Rossi the French ambassador to Rome in 1845. Pope Pius IX made Rossi his prime minister in September 1848. Rossi had few other supporters in Rome.

[3]General Carlo Zucchi was attempting to maintain order in the papal army for Rossi. Giuseppe Garibaldi (1807–1882), an early follower of Mazzini, had won fame as a military leader while in exile in South America between 1834 and 1848. He fought with the Milanese against Austria in the summer of 1848 and organized the defense of the Roman Republic against the French in 1849.

[4]Landlady (Italian).

celleria.[5] He did not know he was entering the place of his execution. The horses stopped; he alighted in the midst of a crowd; it jostled him as if for the purpose of insult; he turned abruptly and received as he did so the fatal blow. It was dealt by a resolute, perhaps experienced, hand; he fell and spoke no word more.

The crowd, as if all previously acquainted with the plan, as no doubt most of them were, issued quietly from the gate and passed through the outside crowd—its members, among whom was he who dealt the blow, dispersing in all directions.—For two or three minutes this outside crowd did not know that anything special had happened.—When they did, the news was at the moment received in silence. The soldiers in whom Rossi had trusted, whom he had hoped to flatter and bribe, stood at their posts and said not a word!—Neither they nor any one asked "Who did this? Where is he gone?" The sense of the people certainly was that it was an act of summary justice on an offender whom the laws could not reach, but they felt it to be indecent to shout or exult on the spot where he was breathing his last. Rome, so long supposed the Capital of Christendom, certainly took a very pagan view of this act, and the piece represented on the occasion at the theaters was "The Death of Nero."

The next morning I went to the church of St. Andrea della Valle, where was to be performed a funeral service, with fine music, in honor of the victims of Vienna; for this they do here for the victims all round—"victims of Milan," "victims of Paris," "victims of Naples," and now "victims of Vienna." But to-day I found the church closed, the service put off— Rome was thinking about her own victims. . . .

Leaving the church I passed along toward the *Piazza del Popolo*. "Yellow Tiber rose,"[6] but not high enough to cause "distress," as he does when in a swelling mood rather than "mantle" it. I heard drums beating, and, entering the Piazza, I found the troops of the line already assembled, and the Civic Guard marching in by platoons; each *battaglione*[7] saluted as it entered by trumpets and a fine strain from the hand of the Carbineers.

I climbed the Pincian to see better. There is no place so fine for anything of this kind as the Piazza del Popolo, it is so full of light, so fair and grand, the obelisk and fountain make so fine a center to all kinds of groups.

---

[5]Chancellery (Italian).

[6]The Tiber, which flows through Rome, is the second largest river in Italy.

[7]Battalion (Italian). Pope Pius IX had granted his subjects the right to form a civic guard (which placed weapons in the hands of Roman citizens for the first time) when he came to power in July 1846. Giovanni Ossoli, the father of Fuller's child, was a member of Rome's Civic Guard.

The object of the present meeting was for the Civic Guard and troops of the line to give pledges of sympathy preparatory to going to the Quirinal to demand a change of Ministry and of measures. The flag of the Union was placed in front of the obelisk; all present saluted it; some officials made addresses; the trumpets sounded, and all moved toward the Quirinal.

Nothing could be gentler than the disposition of the crowd. They were resolved to be played with no longer, but no threat was heard or thought.—They believed that the Court would be convinced by the fate of Rossi that the retrograde movement it had attempted was impracticable. They knew the retrograde party were panic-struck, and hoped to use the occasion to free the Pope from their meshes. All felt that Pius IX. had fallen irrevocably from his high place of the friend of Progress and father of Italy: but still he was personally beloved, and still his name, so often shouted in hope and joy, had not quite lost its *prestige.*

I returned to the house, which is very near the Quirinal. On one side I could see the Palace and gardens of the Pope, on the other the Piazza Barberini and street of the Four Fountains. Presently I saw the carriage of Prince Barberini[8] drive hurriedly into his court-yard gate, the footman signing to close it, a discharge of firearms was heard, and the drums of the Civic Guard beat to arms.

The Padrona ran up and down crying with every round of shot, "Jesu Maria, they are killing the Pope! O! poor Holy Father—Tita, Tita, (out of the window to her husband,) what *is* the matter?"

The lord of creation disdained to reply.

"Oh! Signora, pray, pray, ask Tita what is the matter?" I did so. "I don't know, Signora; nobody knows."

"Why don't you go on the mount and see?"

"It would be an imprudence, Signora; nobody will go."

I was just thinking to go myself when I saw a poor man borne by, badly wounded, and heard that the Swiss were firing on the people. Their doing so was the cause of whatever violence there was, and it was not much.

The people had assembled, as usual, at the Quirinal, only with more form and solemnity than usual. They had taken with them several of the Chamber of Deputies, and they sent an embassy, headed by Galetti,[9] who had been in the late Ministry, to state their wishes. They received a peremptory negative. They then insisted on seeing the Pope, and pressed

---

[8]Prince Francesco-Maria-Barberini-Colona (1772–1853) was a man of wealth and power in Rome.

[9]Giuseppe Galetti (1798–1873) was serving a life sentence for revolutionary activities when the pope issued a general amnesty for political prisoners in July 1846. Galetti became the minister of the interior of the Papal States in 1848.

on the palace. The Swiss became alarmed, and fired from the windows, from the roof. They did this, it is said, without orders, but who could, at the time, suppose that? If it had been planned to exasperate the people to blood, what more could have been done? As it was, very little was shed; but the Pope, no doubt, felt great panic. He heard the report of fire-arms — heard that they tried to burn a door of the palace. I would lay my life that he could have shown himself without the slightest danger; nay, that the habitual respect for his presence would have prevailed, and hushed all tumult. He did not think so, and to still it once more degraded himself and injured his people, by making promises he did not mean to keep.

He protests now against those promises as extorted by violence, a strange plea, indeed, for the representative of St. Peter! . . .

In fact, the only dignified course for the Pope to pursue was to resign his temporal power. He could no longer hold it on his own terms; but to that he clung; and the counselors around him were men to wish him to regard *that* as the first of duties. When the question was of waging war for the independence of Italy, they regarded him solely the head of the Church; but when the demand was to satisfy the wants of his people, and ecclesiastical goods were threatened with taxes, then he was the Prince of the State, bound to maintain all the selfish prerogative of by-gone days for the benefit of his successors. Poor Pope! how has his mind been torn to pieces in these later days. It moves compassion. There can be no doubt that all his natural impulses are generous and kind, and in a more private station he would have died beloved and honored; but to this he was unequal; he has suffered bad men to surround; and by their mis-representations and insidious suggestions, at last entirely to cloud his mind. I believe he really thinks now the Progress movement tends to an-archy, blood, all that looked worst in the first French Revolution. How-ever that may be I cannot forgive him some of the circumstances of this flight. To fly to Naples to throw himself in the arms of the bombarding monarch,[10] blessing him and thanking his soldiery for preserving that part of Italy from anarchy — to protest that all his promises at Rome were null and void, when he thought himself in safety to choose a commission for governing in his absence, composed of men of princely blood, but as to character so null that everybody laughed and said he chose those who could best be spared if they were killed; (but they all ran away directly;) when Rome was thus left without any Government, to refuse to see any

---

[10]The pope, disguised as an ordinary priest, fled Rome on November 24, 1848. Ferdi-nand II, the king of Sicily and Naples, was derisively named "King Bomba" after he bom-barded the people of Naples to quell their revolt.

deputation, even the Senator of Rome, whom he had so gladly sanctioned,—these are the acts either of a fool or a foe. They are not his acts, to be sure, but he is responsible, he lets them stand as such in the face of the world, and weeps and prays for their success.

No more of him! His day is over. He has been made, it seems unconsciously, an instrument of good his regrets cannot destroy. Nor can he be made so important an instrument of ill. These acts have not had the effect the foes of freedom hoped. Rome remained quite cool and composed; all felt that they had not demanded more than was their duty to demand, and were willing to accept what might follow. In a few days all began to say, "Well, who would have thought it? The Pope, the Cardinals, the Princes are gone, and Rome is perfectly tranquil, and one does not miss anything, except that there are not so many rich carriages and liveries."

The Pope may regret too late that he ever gave the people a chance to make this reflection. Yet the best fruits of the movement may not ripen for long. It is one which requires radical measures, clear-sighted, resolute men: these last, as yet, do not show themselves in Rome. The new Tuscan Ministry has three men of superior force in various ways: Montanelli, Guerazzi, D'Aguila;[11] such are not as yet to be found in Rome.

But should she fall this time, (and she must either advance with decision and force, or fall—since to stand still is impossible,) the people have learned much; ignorance and servility of thought are lessened—the way is paving for final triumph. . . .

[11]Giuseppe Montanelli (1813–1862), Francesco Domenico Guerazzi (1804–1873), and Mariano d'Ayala (1807–1877) were pressing for a constituent assembly in Tuscany as Fuller wrote.

35

No. XXXIII. [Rome under Siege]

ROME, July 6, 1849

If I mistake not, I closed my last letter just as the news arrived here that the attempt of the Democratic party in France to resist the infamous proceedings of the Government had failed, and thus Rome, as far as human calculation went, had not a hope for her liberties left.[1] An inland city cannot long sustain a siege when there is no hope of aid. Then followed the news of the surrender of Ancona, and Rome found herself quite alone—for, though Venice continued to hold out, all communication was cut off.

The Republican troops, almost to a man, left Ancona, but a long march separated them from Rome.

The extreme heat of these days was far more fatal to the Romans than their assailants, for, as fast as the French troops sickened, their place was taken by fresh arrivals. Ours also not only sustained the exhausting service by day, but were harassed at night by attacks, feigned or real.—These commonly began about 11 or 12 o'clock at night, just when all who meant to rest were fairly asleep. I can imagine the harassing effect upon the troops, from what I feel in my sheltered pavilion, in consequence of not knowing a quiet night's sleep for a month.

The bombardment became constantly more serious. The house where I live was filled as early as the 20th with persons obliged to fly from the *Piazza di Gesu,* where the fiery rain fell thickest. The night of the 21st–22d, we were all alarmed about 2 o'clock A.M. by a tremendous cannonade. It was the moment when the breach was finally made by which the French entered.—They rushed in, and, I grieve to say, that by the only instance of defection known in the course of the siege, those companies of the regiment Union, which had in charge a casino on that point, yielded to panic and abandoned it. The French immediately entered and intrenched themselves. That was the fatal hour for the city. Every day afterward, though obstinately resisted, they gained, till at last, their cannon being well placed, the city was entirely commanded from the Janiculum, and all thought of further resistance was idle. . . .

Yesterday I went over the scene of conflict. It was fearful even to see the casinos *Quattro Venti* and *Vascello,* where the French and Romans had been several days so near one another, all shattered to pieces, with fragments of rich stucco and painting still sticking to rafters between the great holes made by the cannonade, and think that men had stayed and fought in them when only a mass of ruins. The French, indeed, were entirely sheltered the last days; to my unpracticed eyes the extent and

[1]On March 31, 1849, the French Chamber of Deputies authorized an invasion of Italy. French troops attacked Roman defenses outside the city on April 30 and were defeated by Garibaldi's troops. The French declared a truce until reinforcements could arrive. The French bombardment of Rome began on June 3. French republicans and socialists unsuccessfully protested their government's siege of Rome on June 13, 1849.

thoroughness of their works seemed miraculous, and gave me [my] first clear idea of the incompetency of the Italians to resist organized armies. I saw their commanders had not even known enough of the art of war to understand how the French were conducting the siege.—It is true their resources were at any rate inadequate to resistance; only continual sorties would have arrested the progress of the foe, and to make them and man the wall their forces were inadequate. I was struck more than ever by the heroic valor of *ours,* let me say, as I have said all along, for go where I may, a large part of my heart will ever remain in Italy. I hope her children will always acknowledge me as a sister, though I drew not my first breath here. A *contadini*[2] showed me where thirty seven braves are buried beneath a heap of wall that fell upon them in the shock of one cannonade. A marble nymph, with broken arm, looked sadly that way from her sun-dried fountain, some roses were blooming still, some red oleanders amid the ruin. The sun was casting its last light on the mountains on the tranquil, sad Campagna, that sees one leaf turned more in the book of Woe. This was in the Vascello. I then entered the French ground, all mapped and hollowed like a honey-comb. A pair of skeleton legs protruded from a bank of one barricade; lower a dog had scratched away its light covering of earth from the body of a man, and discovered it lying face upward all dressed; the dog stood gazing on it with an air of stupid amazement. I thought at that moment, recalling some letters received, "O men and women of America, spared these frightful sights, these sudden wrecks of every hope, what angel of Heaven do you suppose has time to listen to your tales of morbid woe? If any find leisure to work for men to-day, think you not they have enough to do to care for the victims here."

I see you have meetings, where you speak of the Italians, the Hungarians. I pray you *do something;* let it not end in a mere cry of sentiment. That is better than to sneer at all that is liberal, like the English; than to talk of the holy victims of patriotism as "anarchists" and "brigands,"—but it is not enough. It ought not to content your consciences. Do you owe no tithe to Heaven for the privileges it has showered on you, for whose achievement so many here suffer and perish daily? Deserve to retain them, by helping your fellow-men to acquire them. Our Government must abstain from interference, but private action is practicable, is due. For Italy, it is in this moment too late, but all that helps Hungary helps her also, helps all who wish the freedom of men from an hereditary yoke now become intolerable. Send money, send cheer—acknowledge as the legitimate leaders and rulers those men who represent the people, who understand its wants, who are ready to die or to live for its good. Kos-

---

[2]Peasant (Italian).

suth[3] I know not, but his people recognize him; Manin I know not, but with what firm nobleness, what persevering virtue, he has acted for Venice!—Mazzini I know, the man and his acts, great, pure and constant,—a man to whom only the next age can do justice, as it reaps the harvest of the seed he has sown in this.—Friends, countrymen, and lovers of virtue, lovers of freedom, lovers of truth!—be on the alert; rest not supine in your easier lives, but remember

"Mankind is one.
And beats with one great heart."

[3]Lajos Kossuth (1802–1894) led the Hungarian revolt against Austria.

36

Italy.[1] [Prophecies]

FLORENCE, 6 January 1850

Last winter began with meteors and the rose-colored Aurora Borealis. All the winter was steady sunshine, and the Spring that followed no less glorious, as if Nature rejoiced in and daily smiled upon the noble efforts and tender, generous impulses of the Italian people. This winter, Italy is shrouded with snow. Here in Florence the oil congeals in the closet beside the fire—the water in the chamber—just as in our country-houses of New-England, as yet uncomforted by furnaces. I was supposing this to be confined to colder Florence, but a letter, this day received, from Rome says the snow lies there two feet deep, and water freezes instantly if thrown upon the pavement. I hardly know how to believe it—I who never saw but one slight powdering of snow all my two Roman winters, scarce enough to cover a Canary bird's wing.

Thus Nature again sympathizes with this injured people, though, I fear me, many a houseless wanderer wishes she did not. For many want both bread, and any kind of shelter this winter, an extremity of physical deprivation that had seemed almost impossible in this richest land. It had seemed that Italians might be subjected to the extreme of mental and moral suffering, but that the common beggar's plea, *"I am hungry,"* must remain a mere poetic expression. 'Tis no longer so, for it proves possible for the wickedness of man to mar to an indefinite extent the benevolent

[1]This was Fuller's final dispatch from Europe.

designs of God. Yet, indeed, if indefinitely not infinitely. I feel now that we are to bless the very extremity of ill with which Italy is afflicted. The cure is sure, else death would follow.

The barbarities of reaction have reached their height in the kingdom of Naples and Sicily. Bad government grows daily worse in the Roman dominions. The French have degraded themselves there enough to punish them even for the infamous treachery of which they were guilty. Their foolish national vanity, which prefers the honor of the uniform to the honor of the man, has received its due reward, in the numberless derisions and small insults it has received from a bitterer, blacker vice, the arrogance of the priests. President, envoys, ministers, officers, have all debased themselves; have told the most shameless lies; have bartered the fair fame slowly built up by many years of seeming consistency, for a few days of brief authority, in vain. Their schemes, thus far, have ended in disunion, and should they now win any point upon the right reverend cardinal vices, it is too late. The seeds for a vast harvest of hatreds and contempts are sown over every inch of Roman ground, nor can that malignant growth be extirpated, till the wishes of Heaven shall waft a fire that will burn down all, root and branch, and prepare the earth for an entirely new culture. The next revolution, here and elsewhere, will be radical. Not only Jesuitism must go but the Roman Catholic religion must go. The Pope cannot retain even his spiritual power. The influence of the clergy is too perverting, too foreign to every hope of advancement and health. Not only the Austrian, and every potentate of foreign blood, must be deposed, but every man who assumes an arbitrary lordship over fellow man, must be driven out. It will be an uncompromising revolution. England cannot reason nor ratify nor criticize it—France cannot betray it—Germany cannot bungle it—Italy cannot bubble it away—Russia cannot stamp it down nor hide it in Siberia. The New Era is no longer an embryo: it is born; it begins to walk—this very year sees its first giant steps, and can no longer mistake its features. Men have long been talking of a transition state—it is over—the power of positive, determinate effort is begun. A faith is offered—men are everywhere embracing it; the film is hourly falling from their eyes and they see, not only near but far, duties worthy to be done. God be praised! It was a dark period of that sceptical endeavor and work, only worthy as helping to educate the next generation, was watered with much blood and tears. God be praised! that time is ended, and the noble band of teachers who have passed this last ordeal of the furnace and den of lions,[2] are ready now to enter their followers for the elementary class.

---

[2]Shadrach, Meshach, and Abednego suffer the ordeal of the fiery furnace in Daniel 3.10–30. Daniel 6.12–24 tells of Daniel's trial in a den of lions.

At this moment all the worst men are in power, and the best betrayed and exiled. All the falsities, the abuses of the old political forms, the old social compact, seem confirmed. Yet it is not so: the struggle that is now to begin will be fearful, but even from the first hours not doubtful. Bodies rotten and trembling cannot long contend with swelling life. Tongue and hand cannot be permanently employed to keep down hearts. Sons cannot be long employed in the conscious enslavement of their sires, fathers of their children. That advent called EMMANUEL[3] begins to be understood, and shall no more so foully be blasphemed. Men shall now be represented as souls, not hands and feet, and governed accordingly. A congress of great, pure, loving minds, and not a congress of selfish ambitions, shall preside. Do you laugh, Editor of the *"Times?"*[4] (Times of the Iron Age.) Do you laugh, Roman Cardinal, as you shut the prison-door on woman weeping for her son martyred in the cause of his country? Do you laugh, Austrian officer, as you drill the Hungarian and Lombard youth to tremble at your baton? Soon you, all of you, shall *"believe* and tremble."[5]

I take little interest now in what is going on here in Italy. It is all leavened with the same leaven, and ferments to the same end. Tuscany is stupified. They are not discontented here, if they can fold the hands yet a little while to slumber. The Austrian tutelage is mild. In Lombardy and Venice they would gladly make it so, but the case is too difficult. The sick man tosses and tumbles. The so called Italian moderates are fighting at last, (not battles, they have not energy for that,) but skirmishes in Piedmont. The result cannot be doubtful; we need not waste time and paper in predicting it.

Joy to those born in this day: In America is open to them the easy chance of a noble, peaceful growth, in Europe of a combat grand in its motives, and in its extent beyond what the world ever before so much as dreamed. Joy to them; and joy to those their heralds, who, if their path was desert, their work unfinished, and their heads in the power of a prostituted civilization, to throw as toys at the feet of flushed, triumphant wickedness, yet holy-hearted in masking love, great and entire in their devotion, fall or fade, happy in the thought that these come after them greater than themselves, who may at last string the harp of the world to

---

[3]Immanuel or Emmanuel, meaning "God is with us," was the name of a child whose birth was predicted by Isaiah. The child was to be a sign to the king of Judah that God would deliver him from his enemies (Isaiah 7:14). The name was applied to Jesus in the New Testament (Matthew 1:23).

[4]The London *Times* took a conservative line on the end of the revolution and the restoration of foreign rule in Italy.

[5]See James 2.19: "The devils also believe, and tremble."

full concord, in glory to God in the highest, for peace and love from man to man is become the bond of life.

THE LAST LETTERS OF MARGARET FULLER

37

To Caroline Sturgis Tappan[1]

Rieti [Italy] 28 August 1849

I have been on the brink of losing my little boy. During all the siege of Rome I could not see him, and though the Physician wrote reassuring letters I often seemed to hear him calling me amid the roar of the cannon, and he seemed to be crying. When I came I found mine own fast waning to the tomb. All that I have undergone seemed little to what I felt seeing him unable to smile or lift his little wasted hand. Now by incessant care day and night I have brought him back (who knows if indeed that be a deed of love?) into this difficult world. I hope that the cruel law of my life will at least not oblige me to be separated from him—

[1]Caroline Sturgis (1819–1888), the daughter of a wealthy Boston merchant, was Fuller's closest, lifelong female friend. She married William Aspinwall Tappan (1819–1905) in 1847. Fuller confided in her friend before telling her family about the birth of her son.

The Letters of Margaret Fuller, ed. Robert N. Hudspeth, 6 vols. (Ithaca, 1983–1994), 5:258–59.

38

To Margarett C. Fuller

[August 31, 1849]

Dearest Mother,

    I received your letter a few hours before leaving Rome. Like all of yours, it refreshed me, and gave me as much satisfaction as anything

The Letters of Margaret Fuller, ed. Robert N. Hudspeth, 6 vols. (Ithaca, 1983–1994), 5:259–62.

could, at that sad time. Its spirit is of eternity, and befits an epoch when wickedness and perfidy so impudently triumph, and the best blood of the generous and honorable is poured out like water, seemingly in vain.

I cannot tell you what I suffered to abandon the wounded to the care of their mean foes; to see the young men, that were faithful to their vows, hunted from their homes, — hunted like wild beasts; denied a refuge in every civilized land. Many of those I loved are sunk to the bottom of the sea, by Austrian cannon, or will be shot. Others are in penury, grief, and exile. May God give due recompense for all that has been endured!

My mind still agitated, and my spirits worn out, I have not felt like writing to any one. Yet the magnificent summer does not smile quite in vain for me. Much exercise in the open air, living much on milk and fruit, have recruited my health, and I am regaining the habit of sleep, which a month of nightly cannonade in Rome had destroyed. . . .

This brings me to the main object of my present letter, — a piece of intelligence about myself, which I had hoped I might be able to communicate in such a way as to give you *pleasure*. That I cannot, — after suffering much in silence with that hope, — is like the rest of my earthly destiny.

The first moment, it may cause you a pang to know that your eldest child might long ago have been addressed by another name than yours, and has a little son a year old.

But, beloved mother, do not feel this long. I do assure you, that it was only great love for you that kept me silent. I have abstained a hundred times, when your sympathy, your counsel, would have been most precious, from a wish not to harass you with anxiety. Even now I would abstain, but it has become necessary, on account of the child, for us to live publicly and permanently together; and we have no hope, in the present state of Italian affairs, that we can do it at any better advantage, for several years, than now.

My husband is a Roman, of a noble but now impoverished house. His mother died when he was an infant, his father is dead since we met, leaving some property, but encumbered with debts, and in the present state of Rome hardly available, except by living there. He has three older brothers, all provided for in the Papal service, — one as Secretary of the Privy Chamber, the other two as members of the Guard Noble. A similar career would have been opened to him, but he embraced liberal principles, and, with the fall of the Republic, has lost all, as well as the favor of his family, who all sided with the Pope. Meanwhile, having been an officer in the Republican service, it was best for him to leave Rome. He has taken what little money he had, and we plan to live in Florence for the winter. If he or I can get the means, we shall come together to the United States, in the summer;—earlier we could not, on account of the child.

He is not in any respect such a person as people in general would expect to find with me. He had no instructor except an old priest, who entirely neglected his education; and of all that is contained in books he is absolutely ignorant, and he has no enthusiasm of character. On the other hand, he has excellent practical sense; has been a judicious observer of all that passed before his eyes; has a nice sense of duty, which, in its unfailing, minute activity, may put most enthusiasts to shame; a very sweet temper, and great native refinement. His love for me has been unswerving and most tender. I have never suffered a pain that he could [not] relieve. His devotion, when I am ill, is to be compared only with yours. His delicacy in trifles, his sweet domestic graces, remind me of E——. In him I have found a home, and one that interferes with no tie. Amid many ills and cares, we have had much joy together, in the sympathy with natural beauty,—with our child,—with all that is innocent and sweet.

I do not know whether he will always love me so well, for I am the elder, and the difference will become, in a few years, more perceptible than now. But life is so uncertain, and it is so necessary to take good things with their limitations, that I have not thought it worth while to calculate too curiously.

However my other friends may feel, I am sure that you will love him very much, and that he will love you no less. Could we all live together, on a moderate income, you would find peace with us. Heaven grant, that, on returning, I may gain means to effect this object. He, of course, can do nothing, while we are in the United States, but perhaps I can; and now that my health is better, I shall be able to exert myself, if sure that my child is watched by those who love him, and who are good and pure.

What shall I say of my child? All might seem hyperbole, even to my dearest mother. In him I find satisfaction, for the first time, to the deep wants of my heart. Yet, thinking of those other sweet ones fled, I must look upon him as a treasure only lent. He is a fair child, with blue eyes and light hair; very affectionate, graceful, and sportive. He was baptized, in the Roman Catholic Church, by the name of Angelo Eugene Philip, for his father, grandfather, and my brother. He inherits the title of marquis.

Write the name of my child in your Bible, Angelo Ossoli, *born September* 5, 1848. God grant he may live to see you, and may prove worthy of your love! . . .

39

To Caroline Sturgis Tappan

[ca. December 17, 1849]
I do not know what to write about him; he changes so much; has so many characters, he is like me in that, his father's character is simple and uniform though not monotonous more than are the flowers of spring, flowers of the valley. He is now in the most perfect rosy health, a very gay impetuous, ardent, but sweet tempered child. He seems to me to have nothing in common with the first baby with its exstatic smiles, its exquisite sensitiveness and a distinction in the gesture and attitudes that struck every body. His temperament seems changed by taking the milk of these robust women. His form is robust but the feet and [ ] quite any [ ] make him some prettier dresses.

He is now come to quite a knowing age (fifteen months.) In the morng, so soon as dressed, he signs to come into our room, there draws our curtain, kisses me, rather violently pats my face, says poor, stretches himself and says *bravo,* then expects as a reward to be tied in his chair and have his play things. These engage him busily, but still he calls to us to sing and drum to enliven the scene. Sometimes he calls me to kiss his hand; he laughs very much at this. Enchanting is that baby laugh, all dimples and glitter, so strangely arch and innocent. Then I wash and dress him; that is his great time. He makes it as long as he can insisting to dress and wash me the while; kicking, throwing the water about full of all manner of tricks that I think girls nere dream of. Then is his walk; we have beautiful walks here for him, Lung-Arno by the bridges, or the sunny walk at the Cascine protected by fine trees always warm in mid-winter the band playing in the distance and children of all ages walking and sitting with their nurses. His walk and sleep give me about three hours in the middle of the day, then at [nig]ht he goes to bed and we have the [ ] otherwise I am always engaged [with] him. Indeed I often walk [with] him, as Italn servants are [not] to be trusted and I feel now [the] need of seeing him at each [mo]ment.

[I] feel so refreshed by his young life. Ossoli diffuses such a peace and sweetness over every day, that I cannot endure to think yet of our future. Too much have we suffered already trying to command it. I do not feel force to make any effort yet. I suppose that very soon now I must do something. I hope I shall feel able when the time comes. I do not yet....

The Letters of Margaret Fuller, ed. Robert N. Hudspeth, 6 vols. (Ithaca, 1983–1994), 5:301–7.

40

To Margarett C. Fuller

FLORENCE, 14 May 1850

My dearest Mother,

I will believe I shall be welcome with my treasures, my husband and child. For me, I long so very much to see you, should any thing hinder it on earth again (and I say it merely because there seems somewhat more of danger on sea than on land) think of your daughter as one who always wished at least to do her duty, and who always cherished you according as her mind opened to discover excellence.

Give dear love, too, to my brothers, first my eldest, and faithful friend, Eugene, God bless him. Love to my kind and good Aunts, my dear cousin Ellen, a sister's love to Ellen Channing, — [1]

We sail in the "Elizabeth," Capt. Hasty, from Leghorn for New York; and I hope we may arrive by the end of June.

I hope we shall be able to pass some time together yet in this world; but if God decrees otherwise, — here and hereafter, My dearest Mother, Your loving child,

MARGARET.

---

[1] Fuller's sister, Ellen Kilshaw Fuller (1820–1856), married the poet William Ellery Channing (1817–1901) in 1841.

The Letters of Margaret Fuller, ed. Robert N. Hudspeth, 6 vols. (Ithaca, 1983–1994), 6:86–87.

15

Contemporary Responses to Fuller

Her contemporaries reacted strongly to Margaret Fuller's life and vision. The documents reprinted here represent the range of responses offered by her admirers (James Freeman Clarke, a Unitarian minister and close friend, and Lydia Maria Child, a successful writer and abolitionist), her critics (Orestes A. Brownson, a conservative opponent of Transcendentalism, and James Russell Lowell, whose poetry Fuller had reviewed negatively), and those who were both fascinated and troubled by her ideas and presence (the prominent American authors Edgar Allan Poe and Henry James). Whatever their reactions, many of Fuller's contemporaries — and the generations to follow — agreed with James that the "unquestionably haunting Margaret-ghost" was impossible to dismiss or to forget.

41

JAMES FREEMAN CLARKE[1]

[Review of *Summer on the Lakes, in 1843*]

The West is our American Romance, our unwritten Poetry, our Eldorado, our Utopia, our Atlantis. It is so changeable in its features that the description of yesterday will not do for to-day; the picture, which a year ago was considered a good portrait, cannot be recognized as a likeness now. Hence the charm and the necessity of new books about the West.

Miss Fuller has given us a charming little volume, full of description

---

[1]James Freeman Clarke (1810–1888) was one of Fuller's closest friends. They studied German literature together while he attended the Harvard Divinity School in the early 1830s. A Unitarian minister in Louisville and Boston, Clarke remained interested in German literature and philosophy and edited a Transcendentalist periodical, *The Western Messenger.*

Christian World 2 (July 6, 1844).

of scenery and manners, in a graceful form. She has done wisely in not making a guide book, which, as we said above, would have become useless in another year; she has not given us a volume of maps, but a portfolio of sketches, some in outline, some filled out and carefully finished. The book is a very interesting one, and we recommend it to all who wish to see our every day life made interesting by the power which belongs to a mind, possessing at once, faculties of keen perception, profound reflection and constructive imagination.

But we should do great injustice to this book in representing it merely as a pleasant book of travels. It belongs to a class of which we can rarely find a specimen. It is full of suggestion, rich in matter, to be read and read again, and to appear new with each new reading. It comes to us with the stores of a mind which has thought much and seen much and experienced much, and which can, therefore, touch no subject without conveying a thousand suggestions and incitements to thought by every word. This is a book for study as well as for entertainment, and we hope that the sale of it will be such as to encourage its author to give the public more of those rich results of genius and study, which her friends have so long known and prized, but which belong, by their nature, to a wider circle than even that which has the privilege of regarding this lady as its light and ornament.

42

ORESTES A. BROWNSON[1]

[Review of *Summer on the Lakes, in 1843*]

The publishers tell us that this book has had a very respectable sale, which we are glad to learn, for the writer's sake. Miss Fuller is a woman of more than ordinary abilities, and, we are told, of rare attainments. She is said to possess remarkable conversational powers, and her conversations, which she has been in the habit of holding, we believe, as a means of meeting her expenses, are represented by her friends to be in the highest degree brilliant, instructive, and inspiring. This we can partly believe, though we have never had the honor of listening to her in her hap-

---

[1]Orestes A. Brownson (1803–1876) was the editor of the *Boston Quarterly Review* from 1838 to 1842. In his youth a political radical and a Universalist, he later became a conservative in politics, a Catholic, and a fierce opponent of Transcendentalism.

Brownson's Quarterly Review 6 (October 1844): 546–47.

piest moments. Her writings we do not like. We dislike them exceedingly. They are sent out in a slipshod style, and have a certain toss of the head about them which offends us. Miss Fuller seems to us to be wholly deficient in a pure, correct taste, and especially in that tidiness we always look for in woman. Then, we detest her doctrines. We know nothing more abominable. She is a heathen priestess, though of what god or goddess we will not pretend to say. She is German, heart and soul, save so far as Germany may retain traditionally somewhat of Christianity. We believe no person has appeared among us whose conversation and writings have done more to corrupt the minds and hearts of our Boston community. For religion she substitutes Art; for the Divinity who has made us, and whom we should worship she would give us merely the Beautiful; and for the stern morality of the Gospel, such principles as we may collect from the *Wahlverwandtschaften,* and Goethe's *Correspondence with a Child.*[2] She is, in fact, the high-priestess of American Transcendentalism, and, happily, ministers now at an almost deserted fane. . . .

[2]The themes of sexual attraction and adultery were central to Johann Wolfgang von Goethe's novel *Wahlverwandtschaften* (Elective Affinities). It was considered one of his most scandalous, immoral works by most readers. Fuller stood almost alone among American critics in praising the novel's deep morality and surpassing artistic beauty; see "Goethe," *Dial,* July 1841, 1–41 (Document 19). For Fuller's review of *Goethe's Correspondence with a Child,* see "Bettine Brentano and Her Friend Günderode," *Dial,* January 1842, 313–57 (Document 21).

43

LYDIA MARIA CHILD[1]

"Woman in the Nineteenth Century"

This is the title of a book now in press in this city, which will be likely to excite a good deal of remark, for and against. It is from the pen of Margaret Fuller, a woman of more powerful intellect, comprehensive thought, and thorough education, than any other American authoress, with whose productions I am acquainted. Her style is vigorous and significant, abounding with eloquent passages, and affluent in illustration; but it is sometimes rough in construction, and its meaning is not always sufficiently clear. This

[1]Lydia Maria Francis Child (1802–1880) had known Fuller since the 1820s in Cambridge but saw little of her after that period. Child was a successful writer of fiction and nonfiction and an ardent abolitionist. She edited the *National Anti-Slavery Standard* in New York City in the 1840s.

Broadway Journal 1 (February 15, 1845): 97.

does not arise from affectation, or pedantic elaboration; it is the defect of a mind that has too many thoughts for its words; an excess by no means common, either in men or women. She is a contralto voice in literature: deep, rich, and strong, rather than mellifluous and clear.

The book in question is written in a free energetic spirit. It contains a few passages that will offend the fastidiousness of some readers; for they allude to subjects which men do not wish to have discussed, and which women dare not approach. But the clean-minded will not sneer; for they will see that the motive is pure, and the object is to ennoble human nature.

There is a great deal of unuttered thought and suppressed feeling, concerning the terrible discords of society, as it now exists. The passion of love, divorced from the pure and elevating sentiment, is felt to be unsatisfactory, as well as degrading. More and more earnestly rise the questions, "Is love a mockery, and marriage a sham? What is woman's true mission? What is the harmonious relation of the sexes?"

This extending murmur of the human heart, this increasing conviction that woman should be the friend, the companion, the real partner of man in all his pursuits, rather than the mere ornament of his parlor, or the servant of his senses, cannot be silenced.

The author of "Woman in the Nineteenth Century," has uttered noble aspirations on this subject, rather than definite theories. She is wise enough to see, that to purify the atmosphere will gradually affect all forms of life. . . .

44

EDGAR ALLAN POE[1]

"Sarah Margaret Fuller"

Miss Fuller was at one time editor, or one of the editors of "The Dial," to which she contributed many of the most forcible, and certainly some of the most peculiar papers. She is known, too, by "Summer on the Lakes," a remarkable assemblage of sketches, issued in 1844 by Little & Brown, of Boston. More lately she has published "Woman in the Nineteenth

---

[1] Edgar Allan Poe (1809–1849) was a leading American author. In the mid-1840s, he and Fuller both reviewed contemporary literature in the New York press.

"The Literati of New York City, No. IV. Sarah Margaret Fuller," *Godey's Magazine and Lady's Book* 33 (August 1846): 72–75.

Century," a work which has occasioned much discussion, having had the good fortune to be warmly abused and chivalrously defended. . . .

"Woman in the Nineteenth Century" is a book which few women in the country could have written, and no woman in the country would have published, with the exception of Miss Fuller. In the way of independence, of unmitigated radicalism, it is one of the "Curiosities of American Literature," and Doctor Griswold should include it in his book.[2] I need scarcely say that the essay is nervous, forcible, thoughtful, suggestive, brilliant, and to a certain extent scholar-like—for all that Miss Fuller produces is entitled to these epithets—but I must say that the conclusions reached are only in part my own. Not that they are too bold, by any means—too novel, too startling, or too dangerous in their consequences, but that in their attainment too many premises have been distorted and too many analogical inferences left altogether out of sight. I mean to say that the intention of the Deity as regards sexual differences—an intention which can be distinctly comprehended only by throwing the exterior (more sensitive) portions of the mental retina casually over the wide field of universal analogy—I mean to say that this intention has not been sufficiently considered. Miss Fuller has erred, too, through her own excessive objectiveness. She judges woman by the heart and intellect of Miss Fuller, but there are not more than one or two dozen Miss Fullers on the whole face of the earth. . . .

[2]Rufus Wilmot Griswold (1815–1857) did include Fuller in his *Prose Writers of America* (1846), 537–38.

45

JAMES RUSSELL LOWELL[1]

[Miranda]

But there comes Miranda, Zeus! where shall I flee to?
She has such a penchant for bothering me too!
She always keeps asking if I don't observe a
Particular likeness 'twixt her and Minerva;

[1]James Russell Lowell (1819–1891) was a respected poet, essayist, and dramatist. A member of an elite social circle in Boston, he had never liked Fuller personally. Her negative review of his poetry in the *New-York Daily Tribune* intensified their differences.

A Fable for Critics (New York, 1848), 53–57.

She tells me my efforts in verse are quite clever;—
She's been travelling now, and will be worse than ever;
One would think, though, a sharp-sighted noter she'd be
Of all that's worth mentioning over the sea,
For a woman must surely see well, if she try,
The whole of whose being's a capital I:
She will take an old notion, and make it her own,
By saying it o'er in her Sybilline[2] tone,
Or persuade you 'tis something tremendously deep,
By repeating it so as to put you to sleep;
And she well may defy any mortal to see through it,
When once she has mixed up her infinite me through it.
There is one thing she owns in her own single right,
It is native and genuine—namely, her spite:
Though, when acting as censor, she privately blows
A censor of vanity 'neath her own nose.

Here Miranda came up, and said, "Phoebus![3] you know
That the infinite Soul has its infinite woe,
As I ought to know, having lived cheek by jowl,
Since the day I was born, with the Infinite Soul;
I myself introduced, I myself, I alone,
To my Land's better life authors solely my own,
Who the sad heart of earth on their shoulders have taken,
Whose works sound a depth by Life's quiet unshaken,
Such as Shakspeare, for instance, the Bible, and Bacon,
Not to mention my own works; Time's nadir is fleet,
And, as for myself, I'm quite out of conceit,"—

"Quite out of conceit! I'm enchanted to hear it,"
Cried Appollo aside, "Who'd have thought she was near it?
To be sure one is apt to exhaust those commodities
He uses too fast, yet in this case as odd it is
As if Neptune[4] should say to his turbots and whitings;
'I'm as much out of salt as Miranda's own writings,'
(Which, as she in her own happy manner has said,
Sound a depth, for 'tis one of the functions of lead.)
She often has asked me if I could not find
A place somewhere near me that suited her mind;
I know but a single one vacant, which she,
With her rare talent that way, would fit to a T.

---

[2]Sibyls were female products of the ancient world. "Sybilline" indicates a prophetic tone.

[3]Phoebus was another name for Apollo, the Greek god of light, music, and poetry.

[4]Neptune was the Roman god of the sea.

And it would not imply any pause or cessation
In the work she esteems her peculiar vocation,—
She may enter on duty to-day, if she chooses,
And remain Tiring-woman for life to the Muses."

(Miranda meanwhile has succeeded in driving
Up into a corner, in spite of their striving,
A small Sock of terrified victims, and there,
With an I-turn-the-crank-of-the-Universe air
And a tone which, at least to my fancy, appears
Not so much to be entering as boxing your ears,
Is unfolding a tale (of herself, I surmise,)
For 'tis dotted as thick as a peacock's with I's.)
Apropos of Miranda, I'll rest on my oars
And drift through a trifling digression on bores,
For though not wearing ear-rings *in more majorum,*[5]
Our ears are kept bored just as if we still wore 'em.

[5]In the manner of our ancestors (Latin).

46

HENRY JAMES[1]

[The Margaret-Ghost]

The unquestionably haunting Margaret-ghost, looking out from her quiet
little upper chamber at her lamentable doom, would perhaps be never so
much to be caught by us as on some such occasion as this. What comes
up is the wonderment of *why* she may, to any such degree, be felt as haunting; together with other wonderments that brush us unless we give them
the go-by. It is not for this latter end that we are thus engaged at all; so
that, making the most of it, we ask ourselves how, possibly, in our own
luminous age, she would have affected us on the stage of the "world," or
as a candidate, if so we may put it, for the cosmopolite crown. It matters
only for the amusement of evocation—since she left nothing behind her,

[1]Henry James (1843–1916) was a leading American author and critic. He wrote this
sketch more than fifty years after Fuller's death. Like Fuller, he was drawn strongly to Europe, living and writing there from 1875 until his death.

Henry James, *William Wetmore Story and His Friends,* 2 vols. (Boston, 1903), 1:127–31.

her written utterance being naught; but to what would she have corresponded, have "rhymed," under categories actually known to us? Would
she, in other words, with her appetite for ideas and her genius for conversation, have struck us but as a somewhat formidable bore, one of the
worst kind, a culture-seeker without a sense of proportion, or, on the contrary, have affected us as a really attaching, a possibly picturesque New
England Corinne?[2]

Such speculations are, however, perhaps too idle; the *facts* of the appearance of this singular woman, who would, though conceit was imputed
to her, doubtless have been surprised to know that talk may be still, after
more than half a century, made about her — the facts have in themselves
quite sufficient colour, and the fact in particular of her having achieved,
so unaided and so ungraced, a sharp identity. This identity was that of
the talker, the moral *improvisatrice*,[3] or at least had been in her Boston
days, when young herself, she had been as a sparkling fountain to other
thirsty young. In the Rome of many waters there were doubtless fountains that quenched, collectively, any individual gush; so that it would
have been, naturally, for her plentiful life, her active courage and company, that the little set of friends with whom we are concerned valued her.
She had bitten deeply into Rome, or, rather, *been,* like so many others, by
the wolf of the Capitol, incurably bitten; she met the whole case with New
England arts that show even yet, at our distance, as honest and touch-
ing; there might be ways for her of being vivid that were not as the ways
of Boston. Otherwise what she would mainly prompt us to interest in
might be precisely the beautiful moral complexion of the little circle of
her interlocutors. That is ever half the interest of any celebrated thing —
taking Margaret's mind for celebrated: the story it has to tell us of those
for whom it flourished and whose measure and reflection it necessarily
more or less gives. Let us hasten to add, without too many words, that
Mme. Ossoli's circle represented, after all, a small stage, and that there
were those on its edges to whom she was not pleasing. This was the case
with Lowell and, discoverably, with Hawthorne; the legend of whose having had her in his eye for the figure of Zenobia, while writing "The
Blithedale Romance," surely never held water. She inspired Mrs Browning, on the other hand, with sympathy and admiration, and the latter, writing of her in 1852, after the so lamentable end of her return-voyage, with
her husband and child, to America — the wreck of the vessel, the loss of
father, mother and small son in sight of shore — says that "her death

---

[2]The heroine of the novel *Corinne* (1807), by the French author Mme. de Staël
(1766–1817), was a wild, exuberant female genius, called an *improvisatrice.*
[3]Literally, a female improviser (French). See note 2.

shook me to the very roots of my heart. The comfort is," Mrs Browning then adds, "that she lost little in the world—the change could not be loss to her. She had suffered, and was likely to suffer still more."[4] She had previously to this, in December 1849, spoken of her, in a letter to Miss Mitford,[5] as having "taken us by surprise at Florence, retiring from the Roman world with a husband and child above a year old. Nobody had even suspected a word of this underplot, and her American friends stood in mute astonishment before this apparition of them here. The husband is a Roman marquis appearing amiable and gentlemanly, and having fought well, they say, at the siege, but with no pretension to cope with his wife on any ground appertaining to the intellect." The "underplot" was precisely another of the personal facts by which the lady could interest— the fact, that is, that her marriage should *be* an underplot, and that her husband, much *decaduto,*[6] should make explanation difficult. These things, let alone the final catastrophe, in short, were not talk, but life, and life dealing with the somewhat angular Boston sibyl on its own free lines. All of which, the free lines overscoring the unlikely material, is doubtless partly why the Margaret-ghost, as I have ventured to call it, still unmistakably walks the old passages.

---

[4]James Russell Lowell (1819–1891), a respected Boston poet, essayist, and dramatist, never liked Fuller; see his poetic satire of her as "Miranda" (Document 45). Nathaniel Hawthorne (1804–1864) was Fuller's neighbor and friend in Concord, but disapproved of her European adventures. Hawthorne's novel *The Blithedale Romance* of 1852, based in part on his experiences at the utopian community of Brook Farm, was widely believed to contain a scathing portrait of Fuller in the character of Zenobia, a fervent feminist. The English poet Elizabeth Barrett Browning (1806–1861), on the other hand, sincerely liked and admired Fuller for her courage in Italy.

[5]Mary Russell Mitford (1781–1855) was an English novelist and dramatist.

[6]Fallen (Italian).

A Fuller Chronology

(1810–1850)

1810 Sarah Margaret Fuller is born in Cambridgeport, Massachusetts, on May 23, the first child of Timothy Fuller and Margarett Crane Fuller.

1817 Timothy Fuller begins serving the first of four terms in the U.S. House of Representatives.

1824–25 Attends Miss Prescott's Young Ladies' Seminary in Groton, Massachusetts.

1831 Spiritual crisis and vision in late November.

1833 Moves to rural Groton, Massachusetts, with her family.

1835 Timothy Fuller dies suddenly of cholera on October 1.

1836 Meets Ralph Waldo Emerson in July. Teaches at Bronson Alcott's Temple School in Boston from December to the following April.

1837 Begins teaching at the Greene Street School in Providence, Rhode Island, in June.

1839 Publishes her translation of *Eckermann's Conversations with Goethe*. Becomes the first editor of the Transcendentalist periodical, the *Dial*. Initiates her first series of Conversations for Boston women in November.

1840 First issue of the *Dial* is published in July. Begins her "Autobiographical Sketch" about her youth. Converses and corresponds with Emerson about the nature and value of friendship.

1841 Publishes "Leila" in the *Dial* in April, and "Goethe" in July.

1842 Publishes "Bettine Brentano and Her Friend Günderode" in the *Dial* in January. Resigns editorship of the *Dial* in March.

1843 Publishes "The Great Lawsuit: Man *versus* Men, Woman *versus* Women" in the *Dial*. Travels with friends through the Great Lakes to Wisconsin Territory in the summer.

1844 Concludes final series of Conversations in April. Publishes *Summer on the Lakes, in 1843* in May. Composes more than thirty poems between April and November. Moves to New York City and becomes literary editor and journalist for Horace Greeley's *New-York Daily Tribune* in December.

1845   Publishes *Woman in the Nineteenth Century* in February.

1846   Sails for Europe with Marcus and Rebecca Spring in August as a foreign correspondent for the *New-York Daily Tribune*. Her first dispatch is published on September 24. Travels through England, Scotland, and France.

1847   Arrives in Italy in February. Meets Giovanni Angelo Ossoli in Rome in April. Travels alone in northern Italy and Switzerland from June to October. Returns to reside in Rome in October.

1848   Gives birth to Angelo Eugenio Filippo Ossoli in the mountain town of Rieti on September 5. Witnesses the flight of the pope from Rome in November.

1849   Roman Republic is proclaimed in February. Siege of Rome by the French begins in April and the bombardment in June. Rome falls; Fuller and Ossoli escape in July. Moves to Florence with her family in September.

1850   Her final dispatch is published in the *New-York Daily Tribune* on February 13. Sails for the United States with Ossoli and Angelo on May 17. Drowns in shipwreck off the coast of New York on July 19.

Questions for Consideration

1. Why did Margaret Fuller's contemporaries react so strongly—and so differently—to her? Why did the "Margaret-ghost" haunt them?

2. Did Timothy Fuller help or hurt his eldest daughter when he educated her as a boy until she was thirteen years old? How did Margaret Fuller's relationship with her father and mother affect her self-image and social vision?

3. How significant were Fuller's spiritual crisis and vision in shaping her life and work? Why did goddess figures continue to fascinate her and fill her writing over the years? Was her mysticism a sign of weakness (as Emerson supposed) or a source of strength?

4. How would you characterize Fuller's theory and practice of education (in the classroom and her Conversation Club) and of friendship? If you were living in New England in the early 1840s, would you have wanted to be one of her students or friends? Would you have found her concept of self-culture liberating or limiting?

5. Why did Fuller create so many quasi-autobiographical fictions? How are we to interpret the contradictions between Fuller's portraits of the heroine of her "Autobiographical Sketch," Leila of her mystical meditation in the *Dial,* Mariana of *Summer on the Lakes, in 1843* and Miranda of *Woman in the Nineteenth Century*? What might these figures reveal or conceal about Fuller's life and aspirations?

6. Why did Fuller reinscribe the basic gender categories of "masculine" and "feminine" in *Woman in the Nineteenth Century, in 1843* if she wished to challenge the social constraints on women's (and men's) development? Why didn't she deny that gender was the "great radical dualism" of the universe? Were Minerva and the Muse different enough from traditional gender roles to be empowering for women?

7. Where and when, if ever, did Fuller become a social radical or revolutionary—in New England, the West, New York, or Rome? Did her social vision gradually unfold over time, or was there a sudden reversal in her thought?

8. Did Fuller ever achieve the harmony and wholeness that she desired and envisioned? Was it possible for anyone in early-nineteenth-century America to unify the divided self and create an identity free of social constructions and limitations? It is possible today?

Selected Bibliography

Nearly 150 years after her death, Margaret Fuller's writings are finally being recovered and restored to their original form. Heavily edited (or suppressed) by her nineteenth-century friends and relatives, her private letters and journals are only now being published as she wrote them. Robert N. Hudspeth has edited the definitive six-volume *Letters of Margaret Fuller* (Ithaca, 1983–1994). Several of Fuller's extant private journals have been published; see especially "Margaret Fuller's 1842 Journal: At Concord with the Emersons," ed. Joel Myerson, *Harvard Library Bulletin* 21 (1973): 320–40; "Margaret Fuller's Journal for October 1842," ed. Robert D. Habich, *Harvard Library Bulletin* 33 (1985): 280–91; and " 'The Impulses of Human Nature': Margaret Fuller's Journal from June through October 1844," ed. Martha L. Berg and Alice de V. Perry, *Proceedings of the Massachusetts Historical Society* 102 (1990): 38–126.

Fuller's published writings have also been reprinted in recent years. Facsimiles of the original edition of *Summer on the Lakes, in 1843* were published by B. De Graaf in 1972 and the University of Illinois Press in 1991. A facsimile of the original edition of *Woman in the Nineteenth Century* was published by the University of South Carolina Press in 1980. *Margaret Fuller's New York Journalism: A Biographical Essay and Key Writings,* ed. Catherine C. Mitchell (Knoxville, 1995), gathers and reprints Fuller's social criticism from the *New-York Daily Tribune* between 1844 and 1846. *"These Sad but Glorious Days": Dispatches from Europe, 1846–1850*, ed. Larry J. Reynolds and Susan Belasco Smith (New Haven, 1991), reproduces all of Fuller's dispatches to the *Tribune* from Europe.

There are now several full-length biographies of Margaret Fuller from which to choose. The feminist authors who rediscovered Fuller in the late 1970s tended to celebrate her movement toward direct political engagement in the 1840s; see especially Bell Gale Chevigny, *The Woman and the Myth: Margaret Fuller's Life and Writings* (New York, 1976; expanded and reprinted, 1994), and Paula Blanchard, *Margaret Fuller: From Transcendentalism to Revolution* (Reading, Mass., 1978). Donna Dickenson, *Margaret Fuller: Writing a Woman's Life* (New York, 1993), follows in this tradition. Two other recent biographies have been somewhat more sympathetic to Fuller's early Transcendentalism; see Charles Capper, *Margaret Fuller: An American Romantic Life. The Private Years* (New York, 1992), the first of a projected two-volume, comprehensive biography, and Joan von Mehren, *Minerva and the Muse: A Life of Margaret Fuller* (Amherst, Mass., 1994). David Watson, *Margaret Fuller: An American Romantic* (Oxford, 1988), offers a brief comparison of the "conversion experiences" of Fuller and Ralph Waldo Emerson.

The development of gender roles and boundaries in the early Republic were first analyzed in Nancy F. Cott, *The Bonds of Womanhood: "Woman's Sphere" in New England, 1780–1835* (New Haven, 1977); Barbara Welter, *Dimity Convictions: The American Woman in the Nineteenth Century* (Athens, Ohio, 1976); and Ann Douglas, *The Feminization of American Culture* (New York, 1977). Lee Chambers-Schiller, *Liberty, a Better Husband: Single Women in America, the Generations of 1780–1840* (New Haven, 1984), discusses an alternative to the norm chosen by many women in New England. Mary Kelley, *Private Woman, Public Stage: Literary Domesticity in Nineteenth-Century America* (New York, 1984), illuminates the conflicts of female authors facing the expectations of domesticity. For an analysis of the American Revolutionary concept of educating girls for "republican motherhood," see Linda K. Kerber, *Women of the Republic: Intellect and Ideology in Revolutionary America* (Chapel Hill, 1980), chaps. 7 and 9.

Early-nineteenth-century Boston politics and society are profiled in Peter R. Knights, *The Plain People of Boston, 1830–1860: A Study in City Growth* (New York, 1971); Ronald P. Formisano, "Boston, 1800–1840: From Deferential-Participant to Party Politics," in *Boston, 1700–1980: The Evolution of Urban Politics*, ed. Ronald P. Formisano and Constance K. Burns (Westport, Conn., 1984), 29–86; William H. Pease and Jane H. Pease, *The Web of Progress: Private Values and Public Styles in Boston and Charleston, 1828–1843* (New York, 1985); and Tamara Plakins Thornton, *Cultivating Gentlemen: The Meaning of Country Life among the Boston Elite, 1785–1860* (New Haven, 1989). On same-sex romantic friendships among the middle class in early-nineteenth-century New England, see Carroll Smith-Rosenberg, "Female World of Love and Ritual: Relations between Women in Nineteenth-Century America," *Signs* 1 (1975): 1–29; and E. Anthony Rotundo, *American Manhood: Transformations in Masculinity from the Revolution to the Modern Era* (New York, 1993).

For students of history, the most interesting studies of Transcendentalism include Lawrence Buell, *Literary Transcendentalism: Style and Vision in the American Renaissance* (Ithaca, 1973), and Anne C. Rose, *Transcendentalism as a Social Movement* (New Haven, 1981). David Robinson, *Apostle of Culture: Emerson as Preacher and Lecturer* (Philadelphia, 1982), and Mary Kupiec Cayton, *Emerson's Emergence: Self and Society in the Transformation of New England, 1800–1845* (Chapel Hill, 1989), introduce and situate the most celebrated American Transcendentalist. For Bronson Alcott's educational philosophy and the Temple School, see Frederick C. Dahlstrand, *Amos Bronson Alcott: An Intellectual Biography* (Rutherford, N.J., 1982).

Fuller's Transcendentalism is the focus of Carolyn Hlus, "Margaret Fuller, Transcendentalist: A Re-assessment," *Canadian Review of American Studies*

16 (1985): 1–13. Laraine R. Fergenson, "Margaret Fuller in the Classroom: The Providence Period," *Studies in the American Renaissance* (1987): 131–42; Judith Strong Albert, "Margaret Fuller's Row at the Greene Street School: Early Female Education in Providence, 1837–1839," *Rhode Island History* 42 (1983): 43–55; and Frank Shuffelton, ed., "Margaret Fuller at the Greene Street School: The Journal of Evelina Metcalf," *Studies in the American Renaissance* (1985), 29–46, treat aspects of Fuller's classroom teaching. Her Conversation Club is profiled in Charles Capper, "Margaret Fuller as Cultural Reformer: The Conversations in Boston," *American Quarterly* 39 (1987): 509–28. For the publication practices of Fuller's *Dial,* see Joel Myerson, *The New England Transcendentalists and the* Dial: *A History of the Magazine and Its Contributors* (Rutherford, N.J., 1980), chaps. 2 and 3.

Fuller's complex relationship with Ralph Waldo Emerson figures centrally in Bell Gale Chevigny, "Growing out of New England: The Emergence of Margaret Fuller's Radicalism," *Women's Studies* 5 (1977): 65–100; and Dorothy Berkson, " 'Born and Bred in Different Nations': Margaret Fuller and Ralph Waldo Emerson," in *Patrons and Protégées: Gender, Friendship, and Writing in Nineteenth-Century America,* ed. Shirley Marchalonis (New Brunswick, N.J., 1988), 3–30. Fuller's influence on Emerson's thought and writing is explored in Judith Mattson Bean, "Texts from Conversation: Margaret Fuller's Influence on Emerson," *Studies in the American Renaissance* (1994): 227–44; and Christina Zwarg, *Feminist Conversations: Fuller, Emerson, and the Play of Reading* (Ithaca, 1995).

For descriptions of the variety of reform activities surrounding the Second Great Awakening, see Ronald G. Walters, *American Reformers, 1815–1860* (New York, 1978); Paul E. Johnson, *A Shopkeeper's Millennium: Society and Revivals in Rochester, New York, 1815–1837* (New York, 1978); and Mary P. Ryan, *Cradle of the Middle Class: The Family in Oneida County, New York, 1790–1865* (Cambridge, Mass., 1981). Carl J. Guarneri, *The Utopian Alternative: Fourierism in Nineteenth-Century America* (Ithaca, 1991), is a good introduction to the American reception of the utopian socialism of Charles Fourier.

For the form and aesthetic context of Fuller's *Summer on the Lakes, in 1843,* see Stephen Adams, " 'That Tidiness We Always Look For in Woman': Fuller's *Summer on the Lakes* and Romantic Aesthetics," *Studies in the American Renaissance* (1987): 247–64; and William W. Stowe, "Conventions and Voices in Margaret Fuller's Travel Writing," *American Literature* 63, no. 2 (June 1991): 242–62. See also Annette Kolodny, *The Land before Her: Fantasy and Experience of the American Frontiers, 1630–1860* (Chapel Hill, 1984). Fuller's poetry of 1844 is analyzed in Jeffrey Steele, "Freeing the 'Prisoned Queen': The Development of Margaret Fuller's Poetry," *Studies in the American Renaissance* (1992): 137–75.

Marie Mitchell Olesen Urbanski, *Margaret Fuller's Woman in the Nineteenth Century: A Literary Study of Form and Content, of Sources and Influence* (Westport, Conn., 1980), examines the literary sources behind *Woman in the Nineteenth Century* and analyzes its form "within the sermon framework." Julie Ellison, *Delicate Subjects: Romanticism, Gender, and the Ethics of Understanding* (Ithaca, 1990), 217–98, sets the book within the context of European Romantic ethics; David M. Robinson, "Margaret Fuller and the Transcendental Ethos: *Woman in the Nineteenth Century*," *PMLA* 97 (1982): 83–98, places it within the boundaries of American Transcendentalism. Jeffrey Steele, "Recovering the 'Idea of Woman': *Woman in the Nineteenth Century* and Its Mythological Background," in *Representation of the Self in the American Renaissance* (Chapel Hill, 1987), 100–33; and Robert D. Richardson Jr., "Margaret Fuller and Myth," *Prospects* 4 (1979), 168–84, discuss the importance of mythology to Fuller. Joel Myerson, ed., *Critical Essays on Margaret Fuller* (Boston, 1980), contains a large sample of the critical responses to Fuller's work from 1845 to 1980.

The politics and culture of New York City in the 1840s are treated in Sean Wilenz, *Chants Democratic: New York City and the Rise of the Working Class, 1788–1850* (New York, 1984); Edward K. Spann, *The New Metropolis: New York City, 1840–1857* (New York, 1981); Christine Stansell, *City of Women: Sex and Class in New York, 1789–1860* (New York, 1986); and Thomas Bender, *New York Intellect: A History of the Intellectual Life in New York City, from 1750 to the Beginning of Our Time* (New York, 1987). Fuller's journalism is analyzed in Paula Kopacz, "Feminist at the *Tribune*: Margaret Fuller as Professional Writer," *Studies in the American Renaissance* (1991): 119–39. Catherine C. Mitchell's introduction to *Margaret Fuller's New York Journalism* sketches Fuller's "work environment" at the *Tribune*.

For an overview of the European revolutions of 1848, see Priscilla Robertson, *Revolutions of 1848: A Social History* (Princeton, 1952); and Charles Breunig, *The Age of Revolution and Reaction, 1789–1850* (New York, 1970). Stuart Woolf, *A History of Italy, 1700–1860* (London, 1979), presents the background, contradictions, and consequences of the 1848 revolts in Italy. Larry J. Reynolds, *European Revolutions and the American Literary Renaissance* (New Haven, 1988), places Fuller's reactions in the context of other American intellectuals' responses to the revolutions. Her life in Rome is discussed in Joseph Jay Deiss, *The Roman Years of Margaret Fuller* (New York, 1969); and Bell Gale Chevigny, "To the Edges of Ideology: Margaret Fuller's Centrifugal Evolution," *American Quarterly* 38, no. 2 (1986): 173–201.

(Continued from p. iv)
standing," 11 December 1832, bMS Am 1569.2 (8), James Freeman Clarke Collection. MF, "Memoranda of interviews, conversations and public discourses," FMW, Box 3. MF to Almira P. Barlow, 19 Nov 1830, FMW, 1:1–5. MF to Frederic H. Hedge, 1 Feb 1835, FMW, 10:99. MF to A. Bronson Alcott, 27 June 1837, 59m–312 (122). MF to Ralph Waldo Emerson, 1 March 1838, bMS Am 1280 (2341). MF to Jane F. Tuckerman, 21 Sept 1838, FMW, 1:89–91. MF to [Sophia Ripley?], 27 Aug 1839, FMW, 9:61–62. MF to Ralph Waldo Emerson, 29 Sept 1840, Os 735Laa 1840.9.29. MF, Journal Fragment, 22 Jan [1840], Os 735Z 1840.1.22. MF to Ralph Waldo Emerson, [Oct 1841?], bMS Am 1280 (2358). MF to Ralph Waldo Emerson, 9 April 1842, bMS Am 1280 (2363). MF to Ralph Waldo Emerson, 9 May [1843], bMS Am 1280 (2365). MF to Ralph Waldo Emerson, 17 Aug 1843, bMS Am 1280 (2371). MF to Elizabeth Hoar, [April 1844?] bMS Am 1280 (111, p. 109). MF to Samuel G. Ward, 29 Dec 1844, bMS Am 1465 (923). MF to Ralph Waldo Emerson, 16 Nov 1846, FMW, 9:216–17. MF to Elizabeth Hoar, Sept 1847, FMW, 2:823–29. MF to Margarett C. Fuller, 16 Oct 1847, FMW, 9:140. MF to Margarett C. Fuller, 16 Dec 1847, bMS Am 1280 (111, p. 129–30). MF to Giovanni Angelo Ossoli, 4 April 1849, FMW, 2:211–215. MF to Emelyn Story, 30 Nov 1849, FMW 9:226. MF to Ellen Fuller Channing, 11 Dec 1849, FMW, 9:171. MF to Caroline Sturgis Tappan, [ca. 17 Dec 1849], FMW, 9:166. MF to Timothy Fuller, 16 Jan 1820, FMW, 9:11. MF to Margarett C. Fuller, 2 Dec 1821, FMW, 9:19. MF to Timothy Fuller, 14 Feb. 1825, FMW, 9:31. MF to Caroline Sturgis, 26 Sept 1840, bMS Am 1221 (241).

The Boston Public Library, Rare Books and Manuscripts Division: MF, Journal, [ca. fall 1839], Ms. Am. 1450 (120), Margaret Fuller Ossoli Collection. MF to Frederic H. Hedge, 6 April 1837, Ms. Am. 1450 (63, 79, 162). MF to [Ralph Waldo Emerson?], 3 July 1837, Ms. Am. 1450 (160). MF to William H. Channing, 22 March 1840, Ms. Am. 1450 (37). MF to William H. Channing, [July 1841?], Ms. Am. 1450 (165). MF to William H. Channing, 16 August 1843, Ms. Am. 1450 (51). MF to William H. Channing, [June? 1844], Ms. Am. 1450 (52). MF to William H. Channing, 17 Dec 1849, Ms. Am. 1450 (58). MF to Caroline Sturgis Tappan, 28 Aug 1849, Ms. Am. 1450 (152).

The Fruitlands Museum Library: MF, "Fragments of Margaret Fuller's Journal: 1844–1845."

The Massachusetts Historical Society: Three poems from Margaret Fuller's Journal of June through October 1844, published in " 'The Impulses of Human Nature': Margaret Fuller's Journal from June through October 1844," ed. Martha L. Berg and Alice de V. Perry, *Proceedings of the Massachusetts Historical Society* 102 (1990), 38–126, on pages 73 ("Leila in the Arabian zone") and 74 ("Patient serpent, circle round" and "Through brute nature, upward rising").

The Thomas Cooper Library, University of South Carolina, Special Collections: Evelina Metcalf, Journal, 7 May 1838.

ILLUSTRATIONS

Page 7: State Street, ca. 1840. Courtesy of the Rare Books Room, the Pennsylvania State University Libraries.

Page 24: A. Bronson Alcott's School of Human Culture. By permission of the Houghton Library, Harvard University, bMS AM 800.23 (246).

Page 25: Greene Street School of Providence, Rhode Island. Courtesy of the Rhode Island Historical Society, RHi X3 690.

Page 31: Ralph Waldo Emerson. Courtesy of the National Portrait Gallery, Smithsonian Institution, Washington, D.C.

Page 52: Margaret Fuller in July 1846. Gift of Edward Southworth Hawes in memory of his father, Josiah Johnson Hawes. Courtesy of the Museum of Fine Arts, Boston.

Page 61: Piazza del Popolo in Rome. Courtesy of the Rare Books Room, the Pennsylvania State University Libraries.

Page 62: Giovanni Angelo Ossoli in the late 1840s. By permission of the Houghton Library, Harvard University, MS AM 1086 box A.

Page 64: Margaret Fuller during the siege of Rome. By permission of the Houghton Library, Harvard University, bMS AM 1086 box 1.

Page 150: Mackinaw Island. Courtesy of the Rare Books Room, the Pennsylvania State University Libraries.

Page 157: Frontispiece of Margaret Fuller's Woman in the Nineteenth Century. Courtesy of the Massachusetts Historical Society.

Index